Successful Marketing
Strategies For
Nonprofit Organizations

NONPROFIT LAW, FINANCE, AND MANAGEMENT SERIES

Successful Marketing Strategies For Nonprofit Organizations

Barry J. McLeish

John Wiley & Sons, Inc.

New York • Chichester • Brisbane • Toronto • Singapore

Copyright © 1995 by John Wiley & Sons, Inc.

Library of Congress Cataloging in Publication Data:

McLeish, Barry, 1956–
    Successful marketing strategies for nonprofit organizations /
Barry J. McLeish.
        p.   cm. — (Nonprofit law, finance, and management series)
    Includes index.
    ISBN 0-471-10568-6.   — ISBN 0-471-10567-8 (pbk.)
    1. Nonprofit organizations—Marketing.   I. Title.   II. Series.
HF5415.M3825   1995
658.8—dc20   95-1657
                                                                  CIP

Printed in the United States of America

10 9 8 7 6 5 4 3 2 1

For
Robin Lynn, Barbara Ann, and David Scott

Acknowledgments

Former president John F. Kennedy wrote, "Victory has a hundred fathers." Certainly the writing of *Successful Marketing Strategies For Nonprofit Organizations* has had a hundred contributors. Some of them knew that they were helping me, while others contributed through their day-to-day actions in their places of business.

Working to change their companies and our society for the better, these nonprofit practitioners tend to have one thing in common. They consistently ask the right types of performance questions. Questions such as:

- What are our distinctive competencies?
- What figures determine success or failure in our marketing endeavors?
- Is our organization bonding correctly with its constituency?
- Does our cause have something of genuine value to offer?
- Is our current strategy the right strategy?

It is this uncommon characteristic—going to the root of issues and measuring their impact both inside their organizations and within society—that differentiates these nonprofit executives from the rest. This book is dedicated to them.

Successful Marketing Strategies For Nonprofit Organizations is written for nonprofit executives wondering where marketing fits within their organizations, for practitioners developing competitive strategies for their nonprofit organizations, and for those seeking to understand how marketing and competition fit in the nonprofit context. The discussion of marketing in the nonprofit world is still a relatively new subject for many nonprofit executives. In some quarters it is hushed over. It is my hope that *Successful Marketing Strategies For Nonprofit Organizations* will further the beginnings of open conversation on the subjects of marketing, strategy, and competition and will help spark continued dialogue among nonprofit directors.

I have had considerable support for this book from The McConkey/Johnston Consulting Group and, in particular, its principles Bill McConkey and Larry Johnston, as well as from the firm's marketing director, Jeff McLinden. Likewise, my writing has benefited from the thoughts of Larry Fuhrer, Richard Karppinen, Jimmy Locklear, Kathy Fitts, John Porter, Bill Chickering, Carolyn Hansen, Judy Packard, John Frank, Mark and Lisa Olson, Pete Sommer, and my Chicago-based Fielding Institute friends.

I also want to acknowledge the help of those within the Professional and Trade Group of John Wiley & Sons, particularly Marla J. Bobowick, who, as acquisitions editor, has been with this project from the start. Marla and all of her staff have been a constant help and a much needed source of encouragement and direction in finishing this project. In addition, I want to thank Julia Willard, without whose expert editing this book would not have been published.

My very close friends James and Roberta McLeish also helped me stay on target in the initial drafts of this project. James died before the manuscript's publication and his encouragement means more in hindsight than I can say. Finally, Deborah Lynn Porter McLeish read and reread countless drafts of this text while maintaining her medical practice.

To all of you I'd like to quote this passage by Frederick Buechner from *The Sacred Journey*:

> To journey for the sake of saving our own lives is little by little to cease to live in any sense that really matters, even to ourselves, because it is only by journeying for the world's sake—even when the world bores and sickens and scares you half to death—that little by little we start to come alive.[1]

Preface

N onprofit organizations account for more than one quarter of the entire American economy. According to Peter Drucker, the non-profit world can be thought of as America's largest employer. "Every other adult—a total of 80 million-plus people—works as a vol-unteer, giving on average nearly five hours each week to one or several nonprofit organizations. This is equal to 10 million full-time jobs." And if these volunteers were paid, their wages, even at a minimum rate, would amount to some $150 billion, or 5 percent of the GNP.[1]

Operating with for-profit businesses on the one hand, and the Unit-ed States Government on the other, the nonprofit sector includes educa-tional institutions, health care providers, houses of worship, social agen-cies, cultural institutions, fraternal organizations, voluntary groups, associations, and societies. Often involved in areas that government and business have chosen to ignore or not provide for, nonprofit organizations pursue socially responsive and service-oriented purposes and objectives.

These same organizations also have audiences they must deal with on a day-to-day basis, and their leaders routinely face product decisions, fund development questions, management tasks, and marketing options. These men and women who manage and control almost one million nonprofit organizations in the United States play a pivotal role in our workforce today. Not surprisingly, they have many of the same problems as their counterparts in government and for-profit companies in keeping their organizations alive in the face of a changing society and rapidly diminishing resources.

This book is principally concerned with those individuals who seek to sharpen their vision, direction, and marketing management savvy to better compete in an increasingly crowded and competitive nonprofit culture. Many nonprofit managers, marketing directors, development directors, annual fund officers, volunteer coordinators, board members, and stewardship officers have come to their tasks with very little prepa-ration for what they face. *Successful Marketing Strategies For Nonprofit Organizations* is written specifically for these people, and for those who have joined the marketing, advancement, stewardship, or fund development office and assumed responsibility for its functions.

In the broadest sense, marketing is a necessary business system that helps an organization develop an interactive approach to its various constituencies; helps evaluate the nonprofit organization's cause, appeal, acceptance, and product satisfaction among targeted audiences; and enables the organization to implement business strategies designed to achieve its goals.

Though seemingly necessary for almost all nonprofit organizations today, the marketing function has not always had a presence in the nonprofit world. As Philip Kotler says in his article, "Strategies for Introducing Marketing Into Nonprofit Organizations":

> Of all the classic business functions, marketing has been the last to arrive on the nonprofit scene. Some years earlier, nonprofit managers began to get interested in accounting systems, financial management, personnel administration, and formal planning. Marketing lagged, except where the nonprofit institution experienced a decline in clients, members, or funds. As long as institutions operated in a seller's market—as colleges and hospitals did throughout the 1960s—marketing was ignored, but as customers and/or resources grew scarce the word marketing was heard with increasing frequency, and organizations suddenly discovered marketing or reasonable facsimiles thereof.[2]

In this text, the idea of "marketing" is defined in terms that the nonprofit organization can use: identifying publics and audiences to help the causes, products, and markets it should offer; the method to communicate to the various audiences of the nonprofit organization; the pricing necessary to sustain the organization's services as well as the charitable dollar amounts needed from its donors; and the sustainable advantages that need to be developed, maintained, or positively exploited to allow the nonprofit organization to compete successfully.

This book attempts to show how marketing philosophies can define three relevant nonprofit issues:

1. the market(s) for the organization;
2. the organization's available resources; and
3. the business the organization is undertaking.

A brief overview follows, along with key objectives of the book.

First, this book makes the case that every nonprofit organization is already deeply involved in some form of marketing activity. But some leaders of nonprofit organizations who read this text may not have an officer assigned to the marketing task or be familiar with some of the language employed. Nevertheless, it becomes necessary for every organization interfacing with the public (or publics) to think in terms of what the organization is saying and asking of its audience; how the intended audience perceives, accepts, and responds to the communication; and the action(s) jointly taken. This is the essence of marketing.

Second, this book presents a strong proactive approach to the field of nonprofit marketing. In particular, the tack taken throughout the book is that marketing is driven by an external analysis orientation first rather than by the internal considerations common to many nonprofit organizations. The practical consequence of this external orientation is to elevate the stature, desires, and importance of constituents, donors, and supporters in a nonprofit organization's marketing strategy.

Third, this book draws on research from within multiple disciplines in order to make the strongest case for a nonprofit marketing orientation. Key concepts, models, and examples are used to give the reader positive insight, theory, and analysis as to how a marketing approach could be helpful to their organization. Case studies from research and real life examples are also used.

Fourth, this book looks at a number of for-profit marketing models and theories and adapts them for nonprofit readers. Nonprofit marketing theory is broken down into core elements that are easily translated to related planning forms and diagrams. A word of caution: what works in the for-profit sector may not always directly apply to the nonprofit sector; likewise, not everything that works for one nonprofit organization will work for another. This is an old excuse. Far more marketing principles work than nonprofit directors often care to admit. Nevertheless, there is a question about how much can be generalized across many different causes and situations. This text addresses principles that cut across broad sectors of the nonprofit world. For each person reading this book, the question will be to what extent these principles can be useful given your nonprofit organization's background, history, and cause.

ORGANIZATION

Chapter 1 provides an overview of marketing, defining it within the nonprofit context, and gives reasons why the marketing task is more important to the life blood of a nonprofit organization today than ever before.

In Chapter 2, after defining the word "strategy" in a nonprofit context, the chapter details why a marketing strategy is important to both the nonprofit organization and the philanthropic community—providing them both with a sense of purpose and movement toward the achievement of organizational and personal goals.

Chapter 3 provides an overview of the nonprofit marketing planning and research program and lays a framework for succeeding chapters.

Chapter 4 introduces the reader to the idea of undertaking external research analysis and the importance such information provides in being able to precipitate strategic events as well as to make strategic decisions. External analysis of the organization's constituency is critical in determining whether the organization is hitting or missing its goals.

Chapter 5 picks up the discussion from Chapter 3 and continues the emphasis upon external analysis as being key to an organization's ability to compete successfully. In this chapter and as part of the external analysis discussion, the reader looks at the competitive boundaries of the cause they are involved in and the environment that surrounds them.

Chapter 6 moves the reader from assessing his or her organization from the outside in to assessing it from the inside out to highlight internal marketing, managerial, or organizational deficiencies that must be corrected and to move the organization closer to its goals.

Chapter 7 is devoted to a discussion of organizational and marketing objectives, particularly as they relate to questions of why the nonprofit organization exists, its intended market, and where constituent goals fit into the organization's objectives.

Chapter 8 helps the reader take the information gathered from both the external and the internal analysis and begin the process of melding the information into a marketing strategy for the organization.

Chapter 9 provides the reader with a number of theoretical strategy frameworks to choose from, shows how they help nonprofit organizations in different ways, and allows the reader to merge his or her organization's past, present, and future into a coherent strategy.

Chapter 10 introduces the concept of public relations and provides insight into how a nonprofit organization can manage its external image.

Chapter 11 demonstrates how a nonprofit marketing practitioner can begin to think strategically and how he or she can implement strategic marketing choices.

As a final summary, Chapter 12 encapsulates the basic theories presented herein and makes a case for a concerted, proactive, and organized approach to marketing that could, possibly, revolutionize the methods of communicating with potential nonprofit volunteers, donors, constituents, and clients.

Contents

Part II THE EXTERNAL ANALYSIS

Chapter 4 External Analysis: Client, Donor, Volunteer, and Competitor Research 55

Chapter 5 Researching Your Nonprofit Organization's Environment 84

Table of Exhibits

xix

Success

To laugh often and much; to win the respect of intelligent people and the affection of children; to earn the appreciation of honest critics and endure the betrayal of false friends; to appreciate beauty; to find the best in others; to leave the world a bit better, whether by a healthy child, a garden patch or a redeemed social condition; to know even one life has breathed easier because you have lived. This is to have succeeded.

—RALPH WALDO EMERSON

PART ONE

Introduction

CHAPTER ONE

A New Way of Doing Business for the Nonprofit Organization

Philanthropy has become much more than simply asking for and receiving gifts, or setting up and supporting charitable causes and purposes. Philanthropy is larger than the good works it performs, and, because it has become a uniquely American tradition, its pervasive presence is largely taken for granted. Today, philanthropy promotes the quality of life, is carried out in a variety of ways, includes the concepts of charity and love towards strangers, and requires voluntary action for the benefit of others.[1]

James M. Greenfield
Fund Raising: Evaluating and Managing the Fund Development Process

Could anyone have predicted some of the changes that have occurred in the nonprofit marketplace in the last 10 years? Nonprofit practitioners today face social, governmental, and economic changes of unprecedented magnitude and variety. Such changes are based on the following facts:

- A global donor community has become a reality for many nonprofit organizations.
- Increased media sophistication has led donors to force nonprofit organizations to change their methods of communication.
- Fund raising has become a battlefield as nonprofit organizations compete for scarce resources.

3

- Data base fund raising has changed the way nonprofit organizations conduct business.
- The growth in the number of nonprofit organizations has caused competition for the same audiences.

These changes forever alter the way nonprofit organizations must operate in the future, requiring innovative responses that past practices simply cannot accommodate. The ideas and actions associated with "marketing" not only have become central to the nonprofit organization's actions and counteractions, but they have become necessities for its survival. This chapter attempts to provide some preliminary concepts and definitions in order to lay a good foundation for a more in-depth discussion of marketing analysis, planning, and implementation.

THE NEED FOR MARKETING ORIENTATION

Traditionally, marketing has not been a popular subject in nonprofit circles; competition is even less so. Marketing issues tend to lay our organizational souls bare and put us on trial. However, with flourishing competition in the nonprofit world, marketing and its attendant strategies *must* be taken into account to ensure the success—even the survival—of most nonprofit organizations. Today, nonprofit organizations are operating under more changes and pressures than ever before. Without closely monitored and implemented marketing strategies designed to take the organization through a particular course of action, and without the ability to change that course should the need arise, an organization risks being lost in the throes of internal and economic upheaval.

It is possible for a nonprofit organization to achieve competitive success despite diminished resources, increased constituent reticence, changing societal needs, and unflagging competition. This book explains how marketing principles can be used to develop a strong market and constituent orientation for a nonprofit organization's cause by providing a series of rational steps and arguments aimed at nonprofit practitioners who, traditionally, have not considered themselves as being part of the "marketing" team.

DEALING WITH NONPROFIT ORGANIZATIONS IN FLUX

Consider the state of most nonprofit organizations in operation today. Many are experiencing both internal and external turbulence. Internally, they may be weighed down by a hierarchy of top-heavy executives, little opportunity for subordinate employee advancement, or a variety of other human resource inequities. Externally, these same organizations are dealing with the need to reorganize, cut costs, improve communications, and involve their constituencies in more profitable ways. Yet the assumption that the nonprofit world is still one of relative calm is a longstanding belief that is not easily replaced.

A Changing Domain: Constituents and Supporters Want More Control

In today's climate of change, nonprofit organizations must serve four distinct groups: *clients, constituents, volunteers,* and *donors.* Clients are the individuals who the nonprofit organization serves directly and who are the immediate beneficiaries of its output. Constituents represent the consuming public that purchases some output from the organization—perhaps a book. Volunteers and donors (also called *supporters* by some organizations) supply or lend the nonprofit organization different types of resources: time, money, knowledge, encouragement, or facilities.

Each of these groups is distinct, yet, it is not unusual to observe some overlapping of the roles. Friends of a nonprofit organization may take on the role of donor, volunteer, constituent, or client by receiving benefits from the organization while providing a volunteer service at the same time.

The problems in serving these groups include their increasing lack of sustained loyalty to a cause as well as an increasing concern about how nonprofit organizations run their day-to-day operations. Given the sea of worthy causes from which an individual can choose to support, volunteer for, or seek services from, nonprofit organizations can no longer assume that today's constituent, volunteer, or donor will be theirs forever. In addition, organizations can no longer assume that the primary concern of their constituency is simply to see the organization "continue as usual." Nonprofit "friends" want to know where their dollar is going. In some cases, these groups want more control or, at least, more say in operational matters.

Networking Systems are Less Reliable

The traditional nonprofit networks are changing as well. Nonprofit organizations can no longer assume that certain individuals or corporations will supply volunteers, money, and publicity for their causes and activities just because they've done so in the past. Time and money have become premium possessions in our society and individuals and corporations are no longer as willing to part with them. For example, church-goers' donations can no longer be counted on to fund any church's many activities and causes. Religious organizations must look elsewhere for support.

New Policy Changes and Lack of Planning Contribute to the Turbulence

External changes also are producing growing uncertainty. One of the most important of these changes is the federal and state governments' new restrictive policies concerning tax deductions, postal subsidies, and what constitutes appropriate nonprofit activity. But the change that affects marketing the most is the growing competition between non-profit organizations for charitable dollars and time. Clearly this new environment in which nonprofits now operate must be taken into consideration before implementing any new plan. Some organizations are confronting these changes with long-range planning, innovation, and a renewed marketing spirit; others are floundering as work patterns and communication styles used for years no longer seem to fit. Both the internal organization and even its external supporters of these flounder-ing organizations have grown up with the view that nonprofit organi-zations are not subject to the economic and market constraints that apply to the rest of the economy and, therefore, need not employ tradi-tional (and maybe unexpected) "marketing" techniques. Nothing can be further from the truth. Today, nonprofit organizations must have a detailed marketing plan to maintain their constituencies.

The Need for a Philosophy of Change

"Today, the idea of modest change everywhere in the corporation is becoming orthodoxy," according to author and former editor of the *Harvard Business Review* Rosabeth Moss Kanter.[2] In essence, management has always assumed a calm environment in its operating style. A com-pany believes it can pretty much go where it wants. However, today, no sooner do you digest one new change and another reappears. There are, as Peter Vaill says, "Lots of changes going on at once." This is true in the nonprofit field as well. Much of the way nonprofits work today, as compared to 10 years ago, must be revitalized. This is no more appar-ent than in the way a nonprofit organization develops, evaluates, and implements strategies of solicitation and service.

Today, the typical nonprofit organization has some degree of momen-tum. It is going somewhere and its mission has either been decided implicitly, through organizational drift, or by individuals inside or outside the cause. A marketing strategy can play a significant role in transforming that momentum into an organization's productive direction. To accomplish this, one must relate an organization's marketing strategies to the surrounding competitive environment, melding the external world into the organization's internal operations, rather than waiting for new programs and new donors to solve all ills. Market and competitive realities can no longer be viewed as an embarrassing undertaking, or an unfortunate consequence: Strategy must be set through purposeful research and planning, to take the organization to the next level.

Adapting to Change

Nonprofit organizations must change the way they operate, the way they view themselves, and the way they manage their resources. Rather than create programs internally and introduce them to unsuspecting publics (as has been done by many in the past), a nonprofit organization must first orient itself to this new environment and then market for that environment. The organization should first build its programmatic, volunteer, and solicitation strategies by assessing and evaluating constituencies and markets, and then build its marketing strategies. This allows the organization to align its programs with the values and interests of its natural constituencies, creating a mutual bond.[3] This kind of competitive marketing strategy is a broad formula for:

1. how a nonprofit organization is going to undertake its business;
2. how it will deliver its services in a manner that gets the organization positively noticed and supported;
3. how it will identify its goals; and
4. outlining the systems and policies needed to carry them out.

MARKETING TO THE EXTERNAL WORLD

Critical to this discussion of marketing is the intended audience's point of view, which must be a part of the quality of service and attitude a nonprofit delivers. Successful nonprofit organizations should be able to bring resources together quickly upon recognizing new audience needs or values. Constituent, volunteer, and donor wants, expectations, and perceptions, taken seriously, can create a competitive edge in the field in which the nonprofit organization operates.

Unfortunately, external points of view do not always seem important, rational, or necessary to many organization executives. W. Edwards

Deming, the American management genius, sadly noted that American industry has become too stubborn to make the changes necessary to boost production, better control quality, and test new management practices.[4] Richard Darman, in a provocative speech made when he was Secretary of the Treasury noted, "Large-scale corporate America has a tendency to be bloated, risk averse, inefficient, and unimaginative."[5]

Both men might just as well have been talking about nonprofit organizations. The financial and managerial pressures facing nonprofit organization directors in the next 10 years will magnify these problems many times in intensity, more than any previous generation ever experienced. The nonprofit world must prepare itself for those pressures and for the competitive environment that will result. The first steps in this preparation are to:

1. define a marketing strategy;
2. define how it operates; and
3. ask why a nonprofit organization needs a marketing strategy.

"MARKETING" DEFINED

Those who have been involved in nonprofit marketing no doubt realize that as little as 10 years ago the word "marketing" was barely uttered aloud at "development" conferences. In fact, practitioners were often encouraged *not* to use the term.

Nonprofit organizations could afford to adopt this attitude as long as there were adequate resources. However, as institutions experienced a decline in funds, students, and members, "the word 'marketing'," according to Philip Kotler, "was heard with increasing frequency and organizations suddenly discovered marketing or reasonable facsimiles thereof."[6] Philip Kotler, author of *Strategic Marketing for Nonprofit Organizations* as well as many other books on marketing, is an internationally renowned expert on marketing and is the S.C. Johnson & Son Distinguished Professor of International Marketing at Northwestern University. In Kotler's text, nonprofit marketing is defined as: "the function of a nonprofit whose goal is to plan, price, promote, and distribute the organization's programs and products by keeping in constant touch with the organization's various constituencies, uncovering their needs and expectations for the organization and themselves, and building a program of communication to not only express the organization's purpose and goals, but also their mutually beneficial want-satisfying products."

This definition's underlying assumption is that if an organization does an adequate job of researching and thereby understanding the needs and wants of its constituents and designs programs and products to meet these needs, then the selling job is greatly reduced. The ease of selling is directly proportional to the internal make-up of the constituent, his or her needs, wants, and values. To get to such a point, however, requires innovation and a willingness to change.

Breaking the Status Quo

Unfortunately, the notion of nonprofit marketing for some has come to mean aggressive promotion, as opposed to aggressive listening to constituent needs. There has been a concentration of effort to communicate the nonprofit's needs first to the public, rather than first listening to its constituents. While promotional programs are a part of a marketing strategy, the strategy must first move away from the point of sale and ask this question: *Who are our constituents and what are their needs and wants?*

Defining the Constituents' Needs

Today's nonprofit supporters are more aware of what good performance means, are more aware of what they want from an organization, and are more concerned about their own values. It is here that marketing must function as the organization's "ear" in an everchanging environment. As such, the organization moves from a "we need" philosophy to a "they need and we can provide" philosophy based on both groups' participation in a commonly agreed upon end. At its most elementary level, nonprofit marketing takes place when an organization and an interested party come together for a mutually beneficial exchange of a service, resource or idea. This is known as *exchange theory;* it will be discussed later in this chapter.

Exhibit 1-1 contains a list of questions which can help to define "marketing" as it relates to all aspects of a nonprofit organization.

Research, in the form of listening to constituents, donors, and clients, allows the organization to uncover what is perceived to be special about its constituents, both in how they think and the benefits they want in relation to the nonprofit organization. In addition, listening to constituents produces more than just information on promotional tactics. Organizations discover whether their "product mix," comprising an organization's causes, style of activity or ministry, and "hard" product offerings like literature, should be maintained, increased, or phased out.

The *product mix* of an organization is the sum total of all of the organization's service outputs on behalf of particular constituencies.

The nonprofit organization's marketing plan should answer the following questions:

1. What are the targeted market(s)?
2. What are the key segments within these markets?
3. What are the needs of each market segment?
4. What "business" do constituents think the nonprofit is in?
5. How much interest or awareness does the organization's activities generate?
6. How satisfied are the current constituents with output?

Concerning resources:

1. What are the major strengths or weaknesses that could either limit or enable expansion?
2. What opportunities are presented that will enable an expanded resource base?

Concerning business orientation:

1. What is the organization's mission?
2. Who are the key constituents?
3. Who are the major competitors?
4. What benefits does the organization have that will allow a different position from competitors?
5. Are there market segments "open" from competition that would allow the organization to excel?

Exhibit 1-1   Defining marketing tasks

Research allows an organization to discover trends affecting its constituents (and ultimately, the nonprofit organization), the values of different market segments, whether constituents are satisfied with the organization's goals, and the benefits they are seeking. Exhibit 1-2 lists the benefits of research.

DEVELOP AN OUTLINE OF MARKETING STRATEGIES

Most nonprofit managers will agree that marketing must become as intrinsic to the nonprofit sector as it is to the for-profit sector. However, we find ourselves in a marketing "preculture," where we have adapted the terminology of for-profit marketers without any of their commensurate systems of evaluation and procedure. This preculture often nega-

Research allows an organization to:

1. assess new or emerging marketing opportunities;

2. furnish information for developing marketing plans, both short and long term;

3. provide information needed to solve problems that arise within an organization's constituencies;

4. know which marketing decisions have been correct and which ones are in need of change;

5. develop new promotional appeals; and

6. assess where it stands vis-à-vis its competitors in the light of marketplace activities.

Exhibit 1-2   Benefits of research

tively impacts the following five arenas of thought and action in the nonprofit world:

1. The *business* or *mission* the nonprofit organization is in and the corporate values and philosophy that are transmitted through its same mission.

2. *Exchange theory:* The notion that each party in the transaction should sense they are receiving more than they are giving up . . . the notion of *self-interest* as it relates to the exchange.

3. The actual *marketing task* itself, which stresses the importance of meeting consumer needs.

4. The *tools* the nonprofit marketer uses (sometimes called the *marketing* or *mix product*) such as advertising, fund raising, pricing, and channels of communication and distribution.

5. The nonprofit organization's *distinctive competencies* in which the organization concentrates on doing what it does best in order to minimize any weaknesses it might have.[7]

The marketing task is fundamentally a transaction in which the self-interest of both parties is key. The promotional tools and marketing mix available to the nonprofit practitioner has only one purpose: to satisfy efficiently and effectively their *half* of the transaction. By further identifying the areas in which a nonprofit excels, it can then strive to better serve individuals seeking competence in those same areas. Each of the above five elements are explained in the sections that follow.

The Organizational Mission

The marketing process begins with a definition of the mission or "business" the nonprofit organization is in. The mission is important for a variety of reasons, not the least of which is that it is the foundation on which all other marketing planning is built. An organization's mission is its purpose and reason for being, and may also serve to determine accurately the types of services it can provide.

The task of determining the mission is especially important because many nonprofit organizations shift their focus as the environment changes. A clear and simple mission statement composed several years ago may or may not still apply. In any case, the mission needs to be defined, re-defined, or at least reconsidered.

Although "mission" can be hard to define, it must be addressed in order to properly develop all of a nonprofit's marketing goals and its plan to meet those goals. Ultimately, mission has ramifications in three important areas:

1. Definition of the constituent groups (sometimes called "stakeholder groups") that will be served. If there is agreement on the organization's mission through an analysis of constituent perceptions and feelings, the effect can be a powerful catalyst for the organization to achieve its goals.

2. Identification of the needs of the constituents that will be satisfied by the nonprofit organization. The organization must know what criteria stakeholders are using to judge the success of its performance.

3. The ultimate strategy by which the needs of the constituency will be satisfied. The strategies and philosophies used by the nonprofit must be in keeping with its core set of values; otherwise there is little chance of achieving stakeholder satisfaction.

In essence, a nonprofit's mission, when well defined, can be translated into a plan that will enable the organization to meet its goals.

The Self-Interest Aspect: Exchange Theory

A nonprofit organization is often consumed with its need for more outside involvement in order to harvest the additional resources it constantly requires. Marketing must answer the problem of how to get the desired response from those groups the organization has targeted for involvement.

Imagine a simple scale. One side of the balance is weighted down by the needs of the organization. The other side is weighted down by the benefits that a person receives by being involved in the organization. Which side is heavier? Which side is heavier in your organization? There should be a balance.

The key to success is to bring about a certain level of satisfaction in its various constituents. This can be accomplished surreptitiously through what is commonly called an "exchange." Under the *Exchange Theory* an individual gives up something (e.g., time, money) in exchange for something else. The individual should perceive the return to be of greater value than that which he or she has given up. *The receiving is thus the motivation for the giving.* The following explanation is offered as an example:

A sense of prestige often plays a major role in convincing people to serve on boards. Similarly, donors are often motivated not only by the feeling that they are part of an exclusive group but by being made to feel generous, important, and central to an organization's success or failure. For a volunteer, the self-image of being essential, being needed, and belonging is often what explains why they work hard for no compensation.[8] Successful exchanges comprise several factors:

- activities
- markets
- prospects
- costs
- benefits
- associated costs
- nonfinancial benefits

Exchanges are *activities* that are engaged in by at least two parties. Each party has a goal. The organization initiating the exchange is the *marketer* and the individual is the *prospect*.

In a pure subsistence economy, each family produces exactly all the goods that it consumes over a period of time. There is no need to look further for other goods or services because each family unit is self-sufficient. Marketing does not occur because marketing is about two or more parties wanting to exchange something for something else. A *market* then is a group of buyers and sellers bargaining in terms of exchange for goods and services.

A *prospect* is someone who is likely to want to be involved with an exchange of some kind. For example, a volunteer prospect might be someone who is willing to give his or her time in exchange for the satisfaction of knowing they helped out in a worthy cause.

There are *costs*, as well as *benefits*, to each party. The individual's costs may be money and/or time. These are relatively easy to calculate. There may also be costs that are more difficult to assess. In the case of a non-profit client, "What are the psychic costs of admitting one's inadequacy, the presumed reason for seeking help?"[9] A donor may also worry about supporting an organization with a potentially controversial or distinct point of view.

The organization also has *associated costs:* in mounting its marketing effort, in managing the client process, in dealing with government regulations, and in dealing with the positive or negative aspects of personalities involved in the process.

Exchanges are not always directly financial; they can also be social or economic exchanges. Social rewards may be internal and not easily delineated or calculated. For example, by being a part of a particular nonprofit and its programs, I may reaffirm particular belief systems I have in how people should be treated or how a cause should be advanced. Economic rewards, on the other hand, are usually clearly spelled out and may have some extrinsic value leading to benefits outside the exchange relationship. For example, a donor participating at a certain financial level may receive name recognition, networking possibilities, invitations to prominent events, all of which have indirect economic impact.

The exchange process is not always simple; it can be complex. Armand Lauffer is a professor of social work at the University of Michigan and author of *Strategic Marketing for Not-for-Profit Organizations.* Lauffer cites the following example:

> When you make a contribution to the United Way, you do not expect thanks from the agencies that are to be recipients of the funds raised or from their clients who are the ultimate beneficiaries. You may, however, experience a sense of well being at having met a social obligation.[10]

Therefore, some degree of less clearly defined "exchange" should be considered.

Exchanges assume that each participant is involved voluntarily. Each participant is free to accept or reject any part of the offer. Successful nonprofit organizations view exchanges as singular events and as a series of events over time. For example, in relationships with donors, nonprofit organizations ultimately assign someone to manage the exchanges in order to maintain the right types of associations with donors over extended time periods.

Exchange partners	Type of exchange sought
A. Donor Nonprofit organization	Recognition, involvement, gratitude Resources, growth potential, service
B. Volunteer Nonprofit organization	Service, community, worthiness Cheap labor, lowering of costs
C. Board member Nonprofit organization	Significant contribution, access to leadership Wisdom, leadership, access to knowledge
D. Client Nonprofit organization	Personal benefits, services, friendship Fulfillment of mission, success, contribution

Exhibit 1-3   A simple listing of exchanges sought between a nonprofit organization and its constituents

Exhibit 1-3 lists exchanges between a nonprofit and different constituents that might be involved with the organization, and each party's reason for involvement.

THE MARKETING TASK

For-Profit vs. Nonprofit

The marketing function in the for-profit sector assumes that good marketing management creates truly satisfied consumers and, ultimately, company profitability. This world assumes a profit motive, a primary constituency (donors, clients, etc.) for the company to work with, and the ability to allocate resources based on the viability of a product or service and its acceptance within a constituency. There are intrinsic characteristics that are unique to nonprofit marketing, however.

First, nonprofit organizations do not seek to make a "profit" yet often find it necessary to generate surpluses of revenue over expenses to fund unpopular or unfundable parts of the organization.

Second, some causes do not lend themselves easily to performance evaluation. For example, a university may want to provide education for all classes of people. Although these organizations may create a psychological or social "profit," actual performance measurement is difficult.

Third, it is difficult in a nonprofit organization to determine how a nonprofit manager allocates resources without an accurate assessment of previous performance levels. Many nonprofits do not charge for services rendered. How does a nonprofit director gauge the correctness of decisions to enhance some programs and curtail others?

Finally, if the essence of the marketing task is meeting the needs of the constituent, how does a nonprofit organization do so if its mission is inconsistent with the desires of at least some of its constituents, as in the case of an anti-drug or anti-tobacco organization?

The differences between for-profit and nonprofit organizations as they relate to the marketing task are most pronounced in three areas:

1. the profit motive;
2. the nature of a nonprofit organization's constituency; and
3. resource attraction.

The Profit Motive

A nonprofit organization, by its definition, does not operate to produce a profit. In other words, nonprofit organizations do not have a *profit motive*. However, the profit motive gives for-profit managers a control tool that is far superior to most nonprofit control tools. The nature of the profit motive allows managers to better measure the efficiency and effectiveness in reaching their objectives. For example, relatively simple mathematical calculations will reveal what percentage of income is actual profit. The nonprofit manager must deal in the area of "services rendered" which, in most nonprofit organizations, is a nebulous concept not easily measured or evaluated. Nonprofit managers try to measure intangibles such as services provided and numbers of large donors, not the "bottom line." In essence, a nonprofit manager must establish a financial model between money spent and services rendered.

The Nature of the Nonprofit Organization's Constituency

To further complicate matters, a nonprofit organization usually deals with two principal constituencies:

1. clients for whom the nonprofit exists and to whom goods and services are provided; and
2. donors (and volunteers) who provide the majority of resources allowing the nonprofit organization's service to take place.

This dual constituency makes the marketing task even more complex.

The profit-motivated company has one marketing function—namely, to facilitate a direct two-way exchange which simultaneously includes both resource allocation (providing goods and services) and resource attraction (obtaining revenue). By contrast, the nonprofit organization must approach these two tasks separately because they involve separate constituencies.[11] (see Exhibit 1-3.)

A fairly common example of this difficulty is the real-life scenario many nonprofit organizations face today: The services the organization is providing, whether the client likes them or not, may not meet the expectations of the organization itself. Likewise, nonprofit organizations may also face a situation in which the resources provided by the donor or volunteer do not meet with the expectations or satisfaction of the recipient.

Nonprofit organizations may provide services to clients because of donor or volunteer pressure that the services be offered and not necessarily because management feels this is the best for either the nonprofit or the clients served. For example, one can easily give money to help build houses in Mississippi or to feed the hungry in Rwanda, without knowing *how well these services are being delivered by the nonprofits to the people that are in need of them.*

Resource Attraction

Resource attraction is the attraction of funding and other resources to nonprofit organizations. A nonprofit organization's resources typically have been obtained by communication of its needs through one or a combination of the following four paths:

1. A "keep quiet" about our needs approach.
2. An advertising and public relations approach.
3. A mass media solicitation approach where the need is made known along with a "hard ask."
4. A strong personal selling approach.

Each path, or combination of paths, requires a different marketing strategy, and each leads to a different outcome. This text does not attempt to cover all the possible marketing and sales approaches since there have been volumes written about what works and what does not, and since "what works" for one industry may not work for another. (See the notes for a listing of books that may prove helpful to the reader in this endeavor.[12]).

There are typically five issues a nonprofit marketer must consider in planning for resource attraction:

1. *Demographic research.* The nonprofit marketer must seek information concerning the demographic nature of either the nonprofit's clients or supportive constituency.

2. *Articulating the mission.* Nonprofit strategy must address "donor fatigue" caused by excessive competition in some industries. The strategy must also specify the mix of resources needed to carry out the organization's marketing task.

3. *Targeting audiences.* Nonprofit organizations are constantly under pressure to be "democratic" in their approach. Internal politics and the fact that a nonprofit organization often deals with multiple constituencies must be set aside in order to target the most appropriate audiences for solicitation or service. This may entail exclusion of other audiences.

4. *Pricing.* Typically, nonprofit organizations have less pricing flexibility than their for-profit cousins. The problem is amplified with those nonprofit organizations which rely solely on contributions and give their services away for free. The nonprofit organization must determine realistically how much money can be raised and how much money can be charged for services.

5. *Resource allocation.* The nonprofit organization should develop a resource allocation strategy. The way funds are distributed in an organization ultimately helps to define its mission. Some nonprofit organizations undertake causes that are tangential to their own mission; other nonprofits undertake causes that constituencies will not support or are perceived as being "outside" the organization's scope of expertise. A clear definition of what is and what is not in keeping with the mission will positively affect the organization's ability to raise funds and solicit volunteers. Mission is discussed in detail in Chapter 7.

MARKETING TOOLS

The marketing tools (or *marketing mix*) with which a nonprofit attracts resources, accomplishes constituent persuasion, and executes appropriate program allocation encompass:

1. the nonprofit organization's communication program;
2. its pricing policy;
3. its causes or products; and
4. its distribution channels.

Houston Elam and Norton Paley are authors of the book *Marketing for Nonmarketers.* Elam is a professor of marketing at Metropolitan State College of Denver and Paley is President of Alexander-Norton, Inc., consultants in marketing planning and strategy. According to Elam and Paley, marketing can be viewed as *a systemic philosophy and approach to doing business.* It is equally important to recognize that marketing requires interacting business activities, reinforcing the premise that each area of management has a stake in the successful operation of the company and depends on every other area if it is to do its part properly.[13] In essence, marketing tools are interdependent with all other aspects of doing business.

The nonprofit organization's marketing mix can be expressed in two different organizational formats. First, marketing can take the form of a *marketing campaign.* A campaign is usually an extended effort by an organization to reach specific financial, membership, or other resource goals within a particular time period. A marketing campaign is often evidenced by a concerted effort on the part of the organization and its supporters.

This specific effort on behalf of a unique organizational goal is in contrast to the second type of marketing, which has to do with an agency's day-to-day marketing operations and its ongoing relationship with its donors, customers, volunteers, and clients in their joint undertakings and interactions. Marketing, in this sense, is the attempt by the organization to accomplish its short-term, day-to-day goals. The lines differentiating "marketing campaigns" and "marketing" can appear to be indistinct because the activities comprising both are similar. They include the following:

- Both marketing operations take into account and target appropriate audiences to accomplish goals. Likewise, target audience members (donors, volunteers, and members) are empowered to achieve their individual goals through personal involvement.

- Messages of encouragement, solicitation, and benefit are sent by those inside the organization to those outside, and messages of acceptance, displeasure, and encouragement are sent from outside the organization to the inside. These messages allow action by both parties.

- Individuals targeted by the nonprofit organization as key to the success of its efforts are given a way to respond appropriately to the offers and/or causes being presented by the nonprofit.

- Both the nonprofit and the individual receive adequate benefits in order to be or feel successful.

- Day-to-day marketing operations and more intensive marketing campaigns have clear, concise goals and objectives; the individual's partnership with the nonprofit organization is stated clearly.
- In every marketing effort, there is a group of nonresponders to whatever is presented.

Appealing to the Constituency

"Marketing campaigns" and "marketing" can appear to be similar, however, each must be considered separately for purposes of planning and execution, for the following reasons:

- There must be some degree of current interest in the subject matter for most people to respond affirmatively to what is being said or asked for by an organization.
- The information presented by an organization must usually be compatible with an individual's prior attitudes in order for an individual to be receptive.
- People respond in different ways to the same material and their response depends on their beliefs and attitudes.

The Importance of a Communications Program

A nonprofit organization's marketing campaign and daily marketing operations depend on its communications program. (See Exhibit 1-4.) Most communications efforts by nonprofit organizations rely heavily on advertising media (direct mail, space advertising, electronic advertising, etc.) to accomplish specific marketing mix goals. These goals typically range from fund raising to client recruitment to volunteer enrollment. Increasingly, nonprofit organizations are using personalized selling techniques to augment this marketing mix.

Pricing

One of the principal goals of a communication program is to relay information about the nonprofit organization's *pricing* policies. Pricing is the amount of resources demanded by a seller.

In a for-profit company, price is the direct link between resource allocation and resource attraction. A company's product price allows it to attract more resources than expended for the product's production. Some nonprofit organizations seek to emulate this system by charging fees for services. In undertaking such a move, a nonprofit organization

1. Annual Report designed for donors, volunteers, and friends.

2. A fact and/or photo book to provide a mid-year update on the organization's operation.

3. Some type of quarterly (minimum) newsletter to discuss subjects of importance to the constituency.

4. Press releases to communicate fast-breaking news of significance.

5. Specialty brochures to promote different aspects of a nonprofit organization's program.

6. Some type of public meetings or gatherings to give management and supportive constituents a chance to interact.

7. Mass marketing efforts like direct mail, advertising, space ads, telemarketing, television specials.

8. Highly targeted events for purposes of conveying special information to preselected audiences.

Exhibit 1-4   Elements of a typical communication program

relies on a single constituency—its clients—to ensure financial viability through the price it charges for its services.

Other nonprofit organizations use more than one constituency— donors and clients—in their day-to-day operations. Two constituencies usually implies two pricing considerations. Donors provide different dollar amounts—some are asked for higher amounts and others lesser amounts. (Technically, donors in this situation are paying different fees.) Clients are also not always charged the same "price." Some nonprofit organizations have different categories of clients, charging different "prices" for services rendered.

For example, a halfway house for drug addiction might offer walk-in treatment at one price, a methadone program at another, and ongoing care at another. Other nonprofit organizations do not charge a fee *per se* for their services; nevertheless, a psychological "fee" is exacted through a "commitment" to the organization and its goals. This outward working of an organization's goals is expressed to the general public through its programs or "products."

Viewing the service as a "product" within the nonprofit context is a relatively new concept. And yet the programs—or products—offered by a nonprofit organization are its most important elements. Programs are what clients and donors accept and help fund. Program goals shape a nonprofit organization's mission.

For most organizations with two primary constituencies (donor and client) "two product" policies should also be in place. Using our previously mentioned halfway house example, donors most likely feel the "product" they are buying is both helping men and women overcome a serious problem, as well as contributing positively to a local or societal problem. The client, on the other hand, is usually buying immediate help for an urgent situation. What is the product provided to a donor? Broadly defined, a donor looks at the cluster of benefits surrounding his or her involvement—intangible items such as being a part of something, being sought out, a feeling of satisfaction and pride—as the "product." The client, on the other hand, looks at the actual services provided and the clients' level of satisfaction with those services as the "product."

Program/Product Distribution

Finally, how does a nonprofit organization deliver or distribute its programs or products to the right audiences? Usually, the following key questions surround a nonprofit organization's distribution system:

1. Where is the best place for a nonprofit organization to sell its services?
2. Where and how will the nonprofit organization collect its donations?
3. Will the nonprofit organization place its programs in the same areas from which it is raising funds? Or in different areas?
4. How will the nonprofit organization access information from its distribution channels in order to improve its services?

USE DISTINCTIVE COMPETENCIES TO ASSESS THE COMPETITION

In another effort to define nonprofit marketing practices in terms that would relate to the for-profit world, the term *distinctive competency* arises. Basically, a distinctive competency is an area of operation in which a nonprofit organization does better than its competitors. The fundamental reason to look at a nonprofit organization's distinctive competencies is to assess the presence of "competitors" offering the same or similar services to the same constituency.

In the for-profit world, competition theoretically forces an organization to better serve its consumers. How, then, does a nonprofit organization distinguish itself from competitors in order to be rewarded by strong consumer confidence and financial viability? By evaluating its role in terms of how it serves its clients and donors, and measuring the programs and services it offers against those of other nonprofit organizations. In this way, an organization can begin to pinpoint the tasks it performs best.

To unlock a nonprofit organization's areas of competence and then "sell" those competencies, an organization undertakes an internal and external analysis of its organization, its delivery systems, the way it charges and raises funds, and the way it promotes itself to publics at large. The goal of this external and internal look is to "audit" every system in light of the organization's mission and the service it provides to its constituents. With this information, the nonprofit organization can then set its goals and develop marketing strategies to meet them.

SUMMARY

Chapter 1 has presented an overview of how the concept of marketing functions in the nonprofit world. Chapter 2 details why a marketing strategy is important to both a nonprofit organization and the philanthropic community in providing each with a sense of purpose and movement towards the achievement of organizational and personal goals.

CHAPTER TWO

Building a Competitive Marketing Strategy

The reality of marketing is that a market consists of consumers strongly or weakly held by a range of competitors. A marketing campaign consists, therefore, of holding onto your customers while at the same time attempting to take customers away from your competition.[1]

Al Ries and Jack Trout

Bottom-Up Marketing

T he following three real-life examples show organizations in difficult situations.

ST. HUGO

St. Hugo of the Hills, a gleaming $7 million edifice of clear glass and white marble, was being officially dedicated. The throng packing the starkly modern church testified to the number of Catholics living in Bloomfield Hills, Detroit's richest suburb.

Standing at the altar, Cardinal Edmund C. Szoka pronounced the new church "a fitting and worthy manifestation" of a vibrant Christian community.

Standing at the back was Joyce Townsend, a retired telephone worker. She and 20 friends, most of them blacks from innercity

Detroit, wore buttons that read, "Let Our Churches Live." They were silently protesting the cardinal's closing 30 innercity Detroit churches last year and his listing 25 more that might get axed.

The sprinkling of black faces at the edge of a sea of whites dramatized the financial struggle confronting 55 million Catholics, the nation's largest religious group. Like many an ossifying corporation, the U.S. Catholic Church isn't working as well as it once did.[2] How does the Catholic church address its black constituency? Its financial issues?

D.A.T.E.

Drug Alcohol Tobacco Education (D.A.T.E.) writes in its December newsletter, "Full-time staff have been reduced from 7 to 6 and pay raises have been curtailed. Printing of classroom handout materials has been stopped. Publication of our new curriculum modules has been shelved. Our prevention specialists have not been assigned to any schools until next year. The Prevention Institute has been postponed indefinitely."[3] Why is this much-needed course in such jeopardy? Clearly, as D.A.T.E. is making great strides, it is experiencing setbacks—How can this be?

SPRING HILL CAMP

Spring Hill Camp has turned away 1,000 or more potential campers for each of its last six camping seasons because each year the camp has filled to capacity. Says camp director Mark Olson, "I'm happy at the support we get from campers, but shouldn't our future direction be to open other camps in different parts of the country so no young person gets turned away from attending?"[4]

A DEFINITION OF STRATEGY

A nonprofit organization needs a marketing strategy in order to provide itself, its volunteers and philanthropic supporters, and those directly benefiting from its work with a substantial sense of purpose and movement toward the achievement of the organization's goals. A marketing strategy is a way for all parties to see effective goal and resource attainment; it is also a way to ensure that limited resources are used wisely in pursuit of those goals. In fact, a nonprofit organization must be an effective strategist if its organization is to fulfill not only its short-term but also its long-term goals and mission.

A Disciplined Effort

As illustrated in Exhibit 2-1, a marketing strategy is a disciplined effort, enacted through a management system with a goal of developing and producing actions that help the organization understand what is needed, and to then determine the marketing strategy to attain those goals. The ensuring strategy includes both a look at the nonprofit organization's *output*—programs, products, and the "markets" available to the organization—to determine within which the organization should compete, as well as a look at its *input*—from supporters and from those it serves—to help initiate sustainable competitive advantages in each market. A course

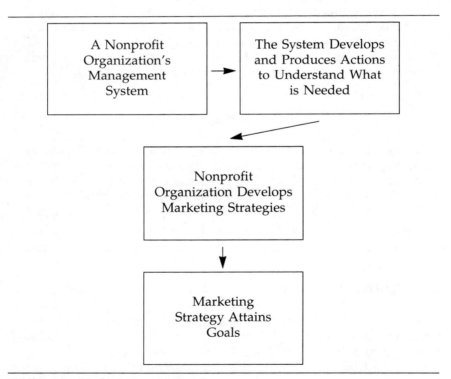

Exhibit 2-1   Marketing strategy process

of rational action, extracted from many alternatives, is then selected, which helps ensure a sense of identity and direction for the organization.

Answers to "Who We Are"

A marketing strategy helps reinforce internally and externally the answers to such fundamental organizational questions as:

- What is the purpose of our organization?
- Who are the people we support and serve and what are the methods of service we value?
- What are our goals in shaping the environment?
- How are we funded and resourced?
- What business are we in?
- What are our goals in shaping the surrounding conditions and influences upon our organization?

An Environment of Cooperation

Such a strategy builds cooperation between the organization's funding and volunteer base, the constituency it serves, and those who lead and influence the organization. The process and presence of a marketing strategy builds a common framework of assumptions and information, and helps differentiate those who support the organization from those who support other competing organizations.

This sense of purpose, embodied in strategy, especially is important as this nation redefines its national and community strategies. As the three authors of *The Nonprofit Organization* put it:

> This is a time of unparalleled opportunity and danger . . . Without a clear sense of identity and a strategic plan, non-profit organizations flounder in a sea of competing sorrows, always at the whim of whatever well-articulated hard luck story motivates action.[5]

Not only has the nonprofit environment drastically changed in the last few years, it has also become increasingly interdependent with the for-profit environment. Changes in both environments tend to have unpredictable consequences. Those changes include demographic changes, value shifts, shifts in federal and state funding priorities, economic, domestic versus international, and political factors, or the increased cultural importance of the nonprofit sector. In addition, the boundaries that traditionally have separated public and nonprofit organizations from the private sector have also eroded. This ultimately has led to a diversification of power.

Sovereignty, for example, is increasingly "farmed out." Weapon systems are produced not in government arsenals but by private industry. Taxes are not collected by government tax collectors but are withheld by private and nonprofit organizations from their employees and turned over to the government. The nation's health, education, and welfare are a public responsibility, yet increasingly we rely on private and nonprofit organizations for the production of services in these areas.[6]

According to John Bryson in his book *Strategic Planning For Public And Nonprofit Organizations:*

> This increased turbulence and interconnectedness requires a three-fold response from public and nonprofit organizations (and communities). First, these organizations must think strategically as never before. Second, they must translate their insights into effective strategies to cope with changed circumstances. And third, they must develop the rationales necessary to lay groundwork for the adoption and implementation of their strategies.[7] (See Exhibit 2-2.)

DEFINING STRATEGY: A FIRST STEP

A nonprofit organization's director might talk about the organization's marketing strategy using words like "vision," "intuition," "judgment," "analysis," and "advantage." Indeed, a competitive strategy may be grounded and developed through a realistic assessment of some of these concerns. More likely, however, it is not.

How, then, would your organization define a marketing strategy? For many nonprofit management professionals, a marketing strategy is the summary of how the organization pursues its objectives. Such a strategy starts with the combination of the organization's mission and a realistic assessment of its ability to realize this mission. This assessment comes from a careful analysis of what the nonprofit organization provides and what its constituents think they are getting in return, as well as a strong sense of organizational conviction.

Many find it helpful to build a marketing strategy by first defining six elements:

1. Mission.
2. Market and services.

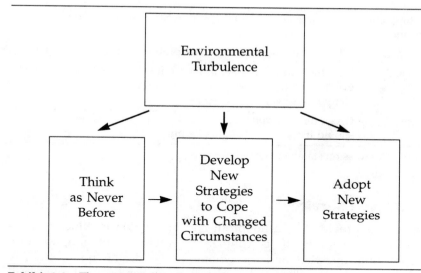

Exhibit 2-2   The organization's response

3. Knowledge of competition.
4. Competitive advantages.
5. Marketing and fund raising budget.
6. Commitment.

Mission

A nonprofit organization may have (or may be able to develop) competitive advantages, but these do not matter unless there are specific organizational objectives toward which the advantages can be directed. A nonprofit organization must compete for a purpose and that purpose should be its mission. Without objectives, competitive advantages are meaningless. In addition, without these same organizational objectives, constituencies and associates don't know where the nonprofit organization is going. Consider the criteria outlined in Exhibit 2-3 and develop a short mission statement. The mission statement should be no longer than one paragraph.

All of your programs should be measured against this mission, and those that do not seek to accomplish the mission should be discontinued.

Developing a mission statement requires a nonprofit organization to answer three questions:

Question 1:	What is the purpose for our nonprofit organization's existence?
Question 2:	Will this purpose change in the future if externally significant events change, such as political, economic, social, or competitive events?
Question 3:	Given the nonprofit organization's response to Question 2, should it consider changing its purpose?

Exhibit 2-3   Mission statement criteria

Market and Services

The services provided by a nonprofit and the market in which it operates define the scope of its competitive environment and, in turn, impose limits on what and for whom it provides. A nonprofit may expand not only its offerings but also the number of constituencies it serves. Each move has competitive consequences, allowing an organization to establish a very narrow marketing approach—limited services appealing to a small audience, a broader based approach, and/or a variety of services appealing to diverse audiences. (Research of market and services are discussed in Chapters 4 and 5.)

Competition

The knowledge of other nonprofit organizations with similar missions, the approach they take with their constituents, and an approximation of the amount they spend on promotions allows a nonprofit organization to evaluate its own programs and eliminate duplication. The process starts by asking how a nonprofit competes:

- What actions are our competitors taking?
- How does our nonprofit develop a strategic position within our field?
- What will our nonprofit industry look like 10 years from now?

Questions like these should form the basis of a nonprofit organization's marketing plans and strategic thinking.

Any organization trying to gain a portion of consumer dollars—philanthropic or otherwise—has competition. And the competition is not only from other nonprofit organizations. It also comes from within the organization's constituency—that is, from the demands made on the dollars and time of each individual involved with the organization.

Competitive Advantages

Competitive advantages are those qualities of programs or services offered that distinguish your nonprofit organization from other organizations offering similar programs or services. These advantages come in a variety of forms:

- Services or programs of the highest quality available.
- The most reasonably priced services or programs.
- The most experienced staff.
- The most variety of services offered.
- The most highly endorsed services or programs.

Nonprofit organizations must be able to identify their competitive advantages; failure to do so puts them at a disadvantage.

How does an organization identify its competitive advantage vis-à-vis other nonprofits? Primarily, one first determines who one's competitors are, the particular strengths and weaknesses of their causes or products, numbers of people involved in supporting their work, the dollar amount that the organization spends on its cause and the revenue or dollars raised that it takes in. Using this information, the marketing director of a nonprofit organization can set up a competitive analysis worksheet, listing each of its competitors' strengths in one column and its own neutralizing responses in the other. Armed with this information, the marketing director then can begin to calculate strategies.

Marketing and Fund-raising Budget

The number of dollars allocated to marketing and to the fund-raising effort contributes significantly to the success or failure of a strategy. This includes not just money, but time, volunteers, and services provided. There are various formulas available to determine how much a marketing department should spend on programs and promotions. Questions like the following should be evaluated:

- Are some programs operating at a loss because organizational conscience dictates them?

- Are some programs operating profitably, allowing the organization to accomplish not only programmatical objectives but other objectives as well?
- Is the organization investing in the growth of other programs, hoping they will break even in the future?
- Should some services and programs be discontinued because they no longer meet the needs they were designed for?

If certain programs are suspect, or elicits statements such as:

"Our measures of success are unclear regarding the program."
"As an organization, we're unsure how we'll accomplish the objectives."
"We do not have enough resources to meet our goals."
"Our constituency is no longer interested in the program."

then they should be carefully evaluated.

Commitment

A successful competitive strategy requires a stated, financially supported commitment from top management down. Without the means and organizational commitment to support a strategy, the nonprofit organization is hamstrung when it comes to necessary activities like coordinating resources, providing a forum to work together organizationally, hiring, and developing a direction. Getting top level commitment for a strategic marketing plan usually involves some or all of the following:

- Tell the absolute truth about the situation using plain talk.
- Be able to clearly articulate the organization's strengths and failures.
- The plan must be simple.
- The plan must have "compromise points."
- The plan needs to be packaged in light of the organization's goals.
- The plan needs to take into account the audience.
- The plan needs to focus on key audience segments critical to the organization's success.

A strategy helps an organization to go where it has decided it wants to go. Without a conscious plan in place, competitive direction ultimately becomes a series of reactions rather than actions—someone asks for organizational help and you help; you are asked to jointly sponsor an event and you do so; another nonprofit organization publishes an annual report so you print one.

The demand for many social services is likely to escalate, as unemployment and its attendant domestic problems affect more Americans. Yet with many states already in economic distress, non-profit social-service groups cannot expect government budgets to cover their growing needs.

More nonprofit agencies may have to join forces to try to influence legislation affecting their budgets and operations.

Chief executives of nonprofits face the prospect of having to spend more of their time raising money.

Organizations that have lost government grants are turning to corporations and private foundations for support—but many of those donors continue to resist making grants for operational expenses or to replace lost government support.

After a decade of bull markets, foundations face the prospect of diminishing returns on their asset portfolios—which may mean less money available for grants.[8]

THE OPERATING ENVIRONMENT'S EFFECTS ON MARKETING STRATEGY

Every nonprofit organization is affected in some way by its competitive strategy or lack thereof. In order to begin to develop a strategy, an organization must first look at the donor, constituent, and supporter environment within which it operates to determine how to proceed. As an example, during the months that the United States was involved in the Gulf War, donations to many nonprofit organizations experienced either an increase or a decrease. Most professionals agreed that the Gulf War had an impact on the attention, support, and giving of hundreds of non-profit donors.

The impact of the war upon nonprofit organizations may have been as simple as diverting people's attention or loyalty away from their favored organizations. Some donors and volunteers to nonprofit organizations may have chosen not to leave their television sets for fear of missing important news. Organizational mail may have gone unnoticed. Or, individuals may have been afraid to part with resources in a world that seemed very uncertain. This is just an example of the potentially great effect that the environment can have on the individual donor, and hence, the nonprofit organization.

The following sections look at individual lifestyles, the situations and organizations they're involved in, and the resultant effect on nonprofit institutions they may or may not support.

The Individual: Dealing with a Lack of Loyalty

An article in *NonProfit Times* entitled "Dealing with a Shifting World" states:

> In essence, everything we do is being touched in one way or another by massive forces of change. It's important for nonprofit organizations to recognize that the future is already in the present. We cannot afford the luxury of a historical perspective.[9]

George Barna, in his book *The Frog in the Kettle,* similarly contends that an individual's beliefs and values will undermine institutional loyalty. A lack of individual loyalty clearly poses a problem for the future of some nonprofit organizations who assume they will get public support for their programs as long as they continue "doing what they have done for years." This expectation of a noninterruption of gifts threatens an organization's future viability. This is also a focus of *The Donor Bond,* which explains that nurturing an organization's donors through a continuous reinforcement process called *relationship marketing* may be one of the few strategies left to offset this lack of donor and institutional loyalty.[10] Relationship marketing is the means by which a nonprofit organization genuinely involves donors, volunteers, customers, and other constituents in all aspects of the organization and serves as an integrator, bringing these interested parties into the organization as active participants in shaping the future of the nonprofit organization.

There are other signs that contribute to individuals' loosening sense of commitment:

- The divorce rate is climbing.
- Studies show that adults feel they have fewer close friends.
- Brand loyalty has dropped in most product categories.
- The proportion of people willing to join an organization as a formal member is declining.
- Fewer people are willing to make long-term commitments.
- The percentage of adults who consider it their duty to fight for their country, regardless of the cause, has dropped.

- The percentage of people who commit to attending events but fail to show is on the rise.

Given some of these indicators, how does an organization build a constituency of "friends" willing to commit to join a cause?

Lifestyle and Demographic Trends

American culture has become increasingly fragmented, and factors such as double-income families and higher divorce rates have blurred demographic lines and forced new thinking on the part of nonprofit marketers.

FORTUNE magazine calls the individuals who contribute to these demographic and lifestyle changes the "Tough Customers."[11] While some would disagree that customers are tougher to sell today than, say, 10 years ago, most certainly would agree that the way a company or nonprofit organization sells customers, volunteers or donors is changing, much of it due to these lifestyle and demographic changes. Says FORTUNE about these customers:

> Meet the paradigm of today's tougher U.S. customers—demanding, inquisitive, discriminating. No longer content with planned obsolescence, no longer willing to tolerate products that break down, they are insisting on high-quality goods that save time, energy, and calories; preserve the environment; and come from a manufacturer they think is socially responsible.[12]

Shouldn't a nonprofit organization expect that many of its donors, volunteers, and clients will exhibit some of these same characteristics? Constituencies are experiencing tremendous change, and it is worthwhile to look at this phenomenon from the point of view of competition. With the bulk of the baby-boomers reaching middle age, a nonprofit organization's administration must expect its marketing and financial cultures to change. Clearly, the nonprofit organization is marketing to a new group of potential donors.

Market researchers use terms like "self-stylers," "materialists," and "nesters" to describe their various market segments. These terms should give nonprofit organization officers an idea of the demographic changes occurring today. These changes in audiences mean that a nonprofit must *throw away any preconceived notions of who it is marketing to* and instead must *constantly* monitor its constituencies in order to match their interests to the services and programs the nonprofit organization provides.

If an organization is marketing to a more mature audience, then issues such as type size and letter length are important, as are appropriate role models and pictures in promotional literature. Fund-raising approaches should emphasize giving to generations of individuals that will be helped after the mature person is gone.

The Institutional Turmoil

As discussed previously, individuals today exhibit less loyalty toward institutions, governments, companies, and products than ever before, which means that there is also less loyalty to nonprofit organizations. For example, one relatively prominent nonprofit organization had changed its operational focus three times in five years. The focus changed each time money dried up. How could the nonprofit organization ask donors, volunteers or clients to be loyal or to make a long-term commitment to an institution that changed its focus so frequently?

The nonprofit organization, by changing its focus opportunistically at the slightest chance at raising more money, forsook the importance of maintaining relationships and interest in long-term goals. Constituents began to feel expendable and not influential in the organization's future.

The monetary crisis faced by savings and loan institutions is another case in point. How can these institutions ever ask their customers to be loyal again given the crushing changes they continue to endure?

One study shows that attitudes toward our government are not positive. George Barna in his book *The Frog in the Kettle*, drawing implications from his own research and from the Princeton Religious Research Center's *Emerging Trends*, Vol. 9, No. 1, Sept. 1987, has said:

> We will continue to have a sense of uneasiness about government and national security. The uneasiness will arise from the feeling that we are truly pawns in a larger, more intense game.[13]

Obviously, this is a game where the rules are not completely disclosed. Everyone is leery, even to give to good causes.

Given this general distrust, and the increasing presence of the "tough customer" described earlier, a nonprofit organization should expect similar feelings from its constituencies and should work to curb this potential attrition of supportive constituencies.

How do you curb this potential attrition of supportive constituencies? *An organization must talk to its constituents more than it has done in the past.* Organizations usually feel they know more about their donors, clients, and volunteers than they really do. There are three pragmatic ways to find out what your constituents are thinking:

1. A mail survey which is both the least expensive but also the least reliable method of research.
2. A telephone interview which allows you to have information immediately but also usually requires you to limit the amount of information you can ask the recipient of the call.
3. A personal interview in which extensive information can be obtained, but which is also the most expensive.

The environment in which a nonprofit organization operates, including the interaction between organization and constituents, is in a constant state of flux today, requiring constant vigilance on the part of the organization as it closely monitors its ongoing relationship with its various constituencies.

As the next section details, the relationship a nonprofit organization has with its competitors also bears watching.

Five Constraining Operating Conditions

There have been major consequences to the nonprofit field as a result of increased market competition. Five operating conditions have arisen to constrain nonprofit marketers today and should be considered as operational "givens" in planning a competitive strategy:

1. More competition
2. New experts
3. Business
4. No longer culturally favored
5. Take off blinders

Increased Competition

Because of an increase in competition, principally in the last 30 years, nonprofit organizations today encounter these five operating conditions that may not have been true when some nonprofits first were incorporated. Many nonprofit organizations that have been in existence for at least 10 years never expected to compete against each other. Some organizations enjoyed monopolizing their fields for many years. They were unprepared for the crowded competitive environment of today. (According to the IRS, in 1993, there were *over 1 million registered tax-exempt North American organizations* of which 546,100 were charitable Section 501(c)(3) institutions.) Because of declining donor and dollar share, many nonprofit organizations are no longer able to afford to specialize in only one service activity. Market and competitive demands mean they must spin off new ventures in order to maximize their competitive stance and acquire new donors and dollars.

New Experts

Many nonprofit organizations now experience *new experts* as competitors who offer similar or the same services. This section refers to competitors who do exactly what your organization does, perhaps employing the same methodology.

As a consequence of the increase in overall number of nonprofit organizations, there is an increase in the number of nonprofit organizations performing the same functions. There are many *expert organizations* now in competition with each other. This results in a market condition known as a *parity situation*, whereby the product or cause being produced is similar to other products or services being produced. This, in turn, results in organizations with similar or overlapping constituencies. (Expert companies are those who say they specialize in one or a few areas.)

What does this mean for the future of these organizations? For many, it could mean trying to determine whether they can survive on their own, merging with another nonprofit organization with similar goals, shutting down due to lack of funding or usefulness, or changing the focus of service.

Nonprofit Organizations are Businesses

Many nonprofit organizations have resisted viewing themselves as businesses. However, all nonprofit organizations are similar with respect to the following:

- **Product lines:** Many nonprofit organizations, especially larger ones, are developing new products and services designed to appeal to only certain parts of their constituencies.
- **Donation level:** Almost all nonprofit organizations are trying to get their donors to give more.
- **Customer and donor convenience:** Technology-based service and receipting delivery systems, 24-hour-a-day, seven-day-a-week oper-

ations are becoming the norm in order to compete. And the individuals manning these systems are increasingly better paid professionals and skilled workers.

- **Marketing:** There is a tremendous "sameness" in style, scope, and delivery of nonprofit promotional materials.

What is the consequence of this? More time should be spent in strategies that differentiate one nonprofit organization from the others.

Nonprofit Organizations Are No Longer Culturally Favored

Nonprofit organizations formerly harbored a sense of being "safe" because, with respect to their donors and each other, they did not view themselves in direct competition. They could expect a certain number of donations or clients each year. Because of this complacency, many nonprofit organizations have not cultivated a *performance mentality*, never having to define formally where they were going and what they were doing. Discussions of competition seemed nonexistent. There seemed to be less concern for the bottom line, less industry urgency placed on proving one's service to those in need, and less looking over one's shoulder. But this has changed. Proliferating nonprofit organizations providing similar services and delivery technologies are forcing these organizations to think more strategically. The speed with which nonprofit services can be duplicated means that donor loyalty continues to diminish. The concept of "market" is changing. The limits to what one nonprofit organization can accomplish are also changing; many today have emerged from small and narrowly focused organizations to nonprofit retailers of services for specific, targeted groups.

Getting Rid of the Blinders

Nonprofit organizations must view themselves as serving different constituencies and not vice versa. For many managers and directors the 1980s were a decade of learning the importance of quality and service, primarily because of Tom Peters and Robert Waterman, Jr.'s influence through their book *In Search of Excellence.*[14] Nonprofit organizations now talk about being in the constituent, donor, or volunteer service business.

However, nonprofit organizations must take the next steps. The organization's concept of markets for services must change. No longer can a nonprofit organization solely define what its market is; rather its constituency (or lack of one) defines the market for the nonprofit organization. This fact forces the constituent, volunteer or donor to become more active in the organization's marketing strategy by helping to define a market—and are thereby more likely to get involved in the activities of the nonprofit.

Given the increasingly crowded nonprofit field, this action helps force organizations to take off their competitive blinders in order to maximize their products and services, accept higher levels of risk in pursuit of donor optimization, spend more time on cost-control byproduct and service, and move away from the character of the old competitive battleground to a new one defined by the values and interests of those served and those who fund the activities. The old competitive paradigm in for-profit and nonprofit cultures was to match competitive move for competitive move with those an organization viewed as a competitor. When an organization focuses on the constituent, volunteer, or donor, their activities define the competition and their interests define the competitive marketplace.

REACHING THE "SHRINKING PIE"

In the process of writing this book, one nonprofit organization's marketing director sent me an interesting note. It says, in part:

> Yesterday we spent the afternoon licking each other's wounds. The director and I had spent the better part of the week calling on our key donors. We concluded that our phone calls did very little to change their minds, increase their giving or persuade them to give now. Furthermore, we had followed up on 100 of our high-end donors who had attended one of our briefings in the last few months. It also appears that events or phone calls do not make much of an impact upon them.
>
> What are we doing wrong?[15]

This one nonprofit organization's survival depends on its strategic response to today's highly charged environment. The nonprofit environment is less sheltered from competition, more high-tech, and more market-driven. It is an environment in which the nonprofit organization can no longer dictate to the consumer. The consumer drives the nonprofit.

Clearly nonprofit organizations need help in achieving their goals or restructuring operations. DATE is being forced to spend less time helping school-age children decide for or against cigarettes and alcohol. The Catholic Church needs help in funding its central city work in Detroit.

And Spring Hill is turning away campers by the hundreds. These are only a few examples among many.

The Customer Focus

Peter Drucker, more than 20 years ago, entitled a chapter in *Managing for Results,* "The Customer is the Business."[16] This statement was true then and it is still true today. The donors, volunteers, and those served by the nonprofit organization represent the building blocks upon which a marketing strategy must rest. Competing for the dollars, time, and talents these individuals offer allows an organization to construct marketing systems that ultimately enable it to achieve its mission. Every strategy must start with the individual, the basis of a nonprofit organization's business. In an age of shrinking donor pools and increased skepticism, the key questions are these: How do we gain an individual's confidence? Who is that individual and how much is he willing to give?

FIRST STEPS TO A COMPETITIVE STRATEGY

A competitive strategy should be built around four central theses which are explained in greater detail in the following chapters. First, a *competitive position* is determined by an analysis of an organization's environment, constituents, donors, and competitors. In other words, an organization looks externally and internally to devise a competitive stance. Many successful nonprofit organizations take the following structured and managed approach to their competitive strategy:

1. The first step is analysis and data gathering of market conditions.
2. Next is donor acceptance of their programs in order to arrive at a competitive position. These organizations constantly check to see where they stand vis-à-vis the competitor tomorrow.
3. The best marketing units within nonprofit organizations view marketing as a function to which every organization member contributes. They seek the advice of members of several disciplines within the organization, not relying solely on the director of development or marketing. A diversified opinion from departments such as data processing, the president's office, and accounting contribute to the overall competitive strategy. Every person and department is viewed as a member of the marketing effort on behalf of the organization.

4. Nonprofit organizations that are growing are usually doing more than effectively selling their organizational products to their constituencies; they are, in fact, meeting the value needs of their donors through organizational programs and are giving the donors, volunteers, and constituents the feeling that they are the ones who are accomplishing the good work.

The nonprofit organization is merely a conduit through which the desires of interested parties to do good are matched with the needs fulfilled by the nonprofit organization. Particularly in the key donor and volunteer arena, value-based selling—the means by which the heartfelt needs of the individual merge with the organization's actions—becomes a priority. This concept of placing the individual's interests first and the organization's second enables the nonprofit organization to become attuned to the donor's interests. Rather than funding an organization's needs, the individual ultimately funds those areas that satisfy his or her own beliefs.

BREAKING WITH TRADITION TO REMAIN FLEXIBLE

Finally, nonprofit organizations competing successfully break a number of time-cherished traditions of nonprofit marketing management:

- They are not constrained by the annual planning cycle (their plans change as information changes).
- They develop multiple strategies that realize high potential, rather than limiting themselves to only one strategy.
- They take a long-term as opposed to a short-term perspective.
- They stop programs that do not deliver expected results quickly.
- They measure progress on every aspect of their organization's operations.
- They reward good behavior and terminate those who exhibit bad performance.

In summary, competitive strategy is built upon the constituent's needs; the belief systems and confidence-gaining tactics of potential donors; the perception desired by the external world; and the services that are needed and that are affected by their recipients.

CHAPTER THREE

The Phased Marketing Plan

There are many ways of building an effective marketing strategy. One suggestion is to divide the task into phases so that concerns are dealt with in a sequential manner. This provides enough time for management to reach a consensus on most issues while building a logical framework from which to construct a marketing strategy.

This chapter presents a six-phase process for building a marketing plan (see Exhibit 3-1) that can be scheduled in succeeding months (with the exception of the "evaluation" phase which is ongoing). These phases include:

1. the external analysis phase;
2. the internal or self-analysis phase;
3. the market development phase;
4. the strategy selection phase;
5. the presentation of the plan to important shareholders; and
6. the evaluation phase.

These phases are discussed briefly in this chapter and they are each discussed in detail in the succeeding Chapters. The final phase, of course, is implementation, which is addressed in Chapter 11.

EXTERNAL ANALYSIS PHASE

In nonprofit marketing, you must consider how the external environment impacts your cause, its products, or your services, either positively or negatively. As identified in Chapters 2 through 4, an organization must first look externally to identify its clients and donors. By undertaking this action first, a nonprofit organization will understand clearly

1. *External analysis phase* in which the organization looks at its competitors, undertakes a SWOT analysis (strengths, weaknesses, opportunities, and threats), and identifies specific competitive scenarios.

2. *Internal or self-analysis phase* which looks internally at the organization in order to determine performance levels, organizational characteristics, costs, and the level of success in different organizational ventures.

3. *Market development phase* where issues of market development like the organization's growth pattern, its investment level in new causal products, and the competitive advantages and disadvantages of each are examined.

4. *Strategy selection phase* where two to three strategies are presented in conjunction with their projections. From this discussion one strategy is selected.

5. *Presentation of the plan* to all important stakeholder groups.

6. *Evaluation phase* of the strategy.

Exhibit 3-1   Six phases in building a marketing plan

the societal segments represented by its clients, its constituents, its volunteers, and its donors. From this analysis, the nonprofit organization can develop a plan to appeal to the motivational needs of each group.

Client, Donor, Constituent, and Volunteer Analysis

As stated previously, nonprofits principally serve four distinct groups: clients, constituents, volunteers, and donors. *Clients* are individuals the nonprofit organization serves directly and who become the immediate beneficiaries of its output. *Constituents* represent the consuming public that purchases some output from the nonprofit organization, for example, a book. *Volunteers* and *donors* (also called *supporters* by some organizations) supply or lend the nonprofit organization different types of resources—usually time, money, knowledge, encouragement, or facilities.

Two critical issues are basic in client, donor, constituent and volunteer analysis:

- Who are the major audience segments involved with the nonprofit?
- What are their motivations and unfelt needs?

Why are these points important? Consider the following trends the United States is currently experiencing: how would they impact the clients, constituents, volunteers, and donors of a nonprofit organization?

1. We are becoming older and, happily, we seem to be getting healthier.

2. Most Americans are single for longer periods of their lives and there are more single people than ever before. People are delaying marriage and children.

3. As of 1990, more than 55 percent of women were in the workforce.

4. Childbirth is being delayed and we are having fewer children. In fact, demographers tell us that, without immigration, the United States would have a zero population growth today.

5. We are now the sixth largest Spanish-speaking country in the world, after Mexico, Spain, Argentina, Colombia, and Peru.

6. There has been a huge growth in environmental consciousness in the last decade.

7. Sociologists are seeing an increased willingness to trade in our incomes and material possessions for meaning in our lives.

If the first step in the external analysis is to assess the impact of the market and environment upon the nonprofit organization and its constituencies, what of those nonprofit organizations who do not engage in regular marketing research to monitor these trends? Unfortunately, some nonprofits in this situation simply make an educated guess.

The process of defining its audience and those trends affecting them should produce client, donor, volunteer, and constituent profiles. The purpose of these profiles is to determine the characteristics a nonprofit organization thinks will help it define its targeted markets. The following questions are important in putting such profiles together.

- Age
- Sex
- Race
- Education
- Family income
- Geographic residence
- Employment
- Buying behavior
- Other

Once an organization develops a profile for each group, it can then begin to look at its competitors to try and determine how they fit into this market. For that, you must develop a competitor profile.

Define Your Competitors

Development of a competitor profile is an important step in the process of forming a marketing strategy, but is all too often neglected by nonprofit organizations. In the end, lack of such knowledge costs them time, energy, money, and individuals they could have helped or reached over the long run.

Today, nonprofit organizations must *assume* they have competition and must get to know their competitors. By developing a competitor profile, the nonprofit industry is addressed as a whole. It can serve to identify the strengths and weaknesses of those who are a part of the same industry.

The critical questions behind a competitor analysis are as follows:

- Who are the competitors to the nonprofit organization today?
- Who will they be tomorrow?
- Can the nonprofit organization identify the strengths and weaknesses of each competitor?
- What are their competitive strategies?
- How many people does the competitor serve; how much money are they raising?

A nonprofit organization's marketing director should start by developing a file or list of the organization's competitors. As part of this listing, and as part of a general competitor analysis, the director must consider the approximate number of people each competing nonprofit organization is serving, the types of services or products being used by each, their approximate budgets, and their likely market share.

A marketing strategy also should map out an action plan to minimize the competitive actions of other nonprofit organizations. While most nonprofit organizations do not have the resources available to respond to all "competitive attacks," remaining passive can severely limit their effectiveness. A look at the overall industry allows an organization to get an overview of some of the general conditions at work.

An Industry Analysis Defines Services Offered and Their Trends

As part of a competitor analysis, a nonprofit organization should assess the likelihood that other nonprofit organizations could provide the same services. In an industry analysis, ask:

- How attractive is this industry to other potential competitors?
- What trends does this industry exhibit?
- Are there key success factors that the marketing strategy will have to take into account in order for the organization to compete effectively?
- Does this industry have a history of stability? This analysis should consider the general trends in the industry—use of technology, changes in leadership, and changes in service delivery—to help a marketing manager anticipate industry changes.

The result of an industry analysis should reveal an environment with both threats and opportunities. It should answer these questions:

- What environmental threats and opportunities exist?
- Does the nonprofit organization expect there to be major shifts in the environment in the next one to three years?

Threats and opportunities to a nonprofit organization can both originate from the legal environment (i.e., new fund-raising regulations), technological trends (i.e., more affordable technology), social and cultural trends (i.e., U.S. citizens seem to identify themselves more and more as "environmentalists" and, as such, seem more open to promoting like-minded values), and economic trends (i.e., if philanthropic giving is charted against population growth, it is declining; if it is charted against age, giving is increasingly reliant on older donors).

INTERNAL ANALYSIS PHASE

Having begun the process of looking internally through a competitor profile, a nonprofit organization needs to take the next step in this process by determining how others view its work. In particular, the organization must assess how its constituency defines what it does. This type of *image survey* seeks to determine constituent answers to the following questions: What work do they think the organization is engaged in? Can they describe it in detail?

Defining your organization this way is counterintuitive to many nonprofit organizations. Most directors believe they are the ones to define what they are doing, and having done so, donors, volunteers, and clients will follow. Wrong!

An image survey helps an organization firm up what is expected of it in the constituents' minds. This creates more loyalty between the two and helps to prevent the organization from trying to become all things to all people. Likewise, knowing what is expected of you allows a nonprofit organization to concentrate its resources, thereby saving money that would be required in a broader market approach.

An internal analysis must begin by asking the following questions:

- Does the organization keep track of its current performance levels, particularly in service delivery?
- If the organization has a strategy, can it identify it for itself and others, along with a sense of how it has performed as an organization? Can you identify its strategy's strengths and weaknesses compared to the strategies of competitors?
- What is the self-image of the nonprofit organization? How does the organization describe its culture, structure, key stakeholders, and operational systems?
- How will all of the above affect the organization's strategy?
- Does the nonprofit organization know its costs of doing business?
- Does it know what its competitors are spending to enact the same services and the same service support?
- Is there any advantage in one cost structure over the other?
- What internal factors constrain the organization and keep it from having a greater success in its market?

These questions are designed to assess the internal "context" from which the nonprofit organization can operate. Geraldine Larkin has managed to describe *internal context.* Author of *12 Simple Steps to a Winning Marketing Plan,* she formerly worked as a program officer for the C.S. Mott Foundation and is currently the Manager of the Emerging Businesses Department at Deloitte and Touche in Ann Arbor, Michigan.[1]

One of the biggest mistakes most people make in marketing is under-valuing the importance of context. Context is everything in marketing. That's because marketing never works in a vacuum. No one can wake up one morning and successfully go out and start selling a new widget without taking two "contexts" into consideration. The first is the company itself, i.e., your business. The second context is the world outside of your business. The more attentive you are to trends going on around you, the more successful you will be in marketing your product.

MARKET DEVELOPMENT PHASE

The market development phase is one that forces the institution to develop a direction for its services, donor relationships, volunteer effort, and its products. In this phase, competitive advantages are studied in relation to the organization's ability to deliver these benefits to clients, constituents, and donors alike. Decisions about growth or maintenance of its current marketing position also are made in this phase, as are decisions about the types of strategies that are compatible with the organization's objectives.

Critical issues in the market development phase are as follows:

- What is the nonprofit organization's business mission vs. what it should be?
- What areas of growth should the organization consider that are not currently pursued?
- What strategies should the organization consider when entering new areas of service or growth?
- What level of investment should the organization consider for each area of current service?
- What competitive strategy options are available to the nonprofit organization given its service portfolio and its product line?
- Given the different strategic options available to the organization, which ones best suit its strengths and weaknesses, particularly its culture and stakeholder expectations?

The goal in looking at these questions is to aim an organization's services and products at very well-defined audiences that will be receptive to the organization's actions. This offers some distinct advantages.

The more successful a nonprofit organization is in defining its mission and the strategies to reach it, the easier it is for clients and donors to understand and like that proposition, join in the cause, or choose to support another institution. Consumers appreciate a clear approach. A nonprofit organization should not try to be "all things to all people." Many nonprofit organizations today have, in their desires to help so many people, forgotten what they do well versus what they do not do well. Any organization that can focus precisely on its goals automatically separates itself from many of its competitors. Clearer goals will produce a stronger client and constituent loyalty.

By taking these steps, a nonprofit organization is in a better position to further penetrate new aspects of the marketplace. Many nonprofit organizations expand their markets and marketing having not fully penetrated one field of service. As a consequence, they often do not have the benefit of knowing all of the potentialities that could arise in their marketing expenditures. By knowing required levels of investment—as well as having to deal with hidden problems that may arise—the organization is not so likely to take an ill-advised move.

STRATEGY SELECTION PHASE

The strategy selection phase is a synthesis of the previous three phases. This phase combines all of the strategic options that have been discussed and, taking into account the nonprofit institution's identity, goals, and its abilities to fulfill its vision, presents the best choices for strategy. There are usually two to three "best" strategic options from which one is selected by going through questions like the following:

- Looking at all of the key performance measures—clients served, sales, investment, dollars raised, donors acquired—which strategy will deliver the best performance in each area?
- Determining which strategy gives the best "overall" performance?

This will be discussed further in Chapters 8 and 9.

PRESENTATION OF THE PLAN

The presentation of the plan presents a selected, refined marketing strategy listing all of the programs and support services, plus client and financial projections for the strategy's performance for the coming year. The presentation of the plan to all levels of management and, ultimately, all levels of employees lists all the programs and support services, plus client and financial projections for the strategy's performance for the coming year. In this phase, the nonprofit institution's senior leadership and marketing management form a group to evaluate the strategy, or strategies, and then make resources allocation and timetable decisions.

In developing a group like this, it is important that a sense of urgency and direction is established early, even as early as in their chartering. Chaired by a senior officer in the nonprofit organization, the group is composed of those whose skills and skill potential, not personalities, will help allow the organization's adoption of the plan. A group like this is represented typically by officers and employees of all levels, as well as some individuals who might be interested outside parties, key board members, donors, or volunteers. In addition, there is often a consultant in place whose job is to point out areas of the plan that may be in jeopardy or need further refinement.

From this leadership group, the strategy plan must be communicated to different management groups and other key insiders, as well as to those who are not formal members of the organization such as key volunteers, some key donors, and some members of the board. These different management groups begin to budget for their activity as part of the plan, while key volunteers, supporters and those within the organization's "insider" network begin absorbing the new direction.

SUMMARY

In this chapter nonprofit executives can get a sense of how important it is for them to have a plan for their organization's research program. Chapters 8 and 9 will show the reader how the gathered information will be crucial in developing a coherent marketing strategy for the organization to implement.

PART TWO

The External Analysis

CHAPTER FOUR

External Analysis: Client, Donor, Volunteer, and Competitor Research

Assess yourselves and your opponents.[1]

Sun Tzu

The Art of War

It is the prospect who is difficult to define and understand, not the product.[2]

John O'Toole

The Trouble With Advertising

The nonprofit world is less a world than a universe—vast, varied, and unexplored.[3]

Fred Setterberg and Kary Schulman

Beyond Profit

In 1989, Americans gave away the equivalent of 2.19 percent of the gross national product. In 1969, not one of the best years for the U.S. economy, we gave away 2.15 percent of the gross national product— .04 percent less. In fact, since 1955, with all the ups and downs of the economy, with growth of not-for-profit groups from roughly 100,000 then to over 900,000 today, from the worst year to the best year, with membership in the National Society of Fund-Raising Executives topping 12,000 at last count, giving as a percentage of the gross national product has varied by less than .5 percent. These numbers are significant: How can so many trained professionals working for so many worthwhile programs have so little effect on philanthropic trends?[4]

The importance of client, donor, volunteer, and competitor analysis in competitive strategy cannot be ignored. For example, the director and creative director of Easter Seals constantly test their direct mail propositions to determine which are motivating to constituents and which are not. Based on research, the Easter Seal Society already knows that plastic pennies or pictures of pennies don't bring in nearly as many donations as the real ones do. But, says Mr. Cleghorn, "We're conducting tests now on concepts, so we may have something in a few weeks or months."

Constant testing of current and new appeals is one of the basics that the director and creative director at Easter Seals consider a necessary expense. Even after finding a successful appeal, testing doesn't end.[5] A recent study by the California-based Barna Research Group indicates 27 percent of American adults plan to reduce giving to nonprofit organizations as a result of the weak economy.[6] As the economy grows more uncertain, donors and potential donors hold their funds in lieu of giving them, to be certain that they can afford to be philanthropic.

THE IMPORTANCE OF CONTINUOUS ANALYSIS

Without external analysis, performed on a continual basis, a nonprofit organization cannot determine accurately which marketing strategies work, which causes should be implemented, which products currently are appropriate for the target markets. External analysis of the client, donor, volunteer, and competitor allow an organization to set company objectives, raise the necessary dollars to accomplish those objectives, and attract interested clients, volunteers, donors, and other key personnel. Analysis also produces a better understanding of the market opportunities, the potential effectiveness of the promotional dollars being spent, and obstacles to overcome.

The Need to Uncover Opportunities and Threats

"Uncover" is the operative word. External analysis is the process of trying to uncover opportunities and threats that could lead to strategic marketing alternatives. Clients, donors, volunteers, and competitors should each be researched separately because these groups' actions disproportionately affect the lifeblood of the organization; more so than any other element. In addition, these groups are also a tremendous source of information and can provide advice on how to better reach and serve them.

GOALS OF THE ANALYSIS

The goals in undertaking a client, donor, volunteer, and competitor analysis are threefold:

1. To determine whether program(s) being proposed truly provide the expected "payback," whether in dollars, organizational benefits, or changed lives.
2. To identify the psychological and pragmatic "fit" between the market and the program in order to determine whether the investment of the organization's time and money is appropriate.
3. To ensure that the organization is not merely duplicating a pre-existing program to its constituency.

Most nonprofit organizations simply cannot afford to do research for research's sake; they need to set goals and objectives for their research. By doing this, the nonprofit organization creates a benchmark from which to judge the way it will use its research.

ADDRESSING OBJECTIONS TO RESEARCH

In organizations where money typically is targeted for very specific programs which serve the public, the idea of embarking on "research" can raise certain objections. Marketing is for somebody else "who is really serious about marketing and has a lot of money to toss around."

Here are some of the typical objections encountered:

- "It sounds so expensive and complex."
- "You have to hire a lot of Ph.D.s to run the whole show, don't you?"
- "Once you've got the data, who really understands it or makes use of it?"
- "Aren't there a lot of different ways to interpret the information you generate?"
- "What donor has time anymore to fill out those long questionnaires?"

- A feeling by managers that they already have enough marketing research information as a by-product of their organization's accounting and control activities.

- Managers feel their decisions are "small potatoes" compared to those of Proctor & Gamble or General Motors and, therefore, cannot justify the expenditures they feel any serious marketing research will require.

The list goes on and on. There are many reasons why nonprofit organizations object to an external analysis and its concomitant, internal, company analysis. Horrendous data collection stories *do* abound. And the cost sometimes *can be* prohibitive. What's more, to the small development or marketing office, research of *any* kind is an intrusive idea and not in step with important issues faced daily—like getting the next mailing out on time or why the brochure's late. Plus, the research field has led us to believe that you really *must* have a Ph.D. if you are to understand the hidden implications of almost any data. And to top things off, consultants, ad agencies, and professional advice-givers speak as though they've already read all the studies ever needed and have perfect solutions to most marketing problems. The truth is that every nonprofit organization has a different operating environment which implies different solutions.

The director or driver of the nonprofit marketing strategy must be able to address the doubts of its constituents and get past them. There are some relatively easy ways to uncover the doubts of donors, volunteers, and other constituents during the market analysis. These will be presented later in this chapter.

The internal organization can process the environmental information in the form of systems, problem-solving methodology, and competitive strategies. Organizational strategies must be tied directly to donor, volunteer, and client needs, or the organization will have no handle on its competitive advantages and how to "sell" to raise more money.

The Need for a Focus When Conducting External Analysis

Another frequently cited concern by nonprofit managers regarding external analysis is uncertainty—when and how to do the research and which issues should be addressed. John Lyons in his book, *Guts,* frames the uncertainty:

> I am not a friend of research. Particularly when it is asked to do what it was never intended to do: predict the future. Research can't

tell us whether an ad is going to succeed any more than a critic can tell us whether a movie will succeed.

Intuition is much more helpful. Not half-baked intuition. Intuition springing from information that triggers an idea.

Research properly used gives me the right information. But I need it before the idea in order to trigger the idea in the first place. And to get the right idea I need research that talks to the right people so I know what they need and feel. For example, did you know that only 20 percent of the beer-drinking population consumes 80 percent of the beer? I can be friendly to research that gives me a fact like this, because now I can put my talent to work and if I'm lucky I can come up with the best beer campaign ever written.[7]

For John Lyons, research is a means for confirming or denying suspicions or hunches about the marketplace. For a nonprofit marketing director, suspicion about how constituents or markets will act, if used as the sole governing stick, is not enough. There needs to be some additional confirmation or denial. This is where marketing research comes in.

In sum, if nonprofit marketers are going to meet their funding requirements of the next few years, objections must be overcome and a focus defined for external analysis.

OTHER PRELIMINARY CONCERNS INCLUDE FLEXIBILITY

The ability to create a flexible competitive strategy is another concern. Constituents', clients', and donors' points of view, whether perceived to be rational or not, will define the scope and quality of service and the performance goals. A nonprofit organization's marketing and competitive advantage is tied directly to meeting its donors' needs, expectations, and perceptions. When market research is not undertaken, donors and constituents themselves are forcing this responsiveness, as opposed to the organization voluntarily making such changes by withholding gifts or volunteerism. With little tolerance for poor corporate performance and a growing expectation for better performance and delivery of services, the constituents—whether board members, volunteers, or large and small donors—are using their opinions and checkbooks to force this change.

Without this type of pressure many nonprofit organizations might leave well enough alone. And because donors cannot judge or see the quality of the service their check is providing, they often make decisions to give, volunteer, or continue their involvement based on reputation, reliability, or even how the service is provided during the donation transaction. It is these impressions guiding donors' actions that non-profit marketers must get to know firsthand.

There is no limit to the amount of external analysis a nonprofit marketer can do or the scope it can take for his or her organization. Historically, external analysis focuses upon four different components:

1. clients, volunteers, constituents, and/or donors;
2. competitors;
3. the industry an organization finds itself in; and
4. the environment in which it operates.

The first elements are treated in this chapter. Items 2 through 4 are discussed in Chapter 5.

START WITH CLIENTS, VOLUNTEERS, CONSTITUENTS, AND DONORS

Pragmatically speaking, most organizations begin with a client, constituent, and donor analysis in order to define the most relevant target markets through a process called *segmentation. Clients* are those individuals who consume the resources or programs that the nonprofit produces. *Donors,* on the other hand, lend the nonprofit resources (money, time, encouragement) in order to allow it to accomplish its goals and objectives. *Constituents* are purchasers of items the nonprofit may produce.

Pitfalls to Avoid

Many nonprofit organizations start incorrectly with their pre-existent products and services and then use external analysis as a vehicle to try to enhance or mandate already agreed-upon promotional decisions. Instead, you should allow an organization to determine strategic alternative products. Without good data that is completely objective and not biased toward existing products, resulting marketing and fund-raising campaigns are less successful. Client and donor analysis should help determine whether the organization is in the right market and is providing the right products and services in that market. (Of course "market" here means those individuals who are either predisposed to support your cause on possess characteristics that would allow them to be interested in your cause.)

Secondly, such an analysis helps to determine the strategic approach to take in selling the organization's values to its constituency. An organization will only achieve a strategic advantage if what it is saying and selling is *perceived* to be of value and use to its constituency. The more this symmetry is achieved in messages that target potential donor values, the more an organization achieves the possibility of superior competitive advantage.

For example, one nonprofit organization has a desire to raise funds on behalf of those who are jailed throughout the world for their religious or political beliefs. The target donor audience has a desire to not see anyone jailed unjustly for their beliefs and responds with gifts to encourage the organization to continue its efforts on behalf of prisoners. Both parties achieve a type of symmetry in their communication.

SEGMENTATION AS THE NEXT STEP

Having taken this first step of defining the needs, finances, motivation, and identity of clients, donors, volunteers and constituents, a nonprofit marketing team then looks for natural groupings or *segments* within each with which to explore its strategy. Most nonprofit organizations don't have to be convinced of the need for segmentation and are quite familiar with analysis of such.

The principles of *recency* (how recently a donor has given), *frequency* (how many times a donor has given in a particular time frame), and *monetary* (how much a donor has given) have been bandied about at so many nonprofit seminars that they are now part of the nonprofit marketing jargon. When you ask a nonprofit director for his or her segmentation strategy, and if they have one, you are more than likely to get one or all three of the aforementioned concepts. These concepts are usually implemented by nonprofit marketing directors. But why, and are they right for the organization?

Segmentation, in the sense that is being presented here, means identifying the most relevant target markets and developing strategies to best reach and influence those targets.[8] Historically, segmentation is a classification system born out of external analysis by which a nonprofit organization identifies viable market segments. From this classification process then emerges promotional, fund-raising, and advertising strategies to reach each segment. Segmentation is built on the needs of constituents and donors. A nonprofit organization must equally address its donors, clients, volunteers, and constituents, for in not doing so the nonprofit is assuming that all constituencies have the same needs. Different audience segments require different product or service attributes, as well as different marketing strategies to be continued to buy or use those.

Henry Ford is reputed to have said to his consumers that they could have any color Model T as long as it was black. At the time, Ford knew his was the only affordable American car. Nonprofit organizations cannot afford to make such assumptions. Partnership with donors thrives when there is relevant communication and when there is a sense of importance attached by both parties. Different audience segments want to be treated differently by the nonprofit organization. It is up to the organization to find out what those different parameters are. By 1940, Henry Ford began to produce cars of different colors.

ENDURING AND DYNAMIC VARIABLES

The external analysis should identify two variables—enduring and dynamic—as a means to its classification or segmentation system. *Enduring variables* are constituent and donor constants such as demographics, geographics, and psychography. *Demographic indicators* describe who people are (i.e., Are they married? What sex are they? Number of children in the household? Do both spouses work? Do they own their own home? etc.). *Geographic segmentation* has to do with where people live, not only in their immediate community, but also the state where they live, and the section of country in which they live. *Psychographic segmentation* divides markets on differences in their lifestyle. It is based on the idea that "the more you know about your audience, the better you can communicate with them." These are known as enduring variables because they are constant within the consumer across all causes and products (at any single point in time). In other words, these variables do not change across nonprofit product classes or cause appeals.

On the other hand, *dynamic variables* are those that would differ for a donor or constituent relative to each donation or act of volunteerism. Dynamic variables are often used in solicitation message creation because a writer is looking at how his or her organization's donors behave in certain situations. (See Exhibit 4-1.)

Enduring Variables	Dynamic Variables
Age	Heavy user of product
Sex	Early user of product
Geographic location	Brand loyal
Working	Autonomous
Single	High self-involvement
Income	Hedonistic
Divorced	Awareness of product

Exhibit 4-1   Enduring and dynamic variables

The following example further explains these two variables:

Mr. and Mrs. Smith support a number of different causes financially. If your job was to raise money from Mr. and Mrs. Smith, you would first look at some of their *enduring variables*. They live in and own a house that is located in the country on 12 acres. Both have white collar jobs—one is a doctor and the other a consultant. Both are college educated and have a combined income of $100,000. These variables are constant. However, a number of different causes, appeals, and dynamic variables influence their "giving" patterns. They support prison reform for political reasons, the Future Farmers of America because of family reasons, some hunger appeals because of compassionate reasons, their church because of spiritual reasons, and a religious worker because of friendship reasons. With each cause, a reason for giving changes based on variables that change as well.

The following section further explores how to use each variable in a strategic manner.

Enduring Variables

The following discussion addresses the enduring variables and suggests ways to uncover them and how to use them strategically.

Demographics. First, consider the enduring demography variable and its characteristics. *Demographic characteristics* are often used by nonprofit organizations to create a client, donor, or constituent profile. Variables like age, sex, income, education, marital status, occupation, race, family dwelling location, regional location, and family size are indicators which help describe potential target markets and allow a nonprofit marketing manager to pursue those segments that yield a better acceptance of one's message. For example, XYZ organization's top 18 donors have the following common demographic characteristics:

- Home values of over $100,000;
- Households with over $80,000 income per year;
- All heads of households have white collar jobs;
- All heads of households are married;

- 14 households have children; 11 of the 14 have at least one child in college or out of college;
- 12 heads of households have jobs in the finance, insurance, and business sectors; two are retired, two are doctors, one is a saleswoman, and one is a professor.[9]

These variables can be determined through survey research or through syndicated studies that are relatively standard; the Simmons Market Research Bureau lists over 65 demographic classifications in its syndicated work.[10] An environmental group recently gathered this type of information by asking their constituents through a mail survey some of the following questions in order to begin to understand who they were in partnership with:

1. How long have you been a member?
2. Why are you a member?
3. How did you hear about us?
4. Is our work helpful?
5. What issues are most important to you?
6. Are you a member of our action network?
7. How would you like to be involved?
8. How do you prefer to renew your membership?
9. Do you read our newsletter?
10. How are you employed?
11. What is your household income?
12. What is the highest level of education you have had?

Some nonprofit organizations personally interview their major donors (or use focus groups) to generate this demographic information. Focus group interviewing is one of the more frequently used forms of qualitative marketing research. A *focus group* is a small grouping of men and women who are brought together for the collaborative purpose of discovering how they feel about some particular issue, trend, or product. This form of group interviewing has been around since World War II and uses a moderator or leader who guides the group in answering certain questions that will provide inferential data to the sponsoring organization.

Demographic data bears mention because it can be an indicator of constant change; for example, dual household incomes have increased dramatically, as have the number of single person households. Both these trends can affect the frequency and size of donation for some groups.

Geographics. A second enduring variable, *geographic characteristics* (or *geodemographics*) relates population and geographic characteristics, specifically relating a particular population and its location (such as a neighborhood) to demographics.[11] Knowledge of geography is important because any nonprofit organization that has less than a national mandate for its services must focus its promotional resources in geographical regions. There is a distinct difference between urban, suburban, and rural areas of the country when it comes to mass media solicitations and their corresponding response rates. This information is also important in order to uncover "who" an organization serves and "who" donates on a national level.

One nonprofit organization realized a fourfold increase in their giving patterns when they segmented their solicitation appeals between rural and urban population centers and developed copy platforms tailored to the concerns of each group.

Books such as *The Nine Nations of North America* and *The Clustering of America* both describe unique socioeconomic groupings in this country, the differences between parts of America and the importance of geodemography in promotional decisions.[12]

Joel Garreau, author of *The Nine Nations of North America*, gives data on regional consumption differences through his geographic segmentation of the United States into nine *nations:*

1. The *Foundry* which encompasses states like Ohio, Pennsylvania, New Jersey, parts of New York, Virginia, Maryland, and Wisconsin. This region is marked by a decaying infrastructure and a dwindling population.

2. *MexAmerica* is the southwest "nation" encompassing parts of California, Arizona, Colorado, and Texas. These states are under heavy Hispanic influence.

3. *Dixie* is an emotion, an idea, and is where one can call themselves "Southern." It encompasses almost 20 states in the South.

4. *New England* encompasses nine states in the northeast with few natural resources, little energy or raw materials, and represents a "poor" nation.

5. The *Empty Quarter* is the intermountain West, rich in materials and natural resources but not rich in population.

6. *Ecotopia* represents the northwestern tier states blessed with adequate water and renewable resources where "quality of life" is a religion.

7. *Breadbasket* is the central part of the country and is marked by agriculture and agricultural-related industries.

8. The *Aberrations* like the Hawaiian Islands and Alaska.

The Clustering of America by Michael J. Weiss looks at the idea of geodemographics through an analysis of 35,600 neighborhood zip codes and over 535 key variables in each, such as education, affluence, mobility, ethnicity, housing, and other urban measures. Nonprofit organizations often receive a significant portion of their major donations from households with dual incomes. The type of contact and approach with these donors should change with the time of year of the fund-raising campaign and certain geographic factors.

How does one "uncover" information about volunteers, donors, clients, and constituents? It may be too simplistic to say "Ask them" but that is essentially true. Depending on the desired information, telephone studies, focus groups, questionnaire sampling, and face-to-face interviewing are all ways of obtaining information. The way these donors view the nonprofit organization and their desire to respond to the appeal made may take on a different light at differing times of year— during the vacation months, the December holiday season, at tax time, etc. It can be critical to find out when you should solicit donations or help, and when you should not.

Some nonprofit organizations such as those with television ministries or disaster relief cause appeals, where the promotional, geographic, and demographic reach can be national, add *behavioral variables* to their segmentation mix. For example, the Claritas Corporation has created a system called PRIZM which sorts the nation's 36,000 zip code zones into 40 *lifestyle clusters* that key in education, ethnicity, affluence, and stage of family life cycle, all based on the principle that "birds of a feather flock together."[13] This data is available for a fee and similar types of data are available through other channels.

By tying in demographic variables and small area geographics, a nonprofit marketer involved in fund-raising decisions can look at potential segments based on multiple variables, not just single variable analysis.

Psychographics.   Having first looked at where a person lives and who he or she is, a nonprofit marketer now looks at how these individuals perceive themselves and the world around them. *Psychographics* is the third enduring variable. Psychographics, according to Arnold Mitchell, who originated the psychographic approach to market segmentation, describes "the entire constellation of a person's attitudes, beliefs, opinions, hopes, fears, prejudices, needs, desires, and aspirations that, taken together, govern how one behaves," and that in turn, "finds holistic expression in a lifestyle."[14] What lifestyle issues do donors, volunteers, and constituents face and how do these groups view themselves as they interact with their world?

The VALS Formulation.   While there are numerous psychographic typologies, perhaps the most famous is the *VALS formulation*, which is an acronym for *Values And Lifestyles*. Values And Lifestyles is a division of SRI International, a not-for-profit research company. VALS grew out of research by Arnold Mitchell in the early 1960s in which four major categories of belief systems and nine lifestyle types were created (in 1989 a new VALS2 typology was created). Mitchell created a holistic approach to consumers and looked at their entire constellation of attitudes, beliefs, hopes, and opinions. These lifestyles were then fit together in what was known as the *VALS double hierarchy*.[15]

True psychographic profiling has usually not been available to the nonprofit world because of its prohibitive cost; and it has not necessarily been the panacea it was thought it could be. However, it remains, as can be seen in the following examples, a powerful tool in experienced hands. First, an example from the for-profit marketplace from the makers of Listerine.

Compared to the light or nonuser of mouthwash, the female heavy user of mouthwash is more likely to agree with the following psychographic statements:

- I do not feel clean without a daily bath.
- Everyone should use a deodorant.
- A house should be dusted and polished at least three times a week.
- Odors in the house embarrass me.
- The kind of dirt you can't see is worse than the kind you can.
- Garbage should be put into a garbage bag before it is thrown out.
- I usually keep my house very clean and neat.
- I am a neat person.
- I usually comb my hair and put on my lipstick first thing in the morning.

- I brush my hair at least once a day.
- When my hair is cleaned and combed, I feel more alive.
- I use one or more household disinfectants.
- Dirty dishes should be washed promptly after each use.
- It is very important for people to wash their hands after eating each meal.

The profile that emerges here led to Listerine's position in the mouthwash market and has allowed it to keep a dominant share of sales for a long period of time against the competing brands that promote "sex appeal" and "fresh breath." This dominance has continued even after the Federal Trade Commission ruled that Listerine didn't kill germs and forced Listerine to put disclaimers in the advertising.[16]

And now, an example for nonprofit organizations:

. . . compared to other types of donors, a conservative donor is likely to agree with the following psychographic statements:

- I do not like to watch violence on television.
- Everyone should vote.
- The greatest threat is from within.
- People should make it on their own and should not receive government handouts.
- I enjoy saying the pledge of allegiance.
- I believe in candidates who go to church regularly.

In 1986, FRA, Inc.—a San Francisco-based fund-raising consulting firm—began offering VALS as part of its fund-raising consulting services. "Market research traditionally has focused on demographics: donor/prospect segmentation by age, income, level of education and other measures," says FRA president Barbara Marion. "What makes VALS different is that it goes *beyond demographics* to put faces on different prospect/donor segments and flesh out lifestyle profiles in order to help you direct your campaign efforts. Since giving is primarily a value-based decision for donors, we're sure that VALS will prove to be a very effective tool in building successful fund-raising campaigns."[17]

By understanding that one's values and beliefs form foundational reasons for many donors, volunteers, and their support of nonprofit causes, Terese Tricamo discovered that some personalities are more likely to respond than others. Therefore, United Way's advertising and fund-raising campaign was aimed at those groups most likely to give and not the entire population.

When United Way of Portland, Oregon needed to develop a campaign, they consulted the ad agency Pihas, Schmidt, Westerdahl, who, in turn, went to a consultant from VALS, Terese Tricamo. "We tried to stress that in the act of giving, donors also receive something," Tricamo said. "The person who looks at the tax benefits of a gift has a values structure that differs from a person who looks at the charity's stand on political issues, and both are different from people who give out of compassion."[18]

Dynamic Variables

Dynamic variables are those that are specific to the relationship a donor, volunteer, or constituent has with a nonprofit organization's cause or products. Not all nonprofit causes and products will involve the donor or volunteer in the same way. The relationship with each changes depending on the values of the donor and the cause or objectives of the nonprofit organization's programs.

Some nonprofit marketers feel dynamic variables are the most valuable information to be had about a constituent because they help in message and solicitation creation. John Lyons is quoted earlier in this chapter regarding beer drinkers and the fact that 20 percent of all beer drinkers consumed more than 80 percent of beer products. The relationship this 20 percent of the beer drinking population has with beer is different in nature than the remaining 80 percent. While this chapter's explanation of enduring variables helped describe the donor and constituent, now the emphasis on dynamic variables helps to define the message you create to get a donor, volunteer, or constituent to "consume" more of your "product," volunteer more of their time, or give more dollars to the nonprofit organization's project.

There are three dynamic variables that bear mentioning: *heavy users* (or major donors), *early adopters,* and *brand loyal* (or core) donors.

Heavy Users/Major Donors.   The heavy user concept is borrowed from product consumption terminology and analogous to a major donor, which may also be termed *affluent donor* or *key volunteer.* Who are these people? Why do they give, purchase, or volunteer the way they do? Do they differ demographically from the rest of the nonprofit organization's audience?

To cite one perspective, Professor Thomas Stanley, an expert on wealth at Georgia State University, says that most millionaires are self-made and hardworking. He says ethnic backgrounds are changing and that only 40 percent of today's millionaires are white Anglo-Saxon Protestants; the rest are of East European, Italian, or Irish descent. The Federal Reserve study shows that nonwhites and Hispanics are beginning to show up in the high-income categories, although very few of them are millionaires. This is quite a jump as compared with 20 years ago when there were hardly any.[19]

How might a nonprofit organization's solicitation message change if it were trying to solicit a wealthy Hispanic couple as compared with an Anglo-Saxon couple? Would there be a significantly different approach? Depending on the product or cause, the answer can be "yes." By looking at the readership profiles of special interest magazines, one can identify distinct groupings of affluent people ... and this information can affect where an organization places its solicitation message in order to attract major donors. Success at solicitation in certain arenas may be dependent on face-to-face presentations, some on mass solicitation or even impersonal media. The critical issue is to recognize that those who consume more of a nonprofit organization's product or give more frequently to its cause usually exhibit peculiar sets of dynamic variables, which should then affect the organization's promotional strategy. Donors and volunteers who might be classified as "heavy users" often give to, or get involved with, very specific and narrow projects that do not enjoy mass following or broad representation.

Early Adopters.   Do you have a group of donors or volunteers that just can't seem to wait for your next program or idea? With one university client, the women's auxiliary was key in getting early support for new fund-raising programs. Early adopters are often the easiest group to sell your activities to; contrast this group with selling those who are more deliberate in their decision making, more skeptical about new ideas or causes a nonprofit organization might propose, and so on. Early adopters frequently enjoy jumping on the bandwagon at an early stage. They are often the first to volunteer for a project that fits their values. And, they tend to be more adventuresome, better educated, and often more socially mobile then other groups. Word-of-mouth campaigns are frequently used with this group.

Brand Loyal and Core Donors.   Although "brand loyalty" is clearly less powerful than it was several years ago, some donors do exhibit loyalty to a cause. This group needs to be approached in a different manner than those who are less loyal and give more sporadically. Those who exhibit loyalty in their giving (i.e., monthly financial partners) or volunteering should be reminded, thanked, and rewarded for their loyalty in order to maintain that loyalty; those who are predisposed to switching their giving loyalty often need to be completely "resold" in order to get each new gift.

In talking about acquisition and message strategy, it is usually not worthwhile to approach donors who are already loyal to a similar cause, while it usually is worthwhile going after those who switch loyalties with some frequency. Acquisition means acquiring new donors, constituents, or volunteers and message strategy is how we are going to say or write something.

DESCRIBING CLIENTS, DONORS, VOLUNTEERS, AND CONSTITUENTS

An organization's external analysis should consist of addressing four sets of broad questions:

1. Donor, client, and constituent segments:
   - Who is donating to our cause (or buying its products)?
   - Who should be but is not giving to or purchasing from us?
   - Who was and is no longer (and why)?
   - How does the market currently segment and how should it?
   - Does the client base we're working with reflect our organization's goals and mission?
2. Donor, client, and constituent financial activity:
   - How are the donors and buyers stratified from largest to smallest financially?
   - What is the time frame of their giving?
   - What is the frequency of their giving?
   - Do fees for services get paid on time?
   - Is there a need for a stronger collection policy?
3. Donor, client, and constituent motivation:
   - What are the primary motivations behind donors, clients, and constituents involved with our products?
   - What are the most important attributes of our cause?
   - What objectives are the donors trying to solve by giving and the constituents by buying?

4. Donor, client, and constituent needs:

- To what degree are our donors, clients, and constituents happy with what our organization is doing?
- What problems regarding our programs must be solved organizationally to bring them in line with donor, client, and constituent needs?

Donor Profile

The following case study is a profile of a donor's involvement with an organization. The profile examines the donor from a number of different ways and with different data elements in order to help the nonprofit marketing director make a decision on how best to pursue a relationship with this donor. To get the best possible sense of how to pursue the continuing relationship with the donor, the donor must be viewed by the nonprofit organization through a number of different lenses:

Donor Demographics

- Regarding the donor, she might be over 50 years of age, living in a home that she owns, vacationing for one month a year in Phoenix with her spouse, with a combined income of over $35,000 a year, attending a Methodist church, living in a suburban community, and giving to more than five other nonprofit organizations besides her church.

Donor Financial Activity

- Her financial activity may show that she gave her second and most recent gift six months ago in response to a direct mail appeal on hunger in an African nation, that her response was $45 though she was asked for $25, she wrote a check from a shared checking account with her husband, and she has been giving to the organization for over four years.

Donor Motivation

- The donor feels her personal needs and motives are fulfilled by the act of giving to this nonprofit organization. She can readily identify the benefits she receives by giving.

Donor Needs

- Donor needs to perceive the cause as having relevance and organization as having credibility in order to stay involved. Because of the nature of her interest, communication needs to be relatively emotional in order to maintain donor involvement. What does the organization gain by making this analysis? A number of key bits of information. For example, depending on how a donor perceives their involvement with a nonprofit organization, some of the following issues have to be addressed:

1. How relevant to the donor is the information that the nonprofit organization is sending on a regular basis? Is there a positive or negative return on this investment of communication?

2. Does the donor's involvement mean that the organization should take a more personal approach to the donor? Are letters starting with the salutation "Dear friend" appropriate to the donor's involvement? Should they be visited personally?

3. Is the donor looking for more accountability by the nonprofit organization in the relationship? Should the nonprofit organization provide more information on its current spending practices?

USING THE EMERGING SEGMENTATION STRATEGIES FOLLOWING AN EXTERNAL AUDIT

Philip Kotler suggests four common strategies that emerge after an organization undertakes an external analysis of its clients, constituents, volunteers, and donors. The four strategies, as shown in Exhibit 4-2, are undifferentiated, wholly differentiated, concentrated, and partially differentiated.

1. *Undifferentiated strategy.* This occurs when an organization decides to treat its market as a homogenous whole, focusing on common needs and concerns of all the members of the market. This is, in essence, no market segmentation. By definition the media strategy for a cause that did not differentiate would be broad, using many different media vehicles to reach as many as possible. For example, when political disaster

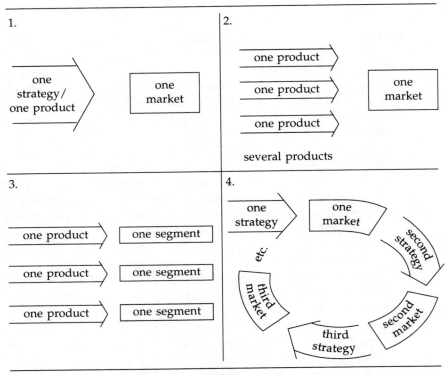

Exhibit 4-2   Four segmentation strategies

and famine struck the African nation of Rwanda in mid-1994, many non-profit disaster relief groups flooded the television and radio airwaves and stuffed the mailboxes of hundreds of thousands of zip codes throughout America looking for an immediate cash response. There was no differentiation in this strategy; all Americans were being asked to give on behalf of the tragedy.

   2. *Wholly differentiated strategy.* In this situation, the nonprofit organization also aims at the whole population, but does so with an array of different products and messages each aimed at a particular market segment. By offering tailor-made messages and products, the nonprofit organization hopes for greater loyalty for its cause. For example, the Red Cross aims its messages at just about all Americans. However, it allows each American to define how they would like to be involved through their message strategies. Some messages are for immediate cash gifts,

some for volunteerism, some for blood for its blood bank, some for the local community drive, and so on. Messages are tailored for different audiences.

3. *Concentrated strategy.* Rather than spreading a message thinly to all, as the previous two strategies do, a concentration effort offers some product to one segment only. The goal here is to achieve strong standing and loyalty within this market, as well as to achieve economies through specialization. Imagine if a nonprofit organization had only one cause (such as a campaign to help individuals stop smoking) and aimed its message at one audience (such as high school girls who smoked). This strategy would be very narrow in scope with highly definable goals.

4. *Partially differentiated strategy.* Having achieved success in one market, the nonprofit organization employing this strategy would next expand into another market with a tailor-made product or project for this market, while confining its marketing goals to just a few segments instead of the entire available market.[20] If this approach (the anti-smoking campaign aimed at high school girls who were currently smokers) worked, then the organizers might wish to aim a campaign at high school boys who were smokers. This would be a partially differentiated strategy.

The following list includes examples of Kotler's common strategies at work in the marketplace.

1. The nonprofit environment is seeing *undifferentiated strategies* at work today on behalf of the many disaster-relief organizations at work in Africa and parts of Eastern Europe. They mail to all the households they can afford and run television commercials in prime time.

2. An example of a *wholly differentiated strategy* is that of the Salvation Army during its Christmas season appeals composed of different messages and products to different audiences through the use of corner and mall solicitation by Santa Clauses, direct mail appeals to many different audiences, localized promotions by area Armies, corporate solicitation, newspaper advertising, and telephone appeals.

3. A camp for young kids with cancer asking its existing donors for scholarship help is an example of a *concentrated strategy.*

4. A capital campaign is an example of a *partially differentiated strategy* as it goes to the public at large for funding after successfully soliciting its own donors.

In some cases, segmentation is successful. Twenty years ago, there was little use of segmentation; everything was a shotgun approach to marketing. Little thought was given to the efficiencies gained by not treating the whole market as a homogenous unit. The assumption to marketing in those years was that everyone had the same resources and interests. Segmentation is the most *critical element* to be learned in marketing management and theory for nonprofit organizations today. It is also the natural outcome of an external analysis of clients, constituents, donors and volunteers.

EXTERNAL ANALYSIS OF COMPETITORS

Having looked at clients, constituents, volunteers, and donors, attention is now given to the second important external factor to consider—competitors. Believe it or not, one nonprofit organization may be competing for the same dollars as several, if not hundreds, of other nonprofit organizations. An analysis that reveals the competitors in one market will help identify who to realistically expect to reach, in every area—donors, volunteers, clients, and constituents. And, more importantly, it will help to identify a realistic market share and realistic, bottom line targets.

Baseball great Dizzy Dean was reputed to have said, "Hit them where they ain't." For some this defines their view of competitive strategy: to create a product or fill a need where there is currently no product or organization by filling an unmet need or tapping an untapped market. Another tack is to build a "better mousetrap" with the hope that clients, constituents, and donors will beat a path to your doorstep.

When a nonprofit director says, "We are doing better this year" perhaps the correct response should be, "Compared to what?" The understanding of where a nonprofit organization stands in relation to others offering similar services is indeed critical. And, with the rise in the availability of information on competitors through increasing technological advances, a nonprofit organization's sales goals, recruitment quotas, returns on investment, and other key financial ratios are measured against similar categories of other companies. Success and value must be defined by the client, donor, and volunteer, not by the opinions of those inside the organization. It is the client's or donor's world that should define the nonprofit organization's strategy, goals, and identification of its competitive edge.

With the donor, the nonprofit organization really only serves as a "middleman" between the donors' desires to do good and the client or cause they wish to help. The client—or the person for whom the nonprofit organization exists—is truly the only party who can assess whether or not the organization has accomplished its mission and objectives.

Nonprofit organizations, and the causes they promote, now live in an age where we are usually no longer the only game in town. Here's an example that illustrates this point.

ADDITION OF A SECOND CAMP AT SPRING HILL

Mark Olson owns a camp. For three months each summer, his non-denominational Spring Hill Camp gives over 4,000 children a tremendous week filled with activities, periods of learning, discovery, and an intense bonding with a team of specially trained counselors. The camp's reputation is so widespread that they have a *tremendous* number of applicants, with more than 1,000 children being turned away each summer. So Mark has decided to open another camp in a nearby state to both relieve some of the load and pressure Spring Hill currently faces and to allow a new section of the country and its youngsters to benefit from the camp's established program.

In thinking through the process of building a new camp, his first step was to define his new "clients" (campers) and determine whether they would come to the new Spring Hill facility. Mr. Olson spent almost a year and a half using many of the concepts talked about previously before the Spring Hill leadership felt comfortable to move to the next step.

Olson's second step identified the organizations, institutions, and activities his new camp would competitively face. In most cases, identifying such primary competitors is relatively straightforward. Here is his partial list, noting that each entry has a varying degree of competitive intensity with Spring Hill:

1. There is one other nondenominational camp within 30 miles of Spring Hill.
2. There are three church camps within 100 miles.
3. There is one YMCA boys camp and one YWCA girls camp within 150 miles.
4. There are still other camps not mentioned within a 200-mile radius.
5. There are many camp-style outings sponsored by service agencies, Boy's Clubs, churches, etc. within a 200-mile radius.
6. Many families vacation, where camping is part of that vacation, within a 200-mile radius of the new camp.

Three Principles in Defining Competition

While there are many other strategic steps the Spring Hill administration will take, some principles can be drawn from the above list.

1. *Competition for alternatives.* Perhaps the most obvious one is that there seems to be an abundance of potential competition for the campers' dollars. The presence of alternatives to one's own programs is often surprising to many nonprofit directors.

2. *Direct vs. indirect competitors.* Many nonprofit organizations are in situations today where they are not the only ones offering a service to a particular audience; there may be other organizations offering the exact, same service. Surprisingly, clients, donors, and volunteers are often more aware of the substitute options than the nonprofit organization. The clients are looking for the particular service and often discover the different options. Donors and volunteers are eager to support those programs that agree with their values.

In fact, the notion of substitute options is very relevant for today's marketer. If the availability of substitute products or causes is the first observation, then the second observation is that, despite competition for the camper's dollar, not every competitor is competing at the same level. There are usually some *direct competitors* (those a nonprofit organization competes with on a day-to-day basis), as there are also some *indirect competitors* (those a nonprofit organization competes with on an irregular basis). A pattern emerges upon analysis and leads to a deeper understanding of how this example of a youth camp market functions.

3. *Defining the key variables.* The third observation is that, "the definition of the most competitive groups will depend on a few key variables. It may be strategically important to know the relevant importance of these variables."[21] With respect to the camp, important variables might include *proximity* of the camp to the potential camper, the *programs offered*, the *availability* of some type of *moral emphasis* at the camp, some type of *referral* from a previous camp attender, and so on.

POSITIONING TO UNDERSTAND "THE MARKET"

The three principles mentioned in the case study allow the nonprofit marketer to develop a conceptual base for identifying potential competitors. The marketer tries to *position the organization* through the eyes of the client (or camper) in order to understand the competitive environment. By doing so, he or she looks at competitors' performance, current and past programmatical strategies, current and past fund-raising strategies, their strengths and weaknesses. The goal is to understand the competitive advantages of its competitors, allowing the nonprofit organization to be prepared to respond to future moves of the competition.

WAYS TO IDENTIFY COMPETITION

David Aaker, the J. Gary Shansby Professor of Marketing Strategy at the University of California in Berkeley, says there are two ways to identify competitors (and potential competitors):

> The first takes the perspective of the customer who must make choices among competitors. The second attempts to group competitors into strategic groups on the basis of their competitive strategy.[22]

For example, a listing of all of the international child sponsorship agencies who function similarly could be considered a *strategic group* based on their competitive strategy. One could define this group by looking at those who use extensive mail list rentals as a source of names and income, who promote their international work through gut-wrenching photographs in general interest magazines, and who use the "sponsor a child for one month at $X" as their predominant message strategy.

So far, we've discussed how a marketer might see competitive options through a client's or constituent's eyes. Now, the notion of marketing strategy continues as competitors are identified on the basis of their strategy grouping.

HOW NONPROFIT ORGANIZATIONS COMPETE

Nonprofit groups compete with each other in roughly four areas: *programmatical or technical superiority, quality of programs or products, better support services,* and *price.* All four bear further examination.

Programmatical or Technical Superiority

In for-profit organizations, research and development activities (often termed "R&D") often provide the basis for competitive advantage. Is technical superiority also an advantage nonprofit organizations can use?

The answer is "yes," especially if the nonprofit organization engages in constant meaningful innovation.

The message is clear with the Spring Hill Camp case study. After 15 years of consistently developing and improving the right programming mix, the fact that the camp's programs *really work* gives Spring Hill a competitive advantage. It positions itself as a "camp that helps parents raise better kids." And the assumption that "we've got the program right where we want it" is never uttered at Spring Hill; there is a continuing commitment to produce the right innovations and to examine every activity of the camp to identify whether it contributes to "helping parents raise better kids." In other words, continually checking each activity against the organization's core mission or purpose is essential. In fact, in any given programming cycle at Spring Hill, fully 20 percent of its programs are new and under heavy evaluation. If new programs do not advance the organization toward its goal, they're discarded and the staff looks for new options.

Quality of Programs or Products

Quality of programs, staff, and products within a nonprofit organization does not simply fall into place. It takes effort to be perceived as reliable. In order to be perceived as such, the organization must possess true quality. But what is true "quality?" Consider the following case studies.

BUFFALO CITY MISSION

The mission created men's and women's housing. Women who were taken into the Mission often were accompanied by children so there was a need to create a different style of housing with larger rooms, play areas, counseling areas, and small classrooms for the children. The men, on the other hand, did not need the same space allocation. Both needed job counseling rooms and on-the-job training areas. Theirs was not to be the normal rundown facility designed for transients and those in trouble as some "missions" can be perceived. Forethought was given to outside appearances and "its subsequent welcome-ability." There was a need to demonstrate to the city that the mission was interested in *doing an excellent job* with the population it served.

SELLING A SMALL ORGANIZATION'S SERVICES

A St. Louis nonprofit organization attacked the issue of communicating quality a unique way. Being a small halfway house, it could not compete financially with the bigger organizations in St. Louis that were offering similar programs. However, in their analysis of the competition and its similar services, the marketing director felt this organization had a distinct programmatical advantage and could differentiate itself by saying to potential clients, "We have been in the treatment business a lot *longer* than anyone else," hence implying that the organization had more experience and a higher degree of success with its patients. The firm used its small size as another selling point: "Since we're not part of a big hospital or organization, we can offer more personalized service." The goal of both of these "sales tactics" is to seem more humane, and appear to offer a higher quality service.[23] Identify the elements offered that are truly quality products of programs and they will sell themselves. Simply provide descriptions—through brochures, through marketing pieces, and by word of mouth—of a message that is true.

Better Support Services

International Business Machines (IBM) has for years stressed customer service as a fundamental guiding principle. One pitfall that nonprofit organizations must overcome is in thinking that improving their products and programs takes priority over improving their services. Products and programs are easier to pin down than services; nonprofit directors may believe an organization's service improvement is more an "artform" than mandated by good management principles. In fact, the management support processes often say more about a nonprofit organization's ability and quality than do its programs. Simple items like receipt turnaround time, answering complaint mail quickly, returning donors' calls promptly, processing paperwork accurately, and the like all speak volumes about an organization.

Richard Schoenberger's book, *Building a Chain of Customers*, encourages everyone in a company to be concerned about organizational processes, under the belief that all employees have a "client" they must serve. One way of accomplishing this is through quality support services. A quality system audit is one answer, and can be relatively straightforward.

Price

Few nonprofit organizations with a lower cost of doing business (or a lower cost of programs offered) use this fact as a competitive advantage. Surprisingly though, many nonprofit organizations take to heart the need for massive productivity improvement. At a time when the output per hour worked for all companies in the United States has increased only an average of .7 percent per year, lower nonprofit price increases or price reductions should be used as a competitive advantage to nonprofit audiences—particularly those that are price or cost sensitive.[24] For some for-profit audiences, the idea of *low price* sometimes translates into low quality. Inversely, the idea of advertising a low service cost to a contributor base or communicating that field personnel costs are actually decreasing in some areas, can be of tremendous value when stated articulately.

All American consumers are accustomed to hearing about price increases. When a nonprofit organization says that it has saved money or kept costs down, this represents a beneficial change from what has become the "norm." Stories like this are often placed in a newsletter or magazine format where the nonprofit organization can be shown taking positive steps to minimize costs. Likewise, a nonprofit organization can also point out this cost containment trend in its solicitations as it asks for new funds. Cost containment efforts can be a good way to attract both volunteer and donor interest.

THE SEARCH FOR THE COMPETITIVE ADVANTAGE

The search for identifying the competitive advantage at any nonprofit organization is a process of uncovering the one thing that the nonprofit organization does better than anyone else. It is almost impossible to be everything to everybody. An organization should determine what its strengths are, the services it best provides for the best value, and then focus on those strengths and services. The following case study shows how one organization identified its competitive advantage.

BABY SHOP AND ITS COMPETITION

Company Background

The nonprofit organization, Baby Shop, was started to provide special day-care attention to infants and toddlers under the age of two. The nonprofit organization had trained counselors and stressed that it was the only day-care that specialized in the under two years of age category. Baby Shop targeted its service to higher income households with significant discretionary income, specifically centering on families with new children where the spouse would most likely want to return to the job market.

Market Analysis

Three day-care companies compete with Baby Shop. One of the competitors is a local franchise of a chain of day-care centers. None of the competitors take the same marketing position as Baby Shop.

Competitor Analysis (Competitors, Strengths, Weaknesses, Our Response)

- Little Kids is a local franchise which has significant national advertising and a national reputation to back it up. However, it will take a cookie cutter approach to how it conducts its business. Our response will be to stress that we are local and tailor our approach to the local environment.
- BabyFace is new, has a nice location and strong staff. It is very expensive, though, and caters through age five. We will position ourselves as cheaper, more experienced staff, and specialists in the under age two category.
- Cute is the oldest day-care in the city. They have lots of experience and, most likely, a good referral system at work on their behalf. The neighborhood around their location has declined. We will stress safety and proximity to higher income neighborhoods.

Summation

Baby Shop has developed a strong competitive position in the market. That position can best be described by the following attributes: specialists, up-scale competitively priced, elegant and clean, and a market leader in its age group.

As can be seen from this case study, competitive advantage grows out of an examination of the strengths and weaknesses of the competition.

CHAPTER FIVE

Researching Your Nonprofit Organization's Environment

The nonprofit world is less a world than a universe—vast, varied, and unexplored.[1]

Fred Setterberg and Kary Schulman
Beyond Profit

There isn't enough money, manpower or sympathy to go around. People worldwide must have the feeling of "African famine again?"

Dr. Tatsuo Hayashi
Japan International Volunteer Center in Tokyo

What accounts for the tepid response from what were once concerned patrons? Some factors are perennial: lack of awareness, an absence of national self-interest, and a shortage of resources. But needy causes must now reckon with another significant factor: *donor fatigue.* Besieged by so many appeals along with countless daily news reports of tragedy after drought, after war, after abuse . . . people grow weary of giving. This is particularly true if they've already dug into their pockets for a cause only to see the trouble continue. Endemic problems, like famine in Sudan and Ethiopia, or seemingly uncontrollable ones, like cyclones and earthquakes, stand little chance of sustained public compassion and support.[2]

Consider the following as an example: One recent advertisement pictures a room full of babies. "America's most endangered species" reads the caption. Another ad raises the specter of crime: "The way we treat our kids is killing us." Another poses a question about the nation's economy: "How can we stay number one, if we put our kids last?"

All of these appeals on behalf of children—to compassion, to fear, to enlightened self-interest—were tested recently by a New York advertising agency. *All* had to be scrapped.

"Nothing worked," says Jack Aaker, associate creative director of Grey Advertising, which is developing a public service campaign on children's issues for the Ad Council. "Very few people wanted to call the toll-free number (given in the ads). Many were suspicious that we would ask for money."[3]

Nonprofit organizations have always been confronted with uncertainty, especially in their dealings with donors and their support, volunteers and their ability to serve, and variations in the demand for the organization's services. But now, they are facing more questions than ever. Questions such as:

- How does the economy affect giving and demand for services?
- Will the budget crisis that affects at least 37 states cause more problems for nonprofit organizations that rely on government funds?
- How will increased postal rates and the latest changes in tax laws affect nonprofit organizations?[4]

THE NATURE OF A NONPROFIT ORGANIZATION'S ENVIRONMENT

As part of a nonprofit organization's ongoing external analysis, it should not only look specifically at clients, volunteers, constituents, and donors, but must also assess the larger competitive boundaries of the philanthropic community it is a part of, and the surrounding environment. When a for-profit company is interested in entering an industry, it performs an analysis of that industry as well as an analysis of the surrounding environment. The primary objective of the analysis is to determine the attractiveness of the industry to current and potential participants. The attractiveness potential is measured by the short- and/or long-term returns on investment that will be provided by the industry.

Other ingredients make up the "attractiveness" of the industry, including the number and quality of competitors, their strengths and weaknesses, and those distinctive competencies the company in question must have in place to succeed in the particular industry. These are termed by University of California Professor of Marketing Strategy David Aaker as *success factors*.[5]

In essence, the for-profit company spends considerable amounts of energy and time scanning a potential environment. This chapter will show why the same rationale needs to be applied to the environment surrounding a nonprofit organization.

Defining the Notion of Profit

Profit is the critical measuring stick over time in a for-profit world. A nonprofit organization, though, must measure a number of different "bottom lines" or "profits" in order to assess its performance in the nonprofit world. Profitability is one factor, but there are others. Nonprofit organizations "deal with balance, synthesis, a combination of bottom lines for performance."[6]

Business management author Peter Drucker reminds nonprofit marketers of the differences between the nonprofit and for-profit worlds:

> Nonprofit organizations have no "bottom line." They are prone to consider everything they do to be righteous and moral and to serve a cause, so they are not willing to say, it doesn't produce results then maybe we should direct our resources elsewhere. Nonprofit organizations need the discipline of organized abandonment perhaps even more than a business does. They need to face up to critical choices.[7]

A look at the philanthropic community, as well as the environment that surrounds both the nonprofit organization and its contributing constituencies, can help in developing a marketing and competitive strategy. A nonprofit agency tends to arrive at its marketing strategy and competitive position largely because "it works," sometimes through research and other times through pure accident.

Competitors and a Nonprofit Organization's Environment

Most nonprofit organizations actually operate in a very competitive environment. There are many other nonprofit organizations operating within the same environments, with similar service/product mixes, often to the same audience.

A nonprofit organization and its competitors are sometimes spoken of as comprising a separate "industry." Though it seems out of context to speak of nonprofit organizations comprising an "industry," it is helpful in order to group nonprofit organizations into the same field(s), cause(s), and to "adjacent" organizations. The nature of the nonprofit organization's industry depends on context. The "industry" boundaries depend to a large measure on *how* the nonprofit organization competes: Is it competing with other like-minded firms in the city, state, national, or international context? A nonprofit organization competing with other nonprofit organizations in the same city serving the same local population, all undertaking like-minded causes, has a much more volatile competitive situation than one whose nearest competitor is 300 miles away.

Nonprofit directors must begin to think in terms that have historically been outside of their normal circumstances. For example, suppose you're interested in developing an international child relief and sponsorship agency. What critical dimensions would you look at to get a sense of the child relief and sponsorship field? The following seven questions serve as a starting point in gathering the necessary data to facilitate your decision:

1. The actual size of the child relief and sponsorship philanthropic environment, including the potential donor universe and the number of organizations in this field.

2. How this environment structures itself (e.g., Do relief organizations work together to deal with problems or do they work separately? Are their headquarters U.S. based or internationally based? Are volunteers critical to the success of their operations?)

3. How nonprofit organizations obtain information in order to choose to enter the child relief and sponsorship "field."

4. How the sponsorship environment prices its services (or the dollar amount it tries to raise for those services) from its supporting constituency.

5. How sponsorship organizations ensure the money they solicit and the help they provide get to those in need.

6. The economic or geopolitical trends that are occurring in the child relief and sponsorship field.

7. The potential for growth in the child relief and sponsorship community.

Each of the previous seven questions—and a nonprofit organization's response to them—will influence its marketing and competitive stance vis-à-vis other child and relief sponsorship organizations. The implications of these questions and the ultimate bearing they have upon the sponsorship example and its competitive stance are discussed fully in the following sections.

THE ACTUAL AND POTENTIAL SIZE
OF THE COMPETITIVE ENVIRONMENT

The principal reason to look at the size of the competitive environment (or industry) is to determine how much money a nonprofit organization will have to spend to gain a portion or share of the market for the cause it represents (in this case, child relief and sponsorship). (See Exhibit 5-1.) This market share includes both those who could support the organization's mission financially, as well as those the organization intends to care for and help. The larger the potential donor pool, the broader the philanthropic nature of the cause or appeal, or the greater the population an organization can care for, the better a nonprofit organization's chances are for success in entering a new market. However, the more narrowly focused the appeal or mission, the smaller the population in need, or the smaller the potential donor pool (especially one crowded with many competitors), the harder it is for the same nonprofit organization to be successful.

In the nonprofit world, the type of marketing and tactical information previously described can be hard to come by. However, actual industry size is often available from trade associations, government or chamber of commerce publications, the financial reports of competing organizations, published financial sources, and even from donors themselves.

Continuing with the child relief and sponsorship example, the primary interest in looking at all child sponsorship organizations (or the "sponsorship industry") is to determine the size of the competition, where it is located, how firmly entrenched (or loyal) donors are to particular organizations, and whether the potential sponsorship nonprofit

Organization	Number of donors	Type of service
Nonprofit A	Approximately 46,000 Budget $22 million	Works through agencies in countries
Nonprofit B	Approximately 800,000 Budget $112 million	Has international divisions, large staff; 21 percent of budget used for fund raising
Nonprofit C	Approximately 120,000 Budget $69 million	Has 1 international office and staff; extensive use of volunteers; wide government support

Exhibit 5-1   Child relief and sponsorship

organization will have enough money to attract a substantially big enough donor supply to accomplish the core goals of the organization.

Identifying a Usage Group

As part of this evaluation, an organization's management must also determine the potential market and how much of it is being tapped by existing sponsorship organizations. This gap in a competitor's strategy, or *usage gap*, is more fully explained in the following case study.

BOOSTING CHURCH ATTENDANCE

In a study done for a specific religious denomination in Wisconsin, in certain cities of the state it was found that attendance for denominational church services was often one half of that of other denominational churches in the same town. Clearly, church attendance for the denomination potentially could be increased by tapping the usage gap by:

- encouraging a greater variety of services covering a broader range of topics;
- finding new church attenders;
- finding new ways to involve local communities through job resource fairs, day-care, providing meals for those in need; and
- increasing the attendance of those nominally aware of the church services.

People might be encouraged to attend the particular church if they saw it addressing a wide variety of issues and being more central to their everyday lives.

Similar logic can be used by nonprofit organizations in analyzing the potential opportunities when entering a new "industry." For example:

- Can a nonprofit organization (such as the suggested child and sponsorship example) find donors for its cause, or can it increase the rate or size of donations given by existing donors to the entire child and sponsorship industry?

- Can the new child and sponsorship nonprofit organization deliver its services, products, opportunities for volunteerism, or solicitation strategies in a new or better way than the competition?

- Are there new ways the sponsorship cause can be introduced, or are there products or variations in the way the cause is being presented to the public currently being ignored by the competition?

- Are there competitive gaps that the sponsorship organization can take advantage of; whether they are gaps in the messages being communicated to the public, audiences being ignored in the marketing process, and the like?

HOW IS THE ENVIRONMENT STRUCTURED?

The ultimate goal in looking at how an environment or industry is structured is to determine whether there is a sustainable competitive advantage for the entering organization. Using the child sponsorship example, the nonprofit organization's management gains an understanding of industry structured by analyzing itself along several different dimensions.

An analysis of past and current marketing, operational strategies, and objectives helps determine a nonprofit organization's stability and marketplace intentions. By looking at size and growth indicators of like-minded nonprofit organizations, management can begin to see how important these measures might be to the overall success of the organization's mission. An organization's culture can provide a clue as to the constraints and potential audiences that may be attracted to the organization. Perceived accumulated costs can be used to project future service costs and fund-raising requirements.

Such information can be derived from annual reports made available by nonprofit organizations in the same or similar industry, talking directly to the marketing or development directors of the nonprofit organizations, talking to their donors when known, and attending a competitor's events. The goal is to give the public something that is not already being provided. Paying close attention to potential competitors' strategies and services is the best way to identify a gap in service that is not currently being filled.

Michael Porter in his book, *Competitive Strategy*, talks about for-profit industries structuring themselves along five basic components: *competitors, potential competitors, substitute products, customers,* and *suppliers.*[8] Porter's thesis is that each of these components has a role in helping determine the intensity of competition in a particular industry.

Competitors

If an environment (like our child sponsorship example) contains a high number of competitors, then one could expect more competition among these organizations for both the philanthropic dollar and actual services provided. The nonprofit organization that is new to an "industry" can expect vigorous and highly committed competitors who are willing to spend money to retain their donors. They will be introducing increased donor services, new twists on existing client services, and tell their story to new publics through intense advertising and fund-raising campaigns.

Most likely, these competitors will also be appealing for similar monthly sponsorship amounts from donors; the donations requested from donors might be similar in their requested amounts because of both high fixed costs the organizations could have in setting up their international sponsorship systems and a similarity of marketing styles. Volunteers may also be drawn from similar groups or pools. In addition, the actual children being helped might be from the *same parts of the world* or channeled through similar organizations.

Therefore, a new organization to the field of child sponsorship would need to ensure that it had enough resources to mount both a vigorous promotional and donor recruitment campaign, as well as enough resources to actually get help to the children it serves. And the question of quality and intent must be addressed: If you cannot rationalize providing service to a group that you will truly be able to help, to reach, to fund, and to sustain, then should you really be entering this industry?

Potential Competitors

When considering a new field of service, an organization should consider competitors who have the *capability* to enter the field successfully. In continuing our example, what would it take for an organization to enter the child relief and sponsorship field? Perhaps:

- A very strong capital investment?
- The ability to attract a large number of donors quickly?
- The ability to either set up an international sponsorship system or work in tandem with an existing system?
- The ability to differentiate the nonprofit organization from other sponsorship organizations?

Most likely it would take some combination of all of these things. In addition, a new organization would have to consider whether the climate was "ripe" for new competitors or whether factors—such as slow growth—have eliminated some of the attractiveness of being in this field.

Substitute Causes, Services, or Products

Substitute causes, services, and products provide potential clients, donors, volunteers, and constituents with alternative choices. Normally a substitute cause or product competes less intensely than the primary cause, service, or product but still influences the marketplace. Obviously, the more attractive and abundant the substitutes to individuals, the harder it is for a new-to-the-field organization to compete in the field.

Using our sponsorship example, there are many forms of child sponsorship used by different organizations. Some of these groups serving children are international in their reach, some are tied to a particular country, and some sponsorship nonprofit organizations are domestic in scope. Regardless of operational style, each substitute competitor possesses a potential challenge to a nonprofit organization's efforts at entering a field by offering a choice; they may all be competing for the same donor's dollar.

Just as an electronic alarm system is available as a substitute for the use of a security agency, support for a local nonprofit adoption agency could be a substitute to a donor for an international child sponsorship organization, especially if the donor's motive for giving is to help defenseless children. A church's initiative at helping children locally could also be a substitute to a potential volunteer who also wanted to be involved with children who are less fortunate. Any organization that is competing for dollars using a similar appeal should be considered as a "competitor." Their marketing and advertising strategies should be studied so as not to replicate appeals.

Clients and Constituents

In a for-profit corporation, the presence or absence of customers usually guides a company's actions. The situation is different in the nonprofit world, although the differences between for-profit and nonprofit organizations continue to narrow. Because clients in the nonprofit world often get services for *free*, or at a greatly reduced price, they are not as quick to complain about their quality and are more likely to forgive or keep quiet about poor service. As a consequence, this most critical indicator of an organization's performance—its services offered—is often not an accurate barometer of performance. How do we measure the level of service provided?

Some of this forgiving attitude on behalf of clients and constituents is changing, especially as other *free* options become available. Churches are a logical example. Today, churches face consumers, customers, and members who are demanding different types of services, mandating different levels of quality and who display a willingness to "shop" churches the way one would "shop" car dealerships. This makes almost any church audience a powerful consumer group because they have the ability to demand many things of the church's administration by virtue of their economic power. In essence, they can demand better service or go elsewhere.

The question remains of how to continually tap into general "feelings" about the services provided. Here are some suggested tactics:

1. Continually poll membership or clients to determine the needs of the congregation and try to tailor services to fill those needs.
2. Monitor the "competition" to see what they are offering their constituents.
3. Former clients should be questioned as to their satisfaction with the services, perhaps in an "exit interview" or mail-in questionnaire.
4. Clients and former attendees ought to be encouraged to vent their feelings and supply suggestions on a regular basis.

Suppliers

Rather than thinking of suppliers in the traditional form as in for-profit organizations, in this case "suppliers" means the impact of the *donating constituency* who supply the needed resources to the sponsorship industry. Of critical importance in the sponsorship example is the question, "Can there be enough *donors* to fund all the sponsorship organizations looking for help, or will donors tend to be concentrated into smaller groups supporting a few well-known agencies?"

An additional key question is, "Will they stay loyal to the organization or will donors quickly change their financial support to another substitute sponsorship organization working in a more attractive part of the world?"

Here are five suggested ways in which to tap into the feelings and possible projected donations of competitors.

HOW NONPROFIT ORGANIZATIONS ENTER AN INDUSTRY

It is relatively easy for a nonprofit organization to enter a certain field, such as the sponsorship field. In fact, it is much easier for a nonprofit organization to enter almost any field than it is for a for-profit company to enter an industry. Why? Usually two variables must be considered and answered before a for-profit company enters an industry—its start-up costs and the competitors it may face. These two factors, however, are usually not as burdensome in the not-for-profit world.

Unfortunately, most nonprofit organizations (like our child sponsor-ship example) look at very few indicators in evaluating the attractive-ness of entering a field. If they do any research in the environment or industry, they primarily focus around potential and real competitors, differences in marketing and fund-raising appeals between groups, the similarity of organizational functions in relation to competitors, and the real or potential donor pool.

There's No Direction Without An Analysis

This lack of analysis may be an error in judgment because most non-profit causes in fact have a *large number of competitors*. Unlike many for-profit industries, the presence of many competitors does not usually pre-vent a nonprofit firm from entering an industry. Perhaps this is because so few nonprofit leaders use the *marketing concept* or *marketing parameters* in making any decision of this type. Marketing concept means the total orientation of a firm's resources toward satisfying the needs of donors, constituents, and/or clients; the presence of a single marketing executive who integrates all marketing functions; and the presence of such staff functions as marketing research and product planning, with all depart-ments contributing to increase profitable volume. (See Exhibit 5-2.)

The major problem plaguing many nonprofit industries is the failure to embrace a marketing orientation in what has become a marketing-dri-ven environment. Let's take a look at how nonprofit organizations decide to enter a field of service, since most nonprofit organizations view entry into a particular environment from a different perspective.

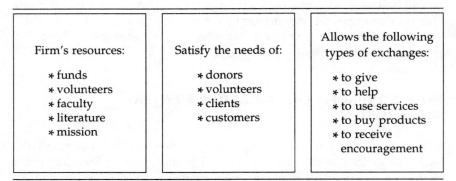

Firm's resources:	Satisfy the needs of:	Allows the following types of exchanges:
* funds * volunteers * faculty * literature * mission	* donors * volunteers * clients * customers	* to give * to help * to use services * to buy products * to receive encouragement

Exhibit 5-2   The marketing concept

Service or Ministry Needs Are Not Everything

Many nonprofit organizations make the decision to enter a field based exclusively on a perceived or imaginary need for their services. This "need" usually is determined by:

- *Inferential data* from the marketplace (often encouragement from current recipients of the organization's services);
- *Entrepreneurial "hunches"* from the director of the organization or board that the organization should move in a certain direction;
- A *"follow the leader"* strategy in which the organization imitates another nonprofit organization's actions;
- *Compassion* on behalf of a societal need that exists; and
- *Strong suggestions* by influential donors to the nonprofit organization promising financial support if the organization enters the field.

In only a few cases has a systematic look at the surrounding community taken place. In a great majority of these cases, the decision to enter a field is not predicated on an industry evaluation or up-to-date market research. Subsequent concerns about the philanthropic environment's structure—such as the realistic donor pool—and real or potential competition are not systematically considered. Yet a systematic look is the key to successful lauching and viability of a new service or product!

Little Research Into Competition Can Spell Disaster

Some environments seem strategically more important than others as measured by the amount of competition. For example, the child care sponsorship world is an extremely competitive field. One would expect, given the high number of competitors in this field, that the competition is more intense.

Issues that inhibit a for-profit firm from entering an industry include the high fixed costs of getting into an industry (the amount of money a company will have to spend to compete effectively) and the cost to the competitors of leaving the industry (called *exit costs*). Such factors should be included in a nonprofit organization's decision to enter a field, but are normally not included.

Nonprofit organizations enter virtually any field they choose with little of the concerns exhibited by for-profit firms. One reason may be the perception of capital investment; the investment required (or perceived to be required) is usually not a big concern for a nonprofit organization. They seldom enter a field having decided to "spend" the required dol-

For-profit organizations	Nonprofit organizations
1. Market research as to opportunities	1. Often one or a few people's initiative
2. Cost factors are taken into account	2. Costs often not analyzed
3. Key stakeholders are polled	3. Key stakeholders usually not polled

Exhibit 5-3 How organizations decide to enter a market

lars needed to do a good job in the respective field. Rather, the average nonprofit organization is interested in both the public relations benefit of being able to say to its constituency that it is at work in a certain field, as well as the personal satisfaction that comes with this, as opposed to the ability to do a truly superior job of working within the field as an overriding management concern. This is not as much a deliberate move as it is a journey into unfamiliar territory.

Likewise, where economies of scale are important in big industries, the issues of obtaining large volumes of business, sales, or services rendered very quickly is usually not given the same weight within a nonprofit milieu, but should be considered. Other issues including product differentiation are also seldom given much strategic thought. In an industry where benchmarks of performance are not usually built into the decision-making apparatus, it often becomes more important to a nonprofit organization to be *perceived* as being involved in a cause than it is to excel or achieve great results in the same cause. Exhibit 5-3 compares the ways in which nonprofit and for-profit organizations enter a new market.

Most likely, clients, constituents, and donors are relatively uninformed with regard to the performance values of a nonprofit organization. Unlike a normal board of directors or governing body of a for-profit company, the informal board of directors of a nonprofit organization (i.e., its donors) actually has little influence—and often little interest—in making the nonprofit organization accountable for its viability.

HOW DOES THE ENVIRONMENT PRICE ITS SERVICES?

In the for-profit sector, firms that sell what consumers want are rewarded by steadily climbing sales. These firms do not sell what they cannot sell profitably because of their dependence on ever-increasing revenues. Likewise, most nonprofit organizations that have been around for a number of years have tailor-made their programs of service to fit the expectations of the donors to the organization. These donors are the "economic demanders of the organization's services."[9]

Given the cutbacks in federal funding to many groups (starting around 1980), donations for many nonprofit entities have had to be supplanted by revenue from engaging in profit-making activities. (The Girl Scouts generate millions of dollars through their cookie sales; revenues well over $200 million.[10]) This is an area that has great potential. Consider other nonprofit organizations that have successfully engaged in profit-making activities in order to raise funds—Unicef's Christmas cards, candy sold by educational institutions, or cookies sold to fund charitable causes. The common thread being that items are sold to customers for a price that includes a built-in profit margin. The effect can be very successful, especially if your image is positive and is recognizable to potential customers. Some degree of "profit" is made here to fund other nonprofit activities.

From the nonprofit organization's point of view, it may make sense when analyzing a field to decide which services can be done at the lowest cost and still demand the highest fees or donations. For example, regarding child sponsorship, it may be that the costs of delivering help and services overseas would require the nonprofit entity to also consider a domestic child sponsorship program, thereby realizing significant cost advantages over its overseas business.

Of course it may not be possible to gain a cost advantage; in fact, many nonprofit organizations do not even concern themselves with costs if they feel a strong or compelling reason to be in a particular field. An organization caring for AIDS victims may feel a moral responsibility to help victims in Africa, as opposed to caring for those in America, regardless of the increase in costs incurred by working overseas.

HOW DOES THE NONPROFIT ORGANIZATION DELIVER ITS SERVICES?

It is important in fast-changing environments to be able to anticipate change. For example, one organization builds medical clinics in Haiti. At the time of this writing many of the organization's workers and operations have been disrupted and forced out of the country in light of Haitian political unrest. Fortunately, this organization has set up channels of operation and delivery of services in other poverty-stricken countries and is transferring operations to these new areas.

There are at least four different concerns for a nonprofit organization in delivering its services:

- Are there inherent *political or environmental problems* in the channels a nonprofit organization uses to distribute its services?
- Are there *alternative channels* available?
- Are there *trends* that indicate a nonprofit organization could deliver services better using a different method?
- Who are the *critical gatekeepers* of the delivery channels or the people who influence service delivery?

David Aaker calls "access to an effective and efficient distribution channel" one of the "key success factors."[11] A nonprofit organization typically deals with many channels simultaneously, both in delivering services and in raising dollars. Alternative channels exist, and some nonprofit organizations sell their wares (or raise their funds) by going directly to the potential donor. Others use "middlemen" like service organizations and churches to attract clients to achieve their distribution or funding goals. Still others count on giant nonprofit retailers like the United Way to cover the bulk of their budget. Some larger nonprofit organizations try to do all of this in varying degrees.

This analysis of emerging changes in distribution or funding channels can be enormously important in understanding the success factors of the environment. For example, a number of city rescue missions in the country that espouse certain theological doctrines expect that between 25 to 40 percent of their funding dollars are coming from constituencies that are either unchurched or affiliated with different theological stances than the city mission in question. Focus group research has indicated many of these new, nontraditional donors to the city missions give because the missions provide benefits to those forced onto the street due to unexpected circumstances. This concern exhibited by those who provide funding overrides the differences in the theological stance some donors may have with the missions. Shouldn't this new constituency force city missions to look at how they communicate with their new donor audiences?

A new constituency can force new channel decisions. The emergence of nonprofit organizations competing with for-profits in the fields of day-care, health-care, and other concerns forces nonprofit management to better control decision making in certain funding channels, how services are chosen, and how this may change in the future.

What Are the Trends in the Environment and Industry?

J. Donald Weinrauch, in his book, *The Marketing Problem Solver,* lists the 10 most colossal marketing mistakes a company can make. The first mistake he lists is "A failure to understand and appreciate trends in the marketplace."[12]

Consider some of the trauma the National Audubon Society is facing in the following case study:

THE NATIONAL AUDUBON SOCIETY LOSES FUNDING

Of all the projects the National Audubon Society has undertaken in its 100 years, none have played to a larger audience and few have drawn more aggressive attacks from opponents than its nationally televised "World of Audubon" specials. Last summer, for instance, its documentary "The New Range Wars" accused ranchers and the government of promoting grazing practices that destroyed millions of acres of fragile drylands.

But Audubon's ability to broadcast its view of the world came under a new threat recently when the General Electric Company said it would not renew its contract to underwrite the productions. The company told Audubon that because of economic pressure from the recession it would not pay for the productions after its three-year, $3 million contract expires next year.

Although Audubon says it will find a way to keep the documentaries on the air, the announcement exposed its vulnerability to sudden cuts in financing from a source that is becoming increasingly important. More than that, it demonstrated the importance of the closer ties between environmental groups and the businesses that are often thought of as their adversaries.[13]

What economic, environmental, or geopolitical trends (see Chapter 3) are occurring that suggest new growth directions or change for the future of nonprofit organizations and their environments? One change or direction may be the practice of nonprofit organizations partnering with other nonprofit organizations to get their work done. Some recent examples of this are a church and a day-care joining forces to provide services to their city ... two food banks joining together to provide broader access and coverage to a city's hungry ... or take the case of a nonprofit publisher working in tandem with an adult rehab center. The net outcome of these mergers is often improved services to the target population, acquired expertise in new market areas, a larger donor pool, and better systems and strategies through joint partnering. Another may be the emergence of database marketing as the flagship of nonprofit marketing strategies.

Another consideration is the bombardment of the U.S. adult population with over 3,000 marketing messages a day and the inability of most nonprofit organizations to have their message stand out in the marketplace. Consider the findings of this recent survey profiling those who donate money in response to specific requests:

- Whites are more likely than ethnic minorities to donate funds.
- Baby-boomers, it seems, have a bad reputation among people as being unwilling to part with their money for good causes. The reality is that boomers are every bit as likely as prior generations were at this stage in their life cycle to donate money to charity.
- Better educated and wealthier people were more likely to have donated money than were people of lesser means and schooling.[14]

It could be disastrous for a nonprofit organization to enter a new industry without taking a look at the trends. Consider this as an example: A group of people wanted to build a horse camp in Colorado for young people. This sounded like a good idea until they found out that Colorado has more camps per capita than any other state in the nation, with many of them not operating to capacity. This fact alone should have a definite bearing on the proposed camp's competitive stance and its potential for success in the future.

How does a nonprofit organization monitor trends?

- By constant monitoring of the economy and the culture at large: Is the economy in decline or growing; is the mood of the country optimistic or desperate?
- By observing shifts in the marketplace, especially jobs that are in decline and those that are promising.
- By monitoring new product introductions into our society, observing their success or failure, and noting how they are changing society at large.
- By observing transformations in community and family structure.

WHAT IS THE POTENTIAL FOR GROWTH IN THE ENVIRONMENT?

There should be a direct correlation between the potential for growth in a particular industry and the attractiveness of that industry to the nonprofit organization considering it. The potential for growth usually means greater opportunity for a company. Today, many nonprofit organizations are looking at the upper plateau of their client and financial growth curves. Their ability to grow translates to their ability to continue to expand the services they exist for; the lack of growth means curtailment of services.

Who Supports the Cause and What Do They Think?

For a nonprofit entity to answer questions regarding the future it must know who it is currently attracting to buy its products or support its causes. By answering this question, a nonprofit organization can begin to address how its client services and products are perceived as contrasted with those of its competitors. (See Exhibit 5-4.) Given an accurate knowledge of client, donor, and constituent perceptions, a nonprofit organization can then determine where there are voids in the competitive strategies it has at work in the environment. This type of *perceptual mapping* allows the nonprofit marketer to look at market niches not occupied by the competition and gives an organization the opportunity to create new products or thrusts to fill these voids. An example of mapping is shown in Exhibit 5-5.

Repositioning to Enhance Growth

Often used in tandem with perceptual mapping is another growth strategy: repositioning the existing client services or product mix in order to enhance growth, sales, or donations and extend the organization's life.

Monthly partners	They like the cause and have budgeted an amount to spend on a monthly basis. They don't need to be re-sold on the importance, but only reminded on a regular basis that what they are doing is important and lifechanging.
Major donors	They tend to give for "strategic" reasons. They are also attracted by others who are giving to the nonprofit organization. They like to interact on a somewhat regular basis with the chief executive officer and some members of the board.
Small, one-time-a-year donors	They give primarily for emotional reasons and in response to an appeal that they could identify with.

Exhibit 5-4   Who supports your cause and why

Monthly sponsorship of children as primary appeal	
Nonprofit Organization A	The oldest child care organization in the field with the largest number of sponsored children throughout the world.
Nonprofit Organization B	Half of the age of Organization A and not as well known. However, Organization B has decided to only center its operation on three continents, therefore not offering as large a choice for constituents as Organization A.
Nonprofit Organization C	Organization C imitates almost everything Organization A does, including how it markets, how it operates organizationally, and how it conducts its sponsorship operations.
Emergency intervention as primary appeal	
Nonprofit Organization D	Organization D is specifically geared to work in highly visible troubled areas of the world. It establishes a network of operations and then begins to slowly transfer the operations to local governments and agencies.
Combination of monthly sponsorship and emergency appeals	
Nonprofit Organization E	This organization undertakes both disaster and famine relief as well as engaging in child care sponsorship as its core missions.
Nonprofit Organization F	This organization is similar in nature to Organization E except it draws its financial support from primarily one denomination, though the organization is not denominationally specific in whom it works with.
Hard to determine	
Nonprofit Organization G	Organization G seems to have gotten into the child care business more for its marketing potential to the organization as a donor acquisition device than for mission reasons.

Exhibit 5-5 Perceptual map of child and sponsorship industry competitors

"Arm and Hammer repositioned its baking soda for the California swimming pool market. While still promoting the traditional application of the baking soda, executives repositioned the product as a good remedy for red, stinging eyes that have been exposed to chlorine. The strategy paid off in a surge of sales."[15] Using market research, the Girl Scouts saw growing numbers of latchkey kids and created the Daisy Scouts, by far one of the more successful programs for preschoolers started in the last 20 years.[16]

PRODUCT LIFE CYCLES

It is not productive for marketing, fund raising, and nonprofit management practitioners to assume a neverending supply of money and interest in the services, products, and causes they are promoting to the public. Every service or product' has a life cycle—with a beginning, a middle, and an end.

For this reason, product life cycle is another important concept to understand, although it is typically a for-profit type of analysis. The product life cycle is certainly applicable to a nonprofit organization's client services and product mix.

There are four generally recognized stages of development for any product or cause (for-profit or nonprofit):

1. Stage 1 is *market development* when a cause or product is brought to market before there is a proven demand for it.
2. Stage 2 is the *market growth stage* where demand for what the nonprofit organization is doing increases and the market as a whole tends to grow.
3. Stage 3 is *market maturity* where there are a number of competitors in the product area, and demand begins to level off.
4. Stage 4 is *market decline* with the cause or product beginning to lose appeal for the client, donor or constituent. (See Exhibit 5-6.)

How do these four stages pertain to the nonprofit world? The question is important because there is little discussion of life cycle theory relating to a nonprofit organization's product planning in nonprofit marketing literature. Projecting a product's life cycle early on could possibly eliminate poor market entry choices and enable a nonprofit organization to choose wise potential competitive moves in advance of market entry.

Stage 1—Market Development

The most critical nonprofit issue in market development is the recognition that demand often has to be "created" for the cause being promoted and sold. This creation of interest has a lot to do with how a product or service offering fits with the potential client and donor

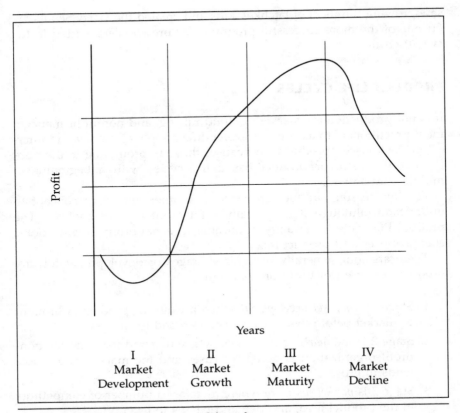

Exhibit 5-6   Stages of the product life cycle

constituency, the equity (or goodwill) associated with the organization's previous performance in the client's and donor's eyes, and the availability of substitute causes for the potential client and donor constituency to be involved with that provide the same psychoemotional rewards.

Most for-profit companies spend millions of dollars and hundreds of man-hours trying to orchestrate new product programs that fit with their consumers. Most new products simply don't make it. According to Theodore Levitt:

> The fact is that most new products don't have any sort of classical life-cycle curve at all. They have instead from the very outset an infinitely descending curve. The product not only doesn't get off the ground; but also it goes quickly underground—6 feet under.

It is little wonder, therefore, that some disillusioned companies have recently adopted a more conservative policy—what I call the "used-apple policy." Instead of aspiring to be the first company to see and seize an opportunity, they systematically avoid being first. They let others take the first bite of the supposedly juicy apple that tantalizes them. They let others do the pioneering. If the idea works, they quickly follow suit. They say in effect, "we don't have to get the first bite of the apple. The second one is good enough."[17]

Because this is the most critical and difficult stage, many nonprofit organizations do not get by the initial market development stage. Those that do, move on to the market growth stage.

Stage 2—Market Growth

The growth stage is the time when a nonprofit jumps into an environment or market, using Levitt's "used apple policy," in order to try to get the client, donor, or constituent to prefer their particular type of service or product, as opposed to building demand for the services and products as is usually the case in stage 1. Or, it is the stage a product naturally moves into after stage 1 when other competitors jump in.

As clients, donors, and constituents accelerate their acceptance level, the number of competitors increases. This "feeding frenzy" can give the appearance of much more client and donor acceptance than there is in reality, thereby luring even more nonprofit companies into the mix. A prime example of this type of behavior is when the national media picks up on a particular tragedy of famine somewhere. The number of nonprofit organizations claiming to help those in distress increases proportionately to the perception of donor acceptance and interest in the crisis.

Stage 3—Market Maturity

The presence of many competitors naturally leads to market saturation and intense competition. Usually, this competition centers around the promoted cost of providing the service to the donating or purchasing constituency, the services that are actually provided to the clients, donors, and constituents, and other promotional practices aimed at establishing a company, name, or brand preference. In this stage, there are usually intense attempts at the acquisition of new audiences, new ways of getting face to face with the donating audiences explored, and intensive differentiation from the competition, often using only marginal differences to appeal to distinctive markets.

Stage 4—Market Decline

Market decline is often a result of oversaturation of competition, client dissatisfaction with the level of services provided, donor or customer boredom with the cause, or some nonprofit organization leaving the environment because of their inability to maintain adequate donor acquisition levels or income-to-expense margins. During this stage, the delivery of services falls to just a few nonprofit organizations who have managed to sustain the "ups and downs" of the life cycle—sometimes successfully and sometimes not so successfully.

DIFFERENTIATING YOUR NONPROFIT ORGANIZATION

Having discussed how nonprofit organizations make decisions to enter a field of service, now attention is turned to how nonprofit organizations differentiate themselves from each other within a field or environment. Nonprofit organizations with similar causes tend to distinguish themselves from others through one, or combinations of, the following:

1. The degree in which they specialize either in their cause, product line, or in the audience segment they work with.
2. The degree to which they try to impress their name upon a given market through advertising, their sales force, or fund-raising field reps.
3. The way they try to accomplish their core mission, either working through a middleman like a church or service group, or going directly to the consumer or donor.
4. The quality or characteristics of their product(s).
5. The leadership status they claim in the development and endorsement of their products using phrases like "new technology" and "cutting edge" programs.
6. The cost position (usually a low cost) they have in delivering their service to clients.
7. The donation amount they request on behalf of client services, which is usually, but not necessarily, tied to their cost position.
8. The amount of leverage they command, often financial, political, or name recognition.
9. Their relationship with a parent company and the objectives, resources, and reputation handed down.

The area of specialization of a nonprofit organization provides *market signals* or competitive information to other nonprofit institutions. The market signals can be used to develop a reactive approach by one nonprofit organization toward another nonprofit organization to develop not only a competitor analysis but also a *strategy formulation*. It is the characterization of these strategies by the nonprofit organizations in question that allows them to be grouped by their specialization.

A curious thing happens when an organization undertakes a group analysis: The individuals undertaking the analysis immediately notice that some nonprofit organizations employ the same client specializations and compete with each other in a very similar manner. Others employ different strategies altogether. Tim Burgess, a principal of the Domain Group, speaks of "specialty or positional mapping" as a way to reposition nonprofit organizations by looking at market signals. Nonprofit organizations who are having trouble gaining significant market share—especially those grouped into similar areas and methods of specialization—undertake this exercise in order to arrive at a strategy for the marketplace.[18]

This strategic "look" allows one to not only view the market as a whole, but also provides the necessary ability to look at a nonprofit organization as it relates to the whole. Significant barriers to competing successfully in a market become clear with this evaluation, and may be tied to the lack of money the institution can spend to attract an audience, the scarcity of programs the nonprofit organization can afford to offer, or the very small donor base available. Just as these barriers prove to limit what a nonprofit organization can do, they also serve to protect those organizations in the environment by keeping institutions out of the competitive arena.

It is the presence of many competitive groups in an environmental analysis that leads to the rivalry and intense competition many in the nonprofit world feel today. Michael Porter, speaking of the for-profit world, says there are four factors that determine how strongly the strategic groupings in an industry will interact in competing for customers:

1. The market interdependence among groups, or the extent to which their customer targets overlap.
2. The product differentiation achieved by the groups.
3. The number of strategic groups and their relative size.
4. The strategic distance among groups, or the extent to which strategies diverge.[19]

Some nonprofit groups choose to enter an environment by announcing their entry through market signals. Two case studies will illustrate the point.

CAMPAIGN TO BUILD A NEW COLLEGE FACILITY HINGED ON CLEAR MARKET SIGNALS

A Canadian college was to engage in a capital campaign to build a new facility. Early on in the campaign, but after the campaign leadership was secured, the college announced to the financial community through the appropriate media that it was contemplating a building and fund-raising initiative. The campus goals and plans were put into a network of financial and political "movers and shakers" within the city.

A substantial effort was also made by the college to network with other institutional heads to try and determine whether the proposed timing of the campaign would put it in competition with other nonannounced campaigns of major fund-raising plans. Likewise, substantial efforts were made through the use of focus groups with donors to help determine the viability of the campaign from their perspective, as well as to assess donor support.

Each signal was designed to send a different message to a portion of the city's potential donation constituency. Each action or market signal was also taken by the college to either provoke a response from other competitor institutions in the same or adjacent field regarding the college's campaign to assess their competitive response, to assess donor response to the announcement, and to let other institutions evaluate their own financial plans given the college's announcement.

The college developed market signals and monitored their response in order not only to send a clear message about its intentions (to commence a building campaign), but also to ensure that their competitors would think twice before announcing their own campaigns or major fund drives during the same period.

A competitor to the college could have responded to the campaign information a number of different ways:

- It could have viewed the announcement as a threat to its own programs.
- It could have seen it as a stimulus to respond to the building program by announcing a bigger, more elaborate building program of its own.
- It could have used it as a gentle prodding to ensure its own donors continued support of the institution given the potential excitement of the campaign.

- It could have chosen to advance or delay its own financial initiatives whatever they were.
- It could have used the campaign to determine which key donors in the community had already committed (or could commit) to the college's project.

Each competitive response is dependent on the position an institution feels it is in with respect to the college announcing its campaign.

A simpler example of how market signals are used concerns a number of different nonprofit organizations that are located in the same city.

TOO MANY BANQUETS, TOO LITTLE TIME

A number of nonprofit organizations are planning fund-raising banquets within a similar time frame and all have overlapping constituencies. In the past years, the announcement of banquet dates by the respective organizations to their constituencies has been made earlier and earlier in the year; invitation committees have been recruited almost the week after the year's previous banquet; and announcements of banquet locations have been made well in advance of the event. All of these actions were taken to try and get a competitive step ahead with the constituency in question.

The multiplication of these fund-raising banquets began as the nonprofit organizations in question developed similar fund-raising tactics; now they are trying new marketing tactics with banquets being held in new locations with different causes being promoted. Each new marketing signal is provoking a mirrored response from a competitor.

How a nonprofit organization competes is the central issue in these case studies. How it views itself internally and assesses its competitive and strategic capabilities is also an important feature of competitive strategy. Chapter 6 continues this discussion by looking at how a nonprofit organization can turn each of its operations into a competitive unit by focusing inward on its own strategy development.

PART THREE

The Internal Analysis

CHAPTER SIX

Competition and Internal Marketing Analysis

At first, increasing information leads to better decisions, but after a while more and more information has less and less effect. There even comes a time when further information makes it difficult to sort out important information from the rest. There is confusion and information overload. Yet, as most data processing (DP) departments will confirm, executives faced with difficult decisions simply ask for more and more information in the hope that somehow the new information will do their thinking for them.[1]

Edward de Bono
Sur/Petition

Without baiting the question with loaded prefaces, ask assembly workers or managers, "Can you tell me, in your own words, where are we trying to take the company?" Then compare the response with the official version.[2]

Tom Brown
Industry Week

One of the great hurdles in nonprofit marketing is getting from the phase of looking outside the organization to looking inward. Achieving closure on the process of looking at an organization's environment requires taking this external information and constructing internal marketing systems to evaluate and use it. This requires discipline. It also requires that an organization create an internal evaluation system to help determine whether or not it is ready to deal effectively with the environment it inhabits.

Just as it was important to examine a nonprofit organization's external marketing elements in the previous chapters, now the nonprofit marketing practitioner's gaze must turned inward to the inner workings of the organization itself, in order to help develop a strategic marketing plan. This look at the internal environment must take into account all of the important organizational issues that ultimately contribute negatively or positively to the organization's marketing strategy. There are many important reasons to undertake this analysis as we will see in the next section.

REASONS FOR AN INTERNAL EXAMINATION

One important reason for this internal examination is the fact that funding constituents are becoming increasingly sensitized to the need for nonprofit organizations to demonstrate performance and efficiency in both their fund-raising and overall operations. Though there are relatively few cases reported in the media in which nonprofit organizations are charged with the misuse of funds or excessive fund-raising costs, these cases nevertheless get enormous coverage, clouding the nonprofit environment by seemingly presenting all nonprofit organizations in a bad light. These media reports send clear signals to all nonprofit organizations as to the need for excellence in their performance and cost-effectiveness, but also to the destructive nature of press coverage should a nonprofit organization stray from acceptable practices.

There is, however, another more important reason for this internal examination. Nonprofit constituencies are changing their buying, support, and purchasing patterns. As a consequence, they are becoming increasingly sensitive to the need for nonprofit organizations to demonstrate increased performance and efficiency in their service offerings and fund-raising practices. They are also changing the ways in which they decide to be involved with a nonprofit organization. Consider these observations on constituents—some of whom may be nonprofit donors and clients—as put forth by *FORTUNE* magazine:

> Here are today's intelligent consumers. All are enthusiasts of a sweeping trend that Grey Advertising calls, "downshifting." Explains Barbara S. Feigin, an executive vice president at Grey: "Americans are taking charge of their lives and their wallets, and are reining in their spending in a major way." They are attempting to justify every purchase and maximize the value of every dollar spent.[3]

Shouldn't a nonprofit organization's administration expect the same type of scrutiny as donors, prospective donors, constituents, and volunteers evaluate appeals, services that are offered, and opportunities for involvement across a wide range of nonprofit organizations?

Frankie Cadwell, co-founder of the Cadwell Davis Ad Agency, calls these analytical consumers "professional customers," and they did not appear overnight. During the 1980s tougher and more demanding shoppers were emerging, but they were focused primarily on product quality. When the recession hit, their concerns shifted to price. In a September, 1992, poll conducted by the Roper Organization in which consumers selected the most important reasons for buying a brand, price surged past quality in the value equation by 17 percentage points. In 1985, by contrast, quality edged out price by two points.[4]

To succeed today, nonprofit entities must understand these intelligent clients, constituents, and donors. Quality of service—both by the nonprofit organization in relation to those it serves and to those who fund its services—is extremely important. The assumption of "blind allegiance" that so many nonprofit organizations seem to believe in as it relates to their clients, volunteers, and donors simply is not present in today's market.

Is this retrenchment by constituents merely a sign of the times? Donors, clients, and constituents are making basic paradigm shifts in how they evaluate their philanthropic involvement. Studies that measure donations as a percentage of per capita wealth have identified those with fixed incomes as the most generous donors in America today, with more affluent families giving a much smaller percentage—less than .5 percent of their available income.[5] Drawing the conclusion that some wealthier constituencies may be leveraging their income as opposed to giving it away, and with fixed income constituent members finding it increasingly difficult to give their dwindling supply of money away, internal analysis becomes even more important as nonprofit organization pursue the correct marketing strategies to these groups.

Organizations begin their internal examination with those areas that either help achieve institutional goals or constrain the institution from achieving them. The objective of this look is to evaluate the viability of the organization's marketing and competitive actions, and to determine whether the findings indicate normal fluctuations of the organization's business cycle or deteriorating situations that deserve immediate attention.

An internal analysis (which goes by many names including *environmental audit, opportunity analysis, marketing audit,* or *development survey*) uses historical data and performance measures to get a sense of seasonal fluctuations and operating patterns in a nonprofit organization's

1. The markets served:
   A. What groups comprise the nonprofit organization's market and constituents?
   B. What are the characteristics of each appropriate segment in each market?
2. The clients, donors, and constituents who support, purchase, and volunteer to the nonprofit entity:
   A. How the clients, donors, constituents, and volunteers feel about the nonprofit's products and services.
   B. What they expect from the nonprofit organization in the future regarding new product development and services.
3. Competitors:
   A. Who are the major competitors to the nonprofit organization?
   B. What does the future hold in terms of increasing or decreasing competition?
4. Competitive environment:
   A. What do the demographics (the characteristics of sub-population groups— age, income, occupation, size, density and so on), psychographics (a study of lifestyle characteristics), and financial data tell the nonprofit organization about the nature of the marketplace?

Exhibit 6-1   Checklist of key elements in a nonprofit organization's external marketing analysis

income and service patterns, as well as identifying historical strengths and weaknesses. This look also allows an organization to take into account changing objectives or marketing strategies that it might have undergone in the past.

How does this internal look fit in context with the previous examination of the external marketing environment? Exhibit 6-1 recaptures the key elements that are a part of an external marketing analysis for the reader. Together, an external and internal analysis provides a nonprofit organization with the information necessary to build its marketing strategy.

An internal organizational analysis uncovers the following key issues:

1. The past and current performance of the organization with respect to clients and donors.
2. The strategic problems that need to be faced by the organization.
3. The organization's ability to overcome these problems.

4. The organization's fund-raising and service costs and their performance.

5. The organization's strengths and weaknesses.

Exhibit 6-2 spells out all of the key elements in an internal organizational analysis in detail.[6]

The first step in the organization's internal analysis is to look at its
past and current performance.

MEASURING PAST AND CURRENT PERFORMANCE

In simple terms, an internal analysis starts with what worked in the past
and what did not. Because an articulated strategy sometimes evolves or
turns out differently than what was planned, the goal in this internal
examination is to determine whether or not a nonprofit organization's
strategy for its clients and/or its donors needs adjustment. Usually, an
organization discovers that some products and services are better supported by a constituency than others. This discovery allows an organization to review its strategy and determine how much it will spend to promote this area of work in the future as opposed to the past, and then be
able to contrast this decision with its spending objectives in other areas.

Likewise, an internal organizational analysis rests upon the organization's objectives. The implication is that objectives need to be both specific and measurable. Objectives, along with their impact upon marketing strategy, are discussed more fully in Chapter 9 which looks at
different types of objectives, how they relate to a nonprofit organization's marketing strategy, and where they fit in the overall marketing
structure. Suffice it to say the pursuit of objectives allows an organization to more readily and ethically attract sufficient resources and, having done this, take these resources and create the types of programs,
products, and services that the awaiting public desires. In addition,
objectives provide a measuring stick of sorts allowing a nonprofit organization to measure its progress towards its goals.

Compare Like Institution Types: Apples to Apples,
Not Apples to Oranges

There are a number of published yearly guides to philanthropy in America. Perhaps the American Association of Fund-Raising Counsel's *Giving
USA* is best known. Inside this report are breakdowns of where philanthropic dollars are going in the United States based on:

1. Past and current performance:

    A. What type of institution does the organization think it is?

    B. Does the organization have a plan?

    C. Are the board of directors helpful?

    D. Is the company's location a burden?

    E. What kind of organizational culture does it have?

2. Strategic problems:

    A. What is the organization's image in the marketplace?

    B. What is the organization's history of marketing, especially in the areas of fund raising and attracting new clients?

    C. How does the organization discover prospects?

3. The organization's ability to overcome these problems:

    A. Does the organization have access to:

    - Prospects for service, volunteers, and fund raising?

    - Existing donors, those needing to be upgraded, and those former donors who need to be renewed financially?

    - An adequate budget for service and fund raising?

    - Professional service and fund raising counsel?

    - A constituent, client and donor relational service mentality?

4. Fund raising, service, product costs and performance:

    A. What is the organization's service portfolio and what cause concepts and services is the organization currently trying to sell to various audiences?

    B. What financial constraints is the organization facing in achieving its goals?

    C. What is the organization's productivity in:

    - Rate of financial return?

    - Average gift size?

    - Average cost per gift?

    - Average cost per client?

    - Service success rate?

    - Program cost percentage?

    - "Bottom line" cost percentage?

5. Organizational strengths and weaknesses.

Exhibit 6-2   Checklist of key elements in a nonprofit organization's internal marketing analysis

- religion;
- education;
- health;
- human services;
- arts;
- culture and humanities;
- public/society benefit;
- environment/wildlife;
- international affairs; and
- undesignated.

Religion constantly outpulls the other categories philanthropically, hovering around the 50 percent of dollars given mark, with education around the 10 percent mark, followed by human services at 9 percent, and other much smaller categories.[7]

Knowledge of one's category is the first step in developing a strategic marketing position. Some categories are simply not as popular as others, philanthropically, resulting in the need for accurate expectations in competing for available resources, potential community involvement, and the ability to attract the right types of donors, volunteers, board members, and the like. These factors become important considerations as a marketing strategy is planned.

The Importance of a "Formal" Plan Cannot Be Overstated

When asked about its marketing strategy, Center City Mission's development director, Tom Evans, looks around his office as if to try to phrase the answer to the question correctly. "It's not so much how Center City is competing with everyone else; it is how they compete with us. The homeless industry in this city is primarily the Salvation Army and Center City Mission. The real question is: how can we retain our presence?"[8]

Tom Evans' predicament captures the essence of market planning and strategy in much of the nonprofit environment. Given the increased homelessness taking place in America's cities and the declining pool of dollars for many philanthropic ventures, nonprofit marketing directors like Tom Evans should consider plans and strategies a very serious undertaking.

The nonprofit environment has become increasingly turbulent and more dependent on economic fluctuations than ever before. Planning as a formalized activity provides a vehicle by which the nonprofit management team can take the constant changes in their economy, environment and society and try to cope with them strategically.

Don't Leave Marketing Strategies Up to the Board of Directors

Perhaps the worst judgment a nonprofit marketer can make is to "leave the service or fund-raising results to the board." Most boards simply cannot and will not pick up the challenge. While there are many reasons for this—ranging from a fear of soliciting to a lack of training and clear expectations—the tragedy for many nonprofit organizations today is keeping a board in place without clearly defined production expectations.

If persistent predictions of shakeups in certain environments hold true, then nonprofit administrations will see a continual thinning of the nonprofit ranks in industries that do not develop and articulate a separate board of directors' strategy in the future. Especially for organizations contemplating a capital campaign or major donor effort, a strong board is often the key to their success in such endeavors.

In addition, given that 83 percent of all gifts are given by individuals, it begins to make sense that the ideal candidates for nonprofit boards are those that come from well-connected backgrounds in their own professional and personal pursuits, as well as those who would not be shy about promoting the organization's cause.[9]

Effective board leadership—the kind that holds organizations accountable for their actions—is one of the best ways nonprofit organizations can outdistance their competition in this environment. Enlist the enthusiasm of the board, and inspire them to work for you by providing a clear focus and a do-able strategy.

A Marketing Strategy Must Take Location into Account

Of course not all nonprofit firms' problems are entirely the fault of marketing, nor can they be solved by marketing. A major problem can occur with the location of an organization in relation to its services and supportive constituency. A marketing strategy must take location into account. See the following case study as an example.

TAPPING INTO THE RIGHT LOCATIONS

A large nonprofit organization is based in a small town in Michigan. The city's population is under 4,000, yet the organization is very successful financially. How can this be? The organization has strategically set up funding offices in Grand Rapids, Ann Arbor, and Detroit—all large metropolitan markets in proximity to the base office. In addition, these cities are where the nonprofit organization draws upon the majority of its clients and donors. Although the three cities are more than two hours away from the actual offices, they contain the bulk of philanthropic dollars. The organization, by way of its regional offices, has overcome a seemingly "bad" location. For this organization's cause, the rural community is not a good market in which to raise the funds needed and to draw in the client population desired as will the larger metropolitan areas.

The demographic profile an organization works with should be an important consideration in its market planning and strategy. Larger communities should not be exempt from the same type of scrutiny.

There is a limit to how many charities a community can support. For example, the greater Boston area has 4 million residents to serve about 70 colleges and universities and 65 hospitals, to name only a few of the 35,000-plus charitable organizations registered in Massachusetts (some of which are renowned national or international centers of excellence). It is not within the realm of possibility that these 4 million people (1 million of whom are students!) can meet the priority needs of these world-class organizations.[10]

Should a nonprofit organization that finds itself in an undesirable location leave and search for new surroundings? For many nonprofits, this is far easier said than done. In fact, most nonprofit organizations in this situation need a marketing strategy to redirect their marketing efforts in the short run in order to cater to both their ideal client population as well as to the national philanthropic population. In the long run, they need to consider a move of some type to a more appropriate setting.

Redefining the Organizational Marketing Culture

With changes in this nation's culture and society moving so swiftly, nonprofit organizations without aggressive marketing strategies are open to more financial problems than those with strong marketing programs.

In a nutshell, a nonprofit entity defines its "marketing culture" when it has someone in charge of the organization's marketing efforts. This person must constantly monitor its service and philanthropic population as to their needs and desires and must bias its programs and promotional efforts to take the comments of its constituencies into account.

However, most nonprofit organizations tend to operate in a sort of "marketing pre-culture," in which nonprofit executives have not yet established a true commitment to marketing. A fear of change is often rooted in resistance to new ideas and ways of doing things, especially in the organization's service and administrative departments.

How does an organization go about creating a strong nonprofit marketing culture? What does it look like operationally? There are general guidelines that every nonprofit organization can adapt in developing its marketing culture:

1. The organization should first strive to create within itself a structure that is highly suitable for the needs of its donors, constituents, and clients, as well as one that is able to carry out the competitive tasks of the marketing enterprise.

2. The culture must have as a basic tenet: the desire to serve the organization's various constituencies as they want to be served.

3. The nonprofit marketing culture must desire to see objectives met through implemented marketing strategies. In particular, these strategies should be of a style and structure that the organization can tolerate.

4. There should be a balance between planning and operating, between long- and short-term goals, and between growth and income goals.

5. The marketing culture should facilitate communication and decision making amongst its members, as well as make an effort that is integrated with the rest of the organization.

6. Such a culture also should have agreed-upon evaluation points and benchmarks of performance.

DEALING WITH STRATEGIC PROBLEMS

Few doctors would prescribe a treatment for a patient without having a good idea of the problems and symptoms. Likewise, facing up to problems and symptoms usually helps a nonprofit organization grow stronger.

Problems are nothing new to nonprofit organizations. In fact, most nonprofit executives are overwhelmed by short-term, tactical problems on a daily basis. However, some of these problems are of a higher profile in the company and, as such, require both dramatic and responsive strategies and programs. It is these types of problems that an internal, organizational analysis tries to uncover.

Considering the Constituents When Defining an Organizational Self-Image

As previously mentioned, taking into account how an organization's constituency is going to feel about certain issues is very important. Even so, many small and medium-sized nonprofit organizations view an image analysis as an unwarranted expense. Chapter 10 will more fully address image analysis.

A backwards analysis of many nonprofit organizations would reveal that a high percentage of them "jumped" into their environment, trying to promote themselves with little thought given to the potential *acceptance* of their service or solicitation message by the community. "Jumping in" efforts may confuse marketing with advertising, and the overall goal is community recognition, rather than the acceptance of the group or of its message. "To make the Center City Mission more of a household name by letting people know we're at work in certain areas" is a typical organization mission statement. In reality it is an *undifferentiated* marketing strategy hoping to be able to attract anyone to its cause, without separating marketing from image relations. Where does the constituent's voice fit in?

Client, donor, and constituent analysis would reveal two major problems with this lack of constituent-based strategy. First, in attempting to attract everyone with one campaign—client and donor alike—a nonprofit organization stands the chance of not attracting anyone. No organization can meet every person's needs adequately. Likewise, such a strategy costs more than most nonprofit organizations can afford because it is too general. It is better to target carefully defined audience segments.

Every institution must assess how its "self-image" fits with the needs of the target markets it serves. A failure to impact the client areas it was created to serve will hurt a nonprofit organization in areas it might not think about initially, including the ability to attract volunteers, to gain community recognition and support, and to get good local services.

How should an organization assess its self-image? The following checklist outlines some basic areas of self-assessment for a nonprofit.

1. Regarding the organization's donors and constituents, consider:
   - their opinion toward the nonprofit and its policies;
   - their acceptance or rejection of the services offered;
   - their regard for the way the organization "serves" them;
   - their feelings toward the organization's communication and fund-raising programs; and
   - their motivations in supporting the organization, its service products, and the fee or fund-raising costs set for them.
2. Regarding markets, consider:
   - the organization's size in comparison with others;
   - its coverage and client size compared to others; and
   - its market expansion and size compared to others.
3. Regarding competitors, consider:
   - service products compared to those of others;
   - the current marketing strategies as compared to others; and
   - the support services provided as compared to others.

Tracking Marketing History Is Important

Most nonprofit organizations lack experience in putting market theories into practice. They also typically have an even shorter history of tracking their results. Consequently, nonprofit organizations cannot really accurately advertise how effective these programs are. Nor can they say with any discernment which areas of untapped monies they are ignoring in the marketplace by using these fundraising methods and not using others.

Many nonprofit organizations are successful today because they run marketing programs year in and out, constantly measuring their outcomes, and never growing tired of *improving* these programs. Once one marketing program is honed to near perfection, another should be started. Good results in one area do not necessarily mean good results in another, though. Marketing requires constant attention to detail and performance. It also means deciding which programs to keep and which to abandon.

Given the difficulty many nonprofit organizations have in staffing and adequately budgeting for marketing ventures, most should fully implement one marketing program at a time, execute it to the best of their ability in accordance with professional norms, constantly monitor and measure the progress, and having done all this, go on to the next program and begin the cycle again.

Discovering New Prospects for Services and Fund Raising

As we all know, the discovery of new prospects with whom a nonprofit organization can initiate and maintain a relationship is a constant strategic issue for nonprofit organizations. Few nonprofits can rely solely on volunteers or a few highly committed donors to meet their service goals and their growing budgets. In fact, one of the key criteria for many nonprofit organizations considering locational moves of their organizational headquarters is the issue of whether the new location will yield better prospect discovery.

In making a judgment to move, or to aggressively pursue new prospects, a company needs an accurate understanding of who it is most likely to attract as a service client, volunteer or donor. This must be based on research and surveys, rather than a stereotyped target or out-of-date notion that does not represent the "target" in today's market.

For many years, most fund raising and development seminars, as well as many books, taught that the only guaranteed donor prospect in America, for almost all nonprofit organizations, was a white woman over the age of 50, coming from a middle-class environment, who has demonstrated an openness to an emotional pitch. Many nonprofit marketers still target all of their appeals with this stereotype in mind!

Today, many nonprofit constituencies, especially in the donor arena, are a very different type of target prospect in age, income, education, and sex. For those organizations who have taken the time to find out and use this new information strategically in their marketing, an immediate improvement in their service, volunteer, and fund-raising programs has occurred.

DEFINING A REHAB CENTER'S CLIENTELE

A major university hospital is interested in expanding the number of clients its rehab unit serves. One group within the hospital is advocating a strong public relations focus in the city. Another is advocating a major paid advertising campaign. A third option was finally chosen.

The hospital took the time to discover where its patients were coming from. Because of the nature of the services it provided, it found out that the majority of its patients came because doctors within a 200-mile radius constantly recommended this hospital's rehab facilities because of their specialized service. What's more, the doctors who served as referrals for this hospital's rehab unit tended to come from smaller metropolitan areas and worked with-in small medical practices.

This information allowed the rehab center to construct a marketing program and strategy that used this type of information.

How does one uncover the same types of strategic information on our markets? What steps should an organization take to accomplish this?

1. A nonprofit organization must first formally establish steps to gather marketing intelligence information on a regular basis, including formulating a budget for gathering the information, appointing a person to run the process, and making a commitment from senior management to use the information strategically on a regular basis.
2. The organization then must establish "sources" of marketing information, and continually cultivate those sources. These sources could include competitors (which would require continuous attention), donors and clients (monitor their opinions on a wide range of issues), and members of the nonprofit organization who should contribute regular submissions of their impression of how the organization's systems of marketing and service delivery are functioning.
3. Third, the organization must collect, interpret, and evaluate the information in order to make some use of the data.
4. Information then must be interrelated with ongoing organizational procedures using the relationships between many research elements.

ASSESSING THE ORGANIZATION'S STRENGTHS AND WEAKNESSES

In order to create an effective marketing plan, an organization must be able to differentiate between its strengths and weaknesses, particularly as they relate to the competition. There are usually four areas in which this type of evaluation is critical: service delivery; methods of raising money and communicating a message to the public; methodology of creating new services; and overall marketing.

The Power of Service Delivery

The delivery of services is a very powerful medium through which to maintain a competitive presence, because of its inherent intense client involvement. The following questions must be answered in order for an organization to ascertain its strengths or weaknesses in this area:

- Is the nonprofit organization delivering its services at a higher or lower than normal cost compared to other like-minded organizations?
- Does the nonprofit organization possess a service array that is distinct or are its services being duplicated by others?
- Does the nonprofit organization possess flexibility in delivery of its services as compared to others?

Communication: The Key to Any Fund-raising Ability

Fund raising, in most nonprofit organizations, has been reduced to a "salesmanship style" of operation. Organizations often find themselves looking for someone who has the "gift of gab" as a spokesperson for the organization, trusting that the ability to make small talk will lead an organization into dollars raised. The ability to raise funds and communicate effectively is crucial to any organization because without it, many great programs for the public never get to their intended audiences. A number of questions help an organization evaluate its fund-raising ability as compared to others:

- Is the organization's force of fund raisers superior in their knowledge of the service industry, as compared to competitors?
- Is the fund-raising force large enough compared to other organizations?
- Does the size and breadth of the services offered allow it to exert more force in its fund raising by appealing to potentially more donors?

Developing New Services

The development of new services is almost exclusively tied to the organization's ongoing assessment of its current services, their impact upon the community, and their need for improvement or curtailment. This monitoring of an organization's services is often called *research and development* in a for-profit organization. The only question to ask in this section is: Are the quality and integrity of the services currently being offered at parity or superior to those of the competitors?

Overall Marketing Function

Determining whether an organization has a particular advantage helps to define its rules when engaging in competition. As more and more organizations see their services being duplicated by competitors, the marketing function often becomes the critical area in which an organization can establish its strengths at the expense of a competitor's weaknesses. For example:

- Does the nonprofit organization have services that are considered the envy of the marketplace?
- Are there established services which draw large numbers of both clients and supportive publics?
- Is the breadth of services offered by the nonprofit organization sufficient enough to withstand duplication by competitors?

IDENTIFYING THE RESIDUAL DONOR

Many nonprofit marketing administrations presume that a second gift from a donor will occur automatically or that a volunteer will return. Unfortunately, this kind of assumption is no longer realistic. Instead, a long-term relationship with a variety of constituents requires constant attention to the needs and wishes of the constituent, meaningful communication, and effective use of marketing strategies designed to renew the relationship on a regular basis. The goal of this variety of tactics is a stable relationship with the constituent. In the case of a donor, this may mean a series of gifts over a period of time including some with upgraded dollar amounts, as well as the potential for future gifts of both capital and estate efforts.

A stable relationship with a competent volunteer can yield hundreds of hours of donated time and effort, thereby reducing the financial strain associated with hiring additional employees. And a successful relationship with a client not only gives the nonprofit organization an opportunity to exercise its services to successful completion, but also gives the opportunity for referrals for its services from satisfied clients.

Managing Long-term Liaisons

Vigilance in the management of constituent relationships is the first precondition for marketing success. Access to the appropriate individuals with whom the nonprofit organization can partner is often the second. Without a supportive community, an organization will have to downscale its service expectations and growth plans.

The ability to recognize and thank clients, donors, and volunteers adequately is an integral criteria for success. No internal analysis would be complete if it did not ask how constituents are being treated and thanked. For many individuals involved in a campaign, recognition is increasingly becoming an important criteria for them in their philosophy of philanthropic involvement. They are interested in seeing their names on the new pool wall, highlighted in a special nonprofit publication, or recognized at the annual banquet. How does your organization thank its constituents?

Of course, all of this requires money in the budget. Professional staff, support staff, space, office systems, and data retrieval systems are all necessary for successful development departments to operate. However, money spent on thanking constituents is the first step in maintaining these all-important relationships.

How does an organization build long-term donor relationships?

1. First, a good marketing team looks for people *already interested in the cause.* Finding someone who is already convinced of the appropriateness of the nonprofit organization's task allows for that donor's values to be affirmed more easily when they give.

2. Second, the *courtship* of a donor is more important in a long-term relationship.

3. All fund raising has to be *personal.* The soliciting organization must always try to be as personal as possible.

4. You must learn to *ask for the gift.* This simple action allows the donor to know exactly what you expect of them.

5. You must frequently *thank all supporters.*

6. Always report on the *progress* of the task at hand, even if the news is not always good. Donors and other supporters want to know what is happening and usually assume the nonprofit organization will encounter some discontinuities in getting its job done.

7. *Don't exaggerate or lie* in any communication. The supporter will never forget this if you do and are subsequently found out.

8. *Don't take "no" personally.* In other words, your supporters cannot say "yes" every time you ask. Some parts of your organization are more appealing to them than others.

9. Let your supporters know *where the money is going.* Always have a budget in plain English with nothing hidden.

10. Assume your job in marketing is always to *build relationships.* Make sure your strategies reflect this philosophy.

COST AND PERFORMANCE ANALYSES HELP DEFINE SUCCESS

The basic goal for a nonprofit organization undertaking a performance analysis is to understand how much it costs for the organization's monies to be raised and how much it costs for the various parts of its services to be performed. Costs and performance can become an advantage or a disadvantage for a nonprofit entity. Determining the biggest costs and the best and worst performing projects, as well as projecting these trends into the future, allows a nonprofit organization to not only improve its own performance, but also to develop strategies vis-à-vis the competition.

Analyzing the Service Portfolio

Most nonprofit organizations undertake different activities on behalf of their supportive constituency and those they serve; activities such as providing shelter, counseling, medical services, food supplies, job retraining, and so on. These "services activities" make up a nonprofit organization's *service portfolio*. A portfolio analysis is very useful in order to determine the attractiveness of some parts of an organization's operation, the causes's ability to either generate cash or simply spend it, and its comparative strength against competitors' services and portfolios.

The determination of how much money and time the nonprofit organization should invest in each service is one of the key elements in any organization's strategic marketing. (See Chapter 8.) This decision is most crucial for those organizations that are involved in multiple causes that aren't necessarily related. Nonprofit management teams cannot be "experts" in every area, and they must determine what is worth focusing on, and what is not.

Dealing with Financial Constraints

Every development director in America knows how painful budget cuts can be—sometimes they are so extensive that they render the development department no longer viable. In reality, however, most nonprofits are not spending enough money or maintaining enough relationships. It is not unusual for a nonprofit organization to spend anywhere from 10 to 25 percent of its operating budget on marketing and fund raising. The financial constraints in an organization can limit the freedom the development department or marketing director has in meeting all constituent needs. The willingness to measure, monitor, and rethink how the organization is undertaking its many work roles, as well as to organize its systems so as to best meet the constituents' needs, usually puts an organization into conflict with those who use financial constraints as a weapon or a control against new ideas.

In an increasingly competitive environment, the future success of many nonprofit organizations lies in developing the necessary controls to monitor their expenditures as well as to master the strategy of marketing their cause or purpose. Every nonprofit organization ought to have a *budget* as its first control. This budget would serve as the financial plan for the organization. A second means of control is for the organization to have a *project budget practice* in place—a process which allows the organization to analyze the income and expense of its various activities on a project-by-project basis. Third, every nonprofit organization ought to have a *contingency or reserve fund* where money is put away. This fund may equal as much as 5 percent of the organization's total budget. (See Exhibit 6-3.)

Accounting is a systematic way of dealing with virtually every piece of financial information. Accounting systems are designed to accommodate most financial activity between any constituent and the nonprofit organization and to ensure that the organization monitors itself and the use of the funds entrusted to it.

In and of itself, accounting is a good controlling and monitoring force; however, in most cases, its data is usually devoid of strategic recommendations and often needs to be converted from raw data into a different form. To accomplish this, the information must be organized into patterns and relationships, with the person doing the work looking for the significance of an apparently disparate element. For example, the majority of supporters for one particular nonprofit organization work in the field of accounting. Tight financial controls may need to be stressed in the selling of the cause to an audience that is composed of accountants.

Income		Expenses	
Speaking fees	6,000	Salaries	72,000
Bookstore sales	48,000	Supplies	11,000
Client services	63,000	Equipment	23,000
Consulting	4,500	Contingency	16,000
Totals	121,500		122,000

Exhibit 6-3 Analysis and budget for xyz nonprofit organization

Accountants tend to look retrospectively at data. Development officers look at data and then use it to estimate prospectively. Who decides when the dollar is spent and how? A balance is necessary so that accountants don't look at development officers as hazards to the financial security of the organization, and so that development officers don't view accountants as narrow in vision and unable to grasp the need to spend money to raise money. This type of trust between staff members is often accomplished through the use of project teams where both the development staff and the accounting staff work side by side on projects together.

Productivity Data Help Define a Strategy

In making decisions today, many nonprofit organizations rely more on financial data than information of any other kind in order to help address their allocations on behalf of services, fund-raising strategies, and long-term investment decisions.

This data can be collected in several ways:

1. *Percentage rate of return:* This is a basic calculation often used in direct mail. Basically, this measurement looks at individuals who respond positively to an advertising or fund-raising message. In the case of direct mail, you divide the number of responses received by the number of solicitations sent. Therefore, if an organization mails 100,000 pieces of mail out to its donor constituency and receives 5,000 affirmative responses, it would have had 5 percent rate of return.

2. *Average gift size:* This is a simple calculation that is arrived at by dividing the total amount of contributions by the number of gifts received. If your organization received $100 in contributions from 5 gifts, your average gift size is $20. This average dollar amount is important when it is coupled with the cost of obtaining a gift, sometimes called the *average cost per gift*. When compared with the average gift size, you are able to calculate the "profit" per gift and get a sense of whether you are raising more money than it is costing you to run the fund-raising process. To reach the average cost per gift, you divide the total fund-raising costs by the number of gifts received.

3. *Program cost:* Each nonprofit program needs to be measured as to its cost effectiveness. The reason for this is very simple. Some programs will cost more than others, some will generate more funds than others, and all will perform differently. Some organizations, including the National Association of College and University Business Officers, have compiled what they believe are reasonable expenses to incur in fund development. Bear in mind that cost averaging ignores those organiza-

tions who undertake programs for ethical or organizational reasons that may incur higher costs than average. However, the idea of measuring programs inside a nonprofit organization for at least three years (and every year after that in order to get a sense of program costs) is very important. Very simply, to reach this percentage, divide the program's total cost by the total contributions received and multiply by 100.

4. *Departmental bottom lines:* The marketing or development department should have a corporate performance measurement on each of its regular programs so that its productivity is measured on a regular basis. This is an inadequate measure on its own; large gifts can be received changing the percentages; new programs can be started that have one-time start-up costs; and some programs may lend themselves to volunteers. However, measuring total fund-raising costs by the total gifts and multiplying by 100 gives a sense of fund-raising performance and verifies how well the development department is doing in raising its share of revenues.[11]

Employing these four data collection methods in an example is the basis of the following case study.

LOCAL RADIO STATION USES MAILER TO RAISE FUNDS

A public broadcasting radio program costs our local station about $4,000 a month to air. This $4,000 represents the program's cost; some programs on the station cost more and some cost less on a monthly basis. The local station decided to send a fund-raising letter to its mailing list (which was composed of previous donors) to see if it could raise enough money from one letter to cover the costs of the program for one month. The letter was sent to 30,000 donor names. The cost for such a mailing was $14,850. Three hundred and forty-eight of those names (or .116 percent) responded with a financial contribution. The total amount of all the contributions was $8,527. This represented an average gift size of $24.50. Was the mailer a success? Exhibit 6-4 illustrates its performance. Management could view the data in two different lights. First, its goal of paying for one month's programming was accomplished by raising more than $8,000. However, omitted in this calculation is that the *costs* of raising the program's money *more than offset any income* the station derived from the mailing. The departmental bottom line is that the mailing lost money.

Number mailed	Number of responses	Percentage of response	Gift income	Average gift	Cost
30,000	348	.116%	$8,527	$24.50	$14,850

Exhibit 6-4   Results of local radio station's mailing program

There are other methods of measurement used by some development departments. For example, departments with a high number of volunteer solicitors or with field or fund-raising representatives often measure the number of potential donor prospects that have been assigned to a volunteer and those who have received a call in order to get a sense of the performance of those volunteers. This number then is often further refined by asking the question, "Of those prospects that were assigned, how many were solicited?" Of course, such a number can be defined even further by asking how many prospects made a gift. Did those who gave a gift upgrade their giving or downgrade? As a group, did we increase in the number of donors we got a gift from this year over last? The ultimate goal in all of this measurement is to begin to forecast how much money development will bring in during a given year, based on a catalog of data and historical trends.

THE INTERNAL AUDIT HELPS DEFINE ORGANIZATIONAL STRENGTHS AND WEAKNESSES

In a very real sense, everything discussed concerning the internal organizational audit has been about "strengths and weaknesses." Organizations that are prospering on a daily basis take their strengths and weaknesses very seriously. In fact, they are often desperate to get rid of their organizational weaknesses. They plan and staff to accomplish this task. Concentration is on their strengths and doing those activities they know how to do best. Marketing issues are evaluated and, ultimately, become issues of cost and time.

A discussion of a nonprofit organization's strengths and weaknesses becomes the summation point in the internal analysis and provides the staging point for the development of a marketing strategy. Nowhere is the issue of strengths and weaknesses more pronounced than in the articulation of a nonprofit organization's objectives. Its objective should provide its reason for existence. This is the subject of Chapter 7.

CHAPTER SEVEN

Marketing and Organizational Objectives

A strategy that doesn't speak explicitly about customers and the competitive environment will surely fail to generate and sustain a proper level of customer and competitive consciousness in your company, especially in the important nooks and crannies where the real work gets done.[1]

Theodore Levitt

Thinking About Management

"Selling and distribution," Thomas Edison told an interviewer in 1910, "are simply machines for getting products to customers. And like all machines, they can be improved with great resulting economy. But it is the plain truth that these machines for distribution have made the least progress of all machines. They are the same in many instances that they were 40 and 50 years ago . . . the average selling machine has become unwieldy and ancient."[2]

Don Wallace

What is the best way to raise money? Many nonprofit organizations still believe that the best way to raise funds is by hawking their needs, regardless of donor interest or feelings. They believe that donors will somehow automatically come flocking in. Unfortunately, the American public does not give in this way. They give in such a way that they must first "buy into" the nonprofit organization's *goals* and results before they buy into the nonprofit organization's *needs*.

Harvard business professor Theodore Levitt says:

> A great many marketing executives today are alert, hardhitting and aggressive. Most of them will quickly admit they wish they got better results. They, like their company presidents above them and their sales managers below them, now fully accept the necessity of being "customer oriented," not "product oriented." They agree that the purpose of business is first to create a customer and then to keep him. Yet we often deny in deed what we affirm in speech.[3]

Simply put, nonprofit organizations, like many organizations, talk better than they act. There is little doubt that a great majority of nonprofit organizations understand the need for marketing; however, what they mean by implementing "it" must be examined more closely.

This chapter continues the inward organizational look at how a marketing strategy begins with an organization's objectives, the resulting way(s) it measures and assesses its past and current performance, and the steps and approaches it uses to reach these objectives.

WHAT ARE OBJECTIVES?

Objectives are those levels of performance labeled by the organization as important areas for effectiveness. This is a more difficult assessment than the previous external assessments because a nonprofit organization, in looking inward at itself, evaluates those organizational areas that constrain it, its strengths and weaknesses, and the need for new action to improve its marketing and service sector activities. Likewise, this inward analysis is richer with data and information than the previous preoccupation with competitors and the operating environment.

A nonprofit organization can analyze its objectives by asking a variety of questions:

1. The first step is to define the objectives, which allow the organization to assess performance and direction. (This may mean that some objectives are changed and others are set.)

2. The nonprofit then analyses past, current, and future strategies that allow it to meet these objectives.

3. Strategies are only worthwhile if they take into account the costs to the organization in both people and dollars and the resulting problems and challenges that may erupt. (See Exhibit 7-1.) Are the organization's strategies correct?

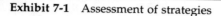

Strategies $\longrightarrow$ Costs $=$ $\left\{\begin{array}{l}\text{People} \\ \text{Dollars}\end{array}\right.$ $\longrightarrow$ Results $\left\{\begin{array}{l}\text{Positive impacts} \\ \text{Negative impacts}\end{array}\right.$

Exhibit 7-1 Assessment of strategies

4. Finally, the nonprofit looks at those areas where donors, clients, and constituents may or may not agree as evidenced by their support and agreement with the direction or lack of it.

The outcome of this inward journey allows an organization to determine whether or not its competitive strategies are working, based on its objectives and the support the nonprofit is receiving. (See Exhibit 7-2.)

WHY DO WE EXIST?

It is helpful to remember the nonprofit director who asked the following question when considering her nonprofit organization's objectives: "Who would miss us if we were gone or didn't exist?"

Without identifying major constituencies or knowing which services offered are most effective and widely received, there is really very little reason to undertake strategy considerations. And while this is not a chapter on planning, nonprofit leadership must first look at the planning process. In particular, this beginning look encompasses the *market* the nonprofit is in, its *purpose*, the way the *future* looks, the *strengths and weaknesses* the nonprofit brings to bear upon the market, and the areas the nonprofit can *excel* in.

Defining the Nonprofit Organization's Market

In order for a nonprofit to develop its mission statement and objectives, the first goal for any organization is to decide *who* its services and products will serve. In essence, what are the markets that will be served and what are the services that will be provided for each of these markets by the nonprofit organization in question in order to meet some need. This vital step also allows the organization to take a backward and forward look at its markets and assess its service (or projected service) performance with each.

On a separate sheet of paper, consider who your market is in one to two sentences. If you don't know the answer to this question, refer to Chapters 4 and 5. Define two "markets"—donors and recipients of your services.

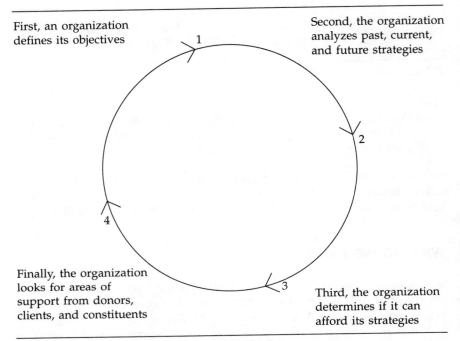

First, an organization
defines its objectives

Second, the organization
analyzes past, current,
and future strategies

Finally, the organization
looks for areas of
support from donors,
clients, and constituents

Third, the organization
determines if it can
afford its strategies

Exhibit 7-2　How organizations analyze objectives

Defining the Nonprofit Organization's Purpose

Sometimes embodied in a finished statement planners call a *mission statement*, the answers to the nonprofit organization's purpose must describe the following:

- A statement describing the environment the organization is currently in, and where it wants to be in the future. In essence, the reason the organization exists.
- The statement is results-oriented and not activity-oriented; it should be realistic.
- It should not state what an organization can do but should state the reason(s) for doing it.
- Mission is the "excelsior" for which an organization exists, although its techniques for reaching its mission may vary by circumstance.
- Mission is outward or client-oriented as opposed to inward or organizationally bound.

- Mission is the essence and the *sine qua non* of organizational activity—the last purpose to be abandoned.[4]

By developing a mission statement, an organization also develops boundaries around its objectives, requiring the nonprofit organization to function within a defined universe of activity aimed at a particular outcome. A mission statement is most forceful when it can be reduced to one sentence; however, some organizations use several paragraphs to describe their mission. If your organization has a mission, review it. If it does not, your next step is to start developing one.

Predicting the Future

It is hard to predict the future. However, in developing organizational objectives, some assumptions about markets, the future political environment, geodemographic changes, economic realities, and competitors must be made. In developing these assumptions, the nonprofit organization must also commit itself to measuring the impact of its assumptions against reality and make the necessary changes in operating style and procedure. This is done for no other reason than to ensure that the organization is on the right course, its resource allocation is correct, and its staffing is adequate for the job it is attempting. Previous chapters have described the ways in which to investigate demographics, and other external factors. How does an organization investigate the future?

1. Noting new trends in society.
2. Looking at new product introductions.
3. Studying demographic shifts, particularly as they relate to the family.
4. Seeing how the economy is running and the mood of the nation toward it.
5. Studying shifts in the workplace and in industries.
6. Studying polls with regard to American attitudes, particularly if those polled are hopeful for the country or not.
7. Following all relevant literature to your cause.

Defining Strengths and Weaknesses

While discussion of strengths and weaknesses is one of the more important activities a nonprofit organization can engage in, it tends to be trivialized in the day-to-day operations. Part of the problem is a practical matter: it is not difficult to talk about those functions an organization does well. It is far more difficult to talk openly and honestly about weaknesses and, for many organizations, it is almost impossible to reconcile those areas that are weaknesses with *solutions* to correct the problem.

An organization may resort to an anonymous survey (see Exhibit 7-3) to achieve an accurate reading of its weaknesses. Others hire an outside consultant who, through interviews, as well as personal and group observation, develops an assessment of organizational strengths and weaknesses. (See Exhibit 7-4.)

Regardless of the method, agreement on what an organization's strengths and weaknesses is an important ingredient in both setting objectives and goals.

AREAS IN WHICH TO EXCEL

This category differs from an organization's strengths. Strengths often tend to be in areas of leadership, fiscal responsibilities, constituent loyalty, and the organization's visibility in the community. Unlike strengths which measure what the organization is currently doing well, this category encompasses tasks that the nonprofit organization does well (and must continue to do well) to survive into the future.

Detailed in length in the next section, these critical or "key result areas" become part of the bedrock for organizational objectives.

Marketing Performance and Objectives

It might seem rather pedantic to many to say a discussion of a nonprofit organization's marketing prowess must first start with a discussion of why it must have clearly defined institutional objectives. Yet marketing practitioners cannot talk about marketing performance in isolation from objectives because performance (and its measurement) rests first upon the direction an organization takes and then the progress it makes toward that end. The simple task of setting objectives allows a marketing director to decide who their donors, volunteers, clients, and constituents should be, what kind of marketing program is required for each, the dollar amounts that will be needed to reach the goal, and the level of marketing expenditure needed. (See Exhibit 7-5.)

Objectives As They Relate to Constituents

First, objectives give clients a reason to be involved and donors and volunteers a reason to give. Most clients avail themselves of a nonprofit organization's services to accomplish objectives of some sort, often in

Here is a sampling of questions you might use to audit the relationships between major donors to a City Mission and the organization itself.

1. How long have you been an active contributor to the City Mission?

Less than 1 Year	1
1–5 Years	2
6–10 Years	3
11–15 Years	4
More than 15 Years	5

2. If you were explaining the Mission to a friend or associate, how would you define its purpose and services?

_____

_____

_____

3. Please tell me the types of services and programs the City Mission operates?

_____

4. Can you please tell me what services offered by the Mission prompts you to continue contributing?

_____

Are there any other reasons why you contribute?

_____

5. In your own words, please describe the personal reward, if any, you feel you get from being involved with the work of the City Mission?

_____

_____

6. If you were considering several charities dedicated to providing care and comfort to those in trouble in your town and could donate to one, what specific qualities of service would help make your decision?

(1) _____

(2) _____

(3) _____

7. Can you tell me how you were originally contacted for a contribution?

_____

8. What has motivated you in the past to contribute to the City Mission?

_____

Exhibit 7-3   Sample survey for relationship audit

their own lives. Likewise, most volunteers and donors do not give time and money simply just for the sake of giving. They wish to accomplish objectives of some sort. Usually objectives for clients, donors, and volunteers are personal in nature; tied to personal belief systems that coincide with the nonprofit organization's goals.

Strengths

The following areas of strength were especially noted in reviewing the organization:

1. *Leadership*—Under the leadership and direction of Debby Director, the City Center Food Pantry has grown steadily for five years achieving a strong donor-based operation.

2. *Constituency*—The Pantry has a nonsectarian emphasis which permits a much wider donor constituency.

3. *Constituency growth*—During the past decade a valuable customer base has been developed with an average 8 percent donor growth rate per year.

4. *Public relations*—A number of positive public relations activities have given widespread visibility to the Pantry beyond its own constituency. This has included a local news interview with Debby Director, three pieces in the local daily newspaper, an op-ed piece on how food is distributed, and a civic award.

5. *Staff growth*—From an initial organization of three people, the staff has grown over the past decade to nineteen full-time and two part-time personnel.

6. *Budget growth*—The budget has grown from $48,000 to $367,000 over a six-year period.

Weaknesses

The following areas of weakness were especially noted in reviewing the organization:

1. *Debt structure*—The presence of debt structure could hinder the organization. At the time of data accumulation for this report the organization had a long-term debt of $78,000.

2. *Fiscal controls*—The absence of a formal fiscal controls system represents a significant vulnerability to the organization. It is not uncommon for nonprofit organizations to have minimal fiscal controls. Among the lack of fiscal controls are: no formal budgeting system; no debt reduction system; lack of contingency, opportunity, capital reserves, or discretionary accounts.

3. *Data processing*—The mailing list has insufficient coding and segmentation capabilities to effectively market the names.

4. *Publications*—In order to communicate to the constituency and motivate donors a number of interpretive materials will be required. They are not available at this time.

Exhibit 7-4 Sample executive summary of strengths and weaknesses, City Center Food Pantry

1. Aids in identifying donors, volunteers, and other constituents.
2. Helps to determine the goals for the marketing plans.
3. Aids in setting the numerical goals for each marketing activity.
4. Enables an organization to set appropriate expenditure levels for all goals.
5. Allows all constituents of the nonprofit organization to have a clear idea of the organization's goals.

Exhibit 7-5 Rationale for objectives

How can an organization tap into these constituent goals? The best way is for an organization to ask its constituents what their goals are, either through research vehicles like questionnaires or telephone interviews, or through face-to-face discussions between organization and constituent. This seeking out of constituent opinions and feelings must be an ongoing, interactive process between the nonprofit organization and those it serves and draws upon for resources.

Second, an organization's objectives help determine the types of volunteer and community support, as well as financial gifts the organization is going to ask for and from whom. Objectives allow the nonprofit organization to judge the various levels of support it will require, from both the service side and the financial side.

Third, according to Thomas Broce, objectives help us "sequence" gifts; that is, large gifts should be secured before our efforts are directed to smaller gifts.[5] Objectives help the organization set the level of support it will need, especially in light of gifts at the higher level of financial support.

Objectives as Decision Drivers

Objectives provide the basis and rationale for nonprofit management to make decisions and develop fiscal controls. In addition, they provide the motivation an organization or department needs to meet their targets. From an institutional and donor perspective, objectives allow the nonprofit organization to communicate across all levels for purposes of planning and evaluating, and likewise allow communication to intelligently pass to a donor, volunteer, client, or constituent and vice-versa.

Clarifying the Objectives to Get to a Mission

Nonprofit executives often feel their missions are very clear. One such organization had as its objective, "To provide mutual understanding and acceptance between the races." Another nonprofit stated that its objective was to, "Assist mankind in its search for God." These may be very worthwhile as missions—but to develop the yardstick by which these organizations may measure their progress in accomplishing these objectives proves to be another matter. Missions such as either of the two described here must be accomplished through very specific objectives.

To be effective, objectives must be both specific and measurable. Otherwise, an organizational mission plays no major role in performance evaluation. Without the establishment of a benchmark measurement, it is impossible to measure results. Without this measurement, who is to say whether the organization has been successful or not?

Reaching the Donor

With clear objectives, an organization can reach substantial funds that might be available from the donor who gives in a thoughtful manner, who needs to find out if he or she is helping to accomplish the objectives the receiver of the grant so forcefully stated in its application. Without a *strong* clarification of *believable* and *saleable* objectives understood by development staff and volunteers alike, the likelihood of attracting new prospects who can give larger sums of money to a cause is diminished.

NOTHING CAN BE DEFINED WITHOUT A PLAN

A nonprofit organization hired a marketing management consulting group to help them. Upon examination, the consulting firm found that they were the third group this nonprofit organization had worked with over the last five years. In reading the previous management reports left by the other consulting groups, the new agency found that neither consulting group had mentioned that the organization in question had no plan for any of the past five years, had no measurable objectives for this time period, and had no plan in place for the future. How could this organization have known whether or not it was ever hitting its objectives?

FORMAL MEASUREMENT OF OBJECTIVES

The measurement of the organization's ability to reach its objectives is as important as setting the right objectives, as stated earlier in this chapter. This is true for both a nonprofit organization's image and donor equity. All of these factors become more salient as the necessity and difficulty of the measurement process increases.

What this means practically to a marketing manager is that the specific purposes of an organization's service programs and/or fund-raising campaigns must be clearly understood before their implementation. Unclear programmatical objectives—whether for fund raising, attracting volunteers, or image projection—translate into unclear research objectives and unclear responses to measurement questions. As a consequence, campaign or program objectives are altered retrospectively to fit the results.

What is a "Bottom Line" for Nonprofit Organizations?

The most common type of for-profit measurement used to measure objectives is profitability, commonly called the "bottom line." This is the point at which nonprofit organizations depart from the for-profit industry. However, the "bottom line" mentality can be operative for many nonprofit organizations. Measuring income against expense allows a nonprofit organization to test whether its nonprofit services or products, fund-raising campaigns, and nonprofit marketing tools are viable both to their constituency and within the competitive environment.

"Profit," for the nonprofit organization, can be measured in numerous ways. Some nonprofit organizations measure their fund-raising efforts because this part of the organization works with an easily definable commodity—money. There are many areas a nonprofit organization could and should measure:

- Growth
- Employee welfare
- Donor movement and financial responsiveness
- Management development
- Financial stability
- Nonprofit service product quality
- New service program investment
- Donor acceptance of programs

How does a nonprofit measure all of those items practically? Consider the evaluation process the following nonprofit organization goes through as evidenced by its year-end report to its board of directors.

SUMMER CAMP EVALUATION

Seven years ago, a summer program operated at 84 percent capacity for 10 weeks with 2,700 people attending. In 1994, we registered participants for 11 weeks at 98 percent capacity; 4,200 people attended, and our waiting list was over 1,100 people. Of the 16 programs offered this year, four of them were new. Three of the four completely filled, and the fourth operated at 80 percent of capacity.

The donor growth has been at 14 percent for the last five years, with this year being the strongest financial year we have ever had. The three focus groups and two listening conferences this year continue to tell the directors that its programming is what donors and campers alike want.

This year the bank has extended to the program a $100,000 line of credit. The relationship with them continues to improve because of the camp's "pay as you go" fiscal policies.

The program's biggest weakness right now is in its middle management area, with the growth of its program outstripping the managers' abilities. The camp has invested in an outside management consultant to help develop a stronger management mentoring program, as well as to identify, through some psychological testing, those individuals who have the capacity to move up in the organization.

This case study is merely a partial report, but it makes a point. Peter Drucker suggests that all business organizations need objectives in *key result areas;* areas where performance and results directly affect the survival and prosperity of the business (or nonprofit organization). These areas have value by virtue of the contributions they make to the organization.[6]

In an informal telephone survey, the following key result areas were articulated by nonprofit directors as being important for purposes of measurement:

- *Marketing and/or fund raising:* Including donor satisfaction and expectations, as well as the traditional tracking of donor financial activity.

- *Programmatical growth:* Traditionally this measures the ongoing programs of the organization. Of equal importance are decisions about programs which are not performing as expected.

- *New nonprofit service programs or products:* New programs can come as the result of new in-house capabilities, data gleaned from constituent research (donors or recipients of service), or in response to outside competitive activity.

- *Internal operations:* The systems an organization mounts to handle its office management, its donor relationship programs, staff and organizational policies, and the distribution of information to donors and clients.

- *Financial resources:* Is the organization in debt? Is it planning for and building revenues for the future?

- *Physical plant and resources:* What capital will be needed to finance the projected growth of the organization and its resultant physical plant needs five to ten years down the road?

- *Internal productivity:* J. Donald Weinrauch says that to neglect answering what makes an effective marketing person in one's industry is to make a colossal management and marketing mistake.[7] One of the harder tasks nonprofit organizations are confronted with is finding well-trained marketing people. Training a marketing staff is an activity that an organization must plan for, and the process must be guided by clear objectives.

- *The costs associated with each program and the manner in which they are funded:* What type of input is required for the organization's programs? What man-hours, dollars, investment are required to deliver the current services and/or products?

- *The ethos (or overall direction) of the nonprofit organization:* What measures will be used to develop the factors associated with the organization's future? How will obligations to society and donors be met in the days ahead? What objectives must be reached in order to ensure long-term organizational health?[8]

TYPES OF OBJECTIVES REQUIRED FOR SUCCESS

Although money tends to dominate the nonprofit marketing measurement process, not all nonprofit measurement is financial. For some organizations, the growth of their programs is measured and discussed as much as their financial status. And for others, intervening objectives serve as a link between the necessities of short-term everyday operations and long-term objectives.

Unfortunately, short-term objectives dominate nonprofit marketing goals, simply because they are not only easier to predict and control, but they are also less risky to the marketing managers involved. As such, they are usually the determining points of whether a nonprofit marketing client service or fund-raising strategy is working. This contributes to the many changed plans some nonprofit organizations have for those they serve, as well as the plethora of emergency appeals and crisis fund-raising management which is all too prevalent today. These actions are often evidence of the organization's short-sightedness in its desperate attempts to fix problems or raise dollars quickly.

Intervening Objectives

How does a nonprofit organization develop objectives that represent where the organization needs to go in the future (long-term success) while retaining a short-term, day-to-day operational performance mentality? Obviously, for many nonprofit organizations, long-term goals simply do not work for day-to-day operational decisions. *Intervening objectives* can be developed that link long-term objectives with current operations. Intervening objectives project a nonprofit organization's operations forward a number of months while linking its current operations to future success. Exhibit 7-6 gives an example of how different types of objectives fit into a cohesive whole.

As explained in Exhibit 7-6, nonprofit marketing management can use both short and intervening objectives to achieve long-term growth concerns. And while most objectives in the nonprofit world project growth, intervening objectives allow a nonprofit entity to structure competitive actions in the form of objectives in a realistic and timely manner to help build a strong competitive position should situations warrant it.

Measuring Intangible Objectives

Many nonprofit organizations have *intangible objectives*. For example, they want to change the public's mind on some issue, they want a client to feel better about themselves, they want to improve the world's condition somehow. How does a nonprofit organization measure these intangible objectives so as to chart its progress toward its goals?

Objectives become meaningless unless there is a measurement tool behind them that translates the objectives into realizable goals. What then of objectives that do not lend themselves easily to measurement? This is obviously not a problem if the goal is easily measurable (i.e., the college needs to build a gymnasium and the financial goal is either met or it is not; the missionary raises his or her deputation support or not; the environmental group buys the land or not; a family of four is given the box of food or not).

In each case the measurement in achieving the objective is easy. It is in areas of intangibility (such as how donors *feel* or the *reputation* of the nonprofit organization) where measurement becomes difficult. An organizational objective may be to encourage conservation thinking or it may seek to persuade groups of people regarding a specific issue or political stance.

Although this type of measurement may be difficult, it is usually not impossible. Many of the same research techniques used by for-profit corporations to measure the marketability of their products can be used in the nonprofit "intangible cause or product" arena.

In this example, a direct mail manager of a nonprofit organization has a number of objectives, some short term, some intervening, and some long term. (In the example the intervening objectives will provide the stair-step linkage to achieving some of the direct mail department's long-term objectives.) The manager may be concerned about the following objectives:

Short-term objectives:

- All direct mail copy done according to editorial calendar and schedule.
- All legal and managerial approval of copy done according to schedule.
- All list requests done according to schedule.
- All copy to design eight weeks before drop date.
- All mailing house materials given three weeks for production
- All drop dates observed.
- All receipting done within 72 hours of gift received.
- All results tracked 16 weeks from date of first response.
- All response data done for weekly managerial summary.

Intervening objectives:

- All direct mail personnel put on a yearly training schedule.
- Incidence of receipt error reduced by 25 percent per year.
- Color monitors installed for 75 percent of the copywriters.
- Management apprised of direct mail strategy through quarterly meetings.
- Instigate research project for a particular mailing list segment.
- Inquire and do research for new software database management system.
- Test four potential rental lists every quarter.

Long-term objectives:

- Maintain overall direct mail department income/expense ratio of five to one.
- Install new database management software in 18 months.
- Hire additional writer in 12 months.
- Hire additional designer in 18 months.
- Grow active donor base by 15 percent.
- Increase capacity to do 25,000 receipts per month.

Exhibit 7-6   Integration of objectives

Use Segmentation.   Perhaps the most common method is the principal of *segmentation* (See Chapter 3.) Segmentation is used to first define a market boundary. In effect, a nonprofit organization tries to identify a fairly homogeneous grouping of people who can be reached effectively with one marketing effort. Segmentation is normally done through geographic, demographic, psychographic, or monetary means. For example, let's say that all Republicans represent a market segment. All Republicans who are male is a further definition of the segment. All Republicans who are male, and are against abortion is the segment even further defined. All Republicans who are male and against abortion and live in Deerfield, Wisconsin creates an even smaller segment.

When nonprofit organizations are unsure of how to segment their market, they may employ a direct questioning method—that is, directly approaching clients, donors, and product buyers, asking them a set of questions and then defining parameters. In addition, projective techniques (formerly called *motivational research*) like word association, sentence completion, and story telling can also be used to augment direct questioning methodology.

Some organizations have used *preference measurements* with audiences through a simple rank ordering or comparison to measure clients, donors, or product buyers' feelings toward nonprofit programs. This can be done in a questionnaire format and then be made available after services are rendered or mailed directly. Exhibit 7-7 is an example of such a questionnaire. Still other organizations have tried to identify donor and client need and their satisfaction with the organization's programs through focus groups and other types of consumer research studies such as product testing, copy testing, comparison testing, and through various preference tests.

Look at Research as Data Base Management.   All nonprofit organizations must conduct market research and, in order to handle the information collected, all nonprofit directors should be proficient in data base management.

For organizations both large and small, marketing managers and directors must listen and talk to their constituents if they are going to build organizations that merit client and donor support. In addition, the data base can be used to direct and manage all parts of the organization and, very specifically, the marketing plan.

Tom Peters and Nancy Austin, authors of *A Passion For Excellence* and members of the Tom Peters Group, have coined the term *naive customer listening* as a process where surveys of customers abound, numerous formal and informal customer feedback devices are used, and all levels of staff are trained to listen and respond better to customer desires.[9] A naive listener in a nonprofit organization is someone inside the group

	Strongly agree 1	Agree somewhat 2	Undecided 3	Disagree somewhat 4	Strongly disagree 5
Television is our primary source of entertainment	☐	☐	☐	☐	☐
I hate to lose at anything	☐	☐	☐	☐	☐
I prefer to participate in individual sports as opposed to team sports	☐	☐	☐	☐	☐
Using credit when you are buying something is a bad habit	☐	☐	☐	☐	☐
A cabin by the lake is a great place to spend the summer	☐	☐	☐	☐	☐
When it comes to recreation, time is more important than money	☐	☐	☐	☐	☐

Exhibit 7-7   Research using simple rank ordering

who tries to see and hear it through the senses of an outsider, as a customer or a potential or current donor or supporter. Customer impressions and satisfaction are measured on a continual basis; and these measurements are integral to gaining future donor and volunteer support as well as maintaining customers and clients.

TRACKING TANGIBLE AND INTANGIBLE OBJECTIVES

In *The Renewal Factor,* Robert Waterman relates an interesting experience he had with the San Francisco Symphony when helping them become one of the "great" symphonies of America. Starting out with their intangible objective of wanting to achieve "greatness," Waterman describes what he helped the Symphony measure:

> We measured by as many parameters as we could find. First, we tackled the financial state of the orchestra, then our own past and that of some of the world's "great" orchestras. We looked at things

like the long tenure of great conductors with the great orchestras. . . . We compared the average weekly salary of our musicians
with the great orchestras. . . . We contrasted the utilization of our
symphony hall (83 percent at the time) with that of the others (all
running in excess of 90 percent). . . . We measured our subscription
ticket sales (70 percent) against those of the others (most running
over 85 percent). . . . We evaluated factors like average ticket revenues and income from broadcasting and recording.[10]

For Waterman and many others the information that was gathered was
ultimately *actionable*.[11] The information that was gathered was used to
help measure (what had started out to be hard to measure) the concept of
"greatness." In this case, market research was the stepping stone to moving into new areas; the existing data base became the historical resource.

Another nonprofit industry that deals in intangible products on a regular basis is that of the religious institution. Their goal is, in some sense,
to facilitate changed lives: a rather intangible product. While this market
has remained relatively stable over the last 20 years (each week about 40
percent of U.S. adults attend church or a synagogue, a percentage that
has remained basically unchanged since 1970), there have been tremendous fluctuations in attendance and membership among churches, individual denominations, and synagogues. In other words, the market for
religion hasn't shrunk; market share has changed dramatically.[12]

What is causing the change in market share? Is it the presence of
more denominational churches, more nomadic churches, or new styles
of worship? A host of factors have been identified and most are intangible—issues like "deepening the constituents' spiritual lives" and "the
quality of religious teaching."[13] This information was obtained by asking the constituents themselves. They were asked by questionnaire, by
individual appointment, by telephone, and in focus groups.[14]

For many organizations their future means moving away from a preoccupation with short-term results into a long-term mentality that takes
into account complex competitive objectives and goals—objectives and
goals that are both intangible and tangible.

There is always going to be a need for "hard copy" decisions that are
predicated upon computer data arranged on computer printouts, reports,
and spread sheets. Likewise though, there is also going to be a need for a
host of other systems and measurements that are concerned with *how marketing information is shared amongst clients and donors,* how these constituents
feel about the information, how they ultimately react, and how employees
handle their reactions. Tangible and intangible measurements will be used
side by side. The measurement of all of a nonprofit organization's objec-

tives will become the driving force behind not only the successful attainment of these goals, but the organization's viability into the future.

WHY RESIST BUSINESS PRACTICES?

A final question: If measuring progress towards an objective can be done, then why don't more nonprofit organizations try to do it? Fred Setterburg and Kay Schulman in their book, *Beyond Profit*, suggest the following:

> Many of us have actually shunned accumulated knowledge and routine business methods that allow the private sector to function efficiently. Today you can still find nonprofit workers who feel that there is something inherently undemocratic about learning to read a financial statement. And nonprofit managers and boards alike sometimes fear that rigorous planning and evaluation might turn their half-million-dollar community organization into IBM.[15]

There is still a holdover for many organizations that the privilege of undertaking "good works" on behalf of society excludes an organization from the day-to-day need for cost controls and budgets. Some view the idea of measurement as unethical, base, or unspiritual. Others fear that they will become like those on "Madison Avenue."

In the end, all nonprofit organizations will participate in data measurement. The competition for philanthropic dollars in some quarters is intense, and for many organizations there is tremendous pressure to decide which programs to cut and which to keep; which staff to fire and which staff to keep. On top of that, add the pressure to find dollars (and sometimes the failure to do so). Some programs do not work as intended. For some nonprofit leaders, to let donors know that a program is not working also means giving the donor a chance to no longer support the institution, thereby causing a loss of revenue and the potentiality of putting people out of work.

TIPS FOR STAYING COMPETITIVE

To be competitive a nonprofit organization must use past and projected future performance analysis and mold it into a strategy. Nonprofit organizations must embrace marketing as a meaningful exchange between the nonprofit organization and the client, constituent, or donor and translate this orientation into action. One small example of this type of thinking comes from one nonprofit company that has taken job descriptions from every level and given all employees marketing parameters that they need to fulfill or work within.

Looking inside a nonprofit's operations is important in order to objectively assess a past and to fruitfully plan for the future. Specifically, it is important to look at from a client, donor, volunteer, and constituent perspective. The review should include:

1. past performance and projected future performance;
2. past and current strategy;
3. strategic problems in the internal organization;
4. costs; and
5. various causes the organization is involved in.

Gap Analysis

One very specific and "organizationally friendly" way to get at these answers is through *gap analysis*. An analysis of the cause or reason why the five items specified in the previous list can be derived through a variety of means and through many different types of audit and measurement tools. These tools can be as simple as comparing the organization's objectives to those actually achieved and looking for the reasons why there is a variance; or as complex as comparing the benefits donors are looking for with those offered by the organization, and then looking at the effects of any variance upon the organization.

Gap analysis is also one tool used by nonprofit organizations as they look for "answers" to problems in their performance. Its purpose is to look at the "gap" between what was hoped for in an organizational objective or strategy component and what actually occurred. See the following case study as an example.

USING GAP ANALYSIS WITH A TEST MAILER

An organization develops a test mailing package for use in mail list rentals. In mailing the test package to portions of selected lists, a 1.1 percent response rate is gained. The organization decides to roll out the mailing package to the rest of its lists. A .6 percent response rate is achieved. Why was there a gap between the test and the actual roll out of the lists? This gap leads the organization to explore a variety of reasons including seasonal factors, other direct mail tests using the same list going out prior to its own mail drop, and approximate delivery times for the mailing pieces. All of this effort is to develop procedures so that the "gap" between testing and the actual mailing roll out is reduced.

Gap analysis is used by many organizations. If "gaps" appear between the projected future performance and the current operational performance, then an organization undertakes a change in its strategy to remedy the situation. Gap analysis can also be used today to look for a gap or hole in a market not currently being filled or serviced sufficiently by other organizations.

Other Alternatives

There are other ways for marketing managers to take a look inside their strategies and organizations. A *benefit/features matrix* is just one example. (See Exhibit 7-8.) Very simply, a benefit/features matrix looks at those benefits being offered by a nonprofit organization and those benefits being sought by donors. The goal of such a matrix is to identify areas where programmatical aspects of the nonprofit organization do and do not fulfill those benefits being sought by the donors.

An organization first determines those benefits being sought by donors through a marketing research study of its donors and the reasons for their involvement. It then matches these reasons with the organizational hunches it has made regarding the reason for donor involvement, and tries to ensure a sufficient match up of both. If there isn't, then the nonprofit could find that its donors will not remain loyal for very long with an organization that does not meet their needs.

| | *Features offered* | | | | |
	Efficiency	*Counseling*	*Emotional support*	*Community*	*Advice*
Benefits sought					
Efficiency					
Convenience					
Prestige					
Advice					
Friendship					

Exhibit 7-8 A benefit/features/matrix

Still another way for an organization to look at its internal marketing program vis-à-vis its constituency is to look at characteristics of the audiences the organization is serving and contrast them with the characteristics of the ideal audience the nonprofit organization would like to serve.

DEFINING REGULAR THEATERGOERS

A nonprofit theater group is trying to identify what common characteristics comprise audience members who see more than one play per year. To this end, they began to profile regular attendees vs. sporadic attendees. They did this to see if there were any lifestyle differences between the two groups. Having developed a profile of what a theater presentation attendee looked like (and what a nonattendee looked like) they then looked at why some attendees come to more than one performance. Issues such as the timing of performances, their cost, and the attendees' presence at other art events were considered. A profile of attendees who came to more than one event per year was drawn up and a marketing program initiated that culled audience members with similar characteristics and offered them discounts to attend another event.

SUMMARY

Internal nonprofit analysis first identifies the organization's needs, then determines what clients and constituents want, and what donors will support. These are turned into programs, products, and services. The goal is to help the nonprofit organization determine where its strategy should go in order to achieve a stronger client and donor perspective. To accomplish this, it must look at internal variables that are either positively or negatively affecting this client and donor orientation. This information then contributes directly to developing a nonprofit organization's strategy, which is the subject of the next chapter.

CHAPTER EIGHT

Competition as Strategy

The world does not automatically beat a path to the man with a better mousetrap. The world has to be told, enticed, coddled, romanced, and even bribed (as with, for example, coupons, samples, free application aids, and the like).[1]

Theodore Levitt
Marketing for Business Growth

THE FORMATION OF A NEW NONPROFIT ORGANIZATION

John Peter works for a $22 million nonprofit organization. He has been with them for almost 22 years. The organization's primary objective is to help improve the moral and spiritual condition of collegians. The company accomplishes this rather open-ended goal by running conferences on college campuses and publishing books and magazines aimed at college audiences that provide a particular perspective on remedying our nation's moral ills; it employs a group of men and women who travel to the country's college campuses helping students and others in this task. In fact, it was as a staff worker (this is what the itinerants are called) where John Peter started his career with the parent company.

Over a period of years, John Peter noticed that business people seemed extremely open to the message of ethics, especially as it applied to their work situations which were not always easy to deal with from an ethical standpoint. John Peter decided there was enough business interest for him to create his own nonprofit organization that dealt solely with business people on the issue of ethics in their jobs. He talked to some of his friends, secured a few financial commitments from others, and began. The first thing John Peter did in his new business venture was to get a brochure and logo designed, as well as business cards that labeled him as the director of the organization. He also prepared an approximate budget, and let his parent company know what he was doing.

When his parent company found out what was happening, they were in a quandary. John Peter had been with them for so long that they couldn't imagine not having him around. And yet, they hadn't known quite what to do with him these last years. His current position in the organization was Director-at-Large, which was as much a ceremonial position as anything else. So after relatively short deliberation, the parent company offered to have John Peter's start-up organization subsumed under them as one of their divisions, with him listed as the director, even though his new company's goals didn't fit the parent company's "objectives."

John Peter now has a newsletter and a magazine, and runs conferences on ethical issues in business across the country for those business people who want to attend. Though there is no formal evaluation mechanism between he and his parent company they feel he is "doing quite well." Besides, some donated funds are coming in, as well as revenue from John Peter's seminars. The parent company's board of directors seem relatively happy, and John Peter feels he is fulfilling his goals of helping business.[2]

Did John Peter have a strategy? Did he need one or was it sufficient to allow an organizational direction to develop somewhat haphazardly? What would he have done if his funding had dried up or if his parent organization had blocked attempts to start his own company? And was there any difference in attitude and thought between John Peter's business strategy and that of his parent company's corporate strategy?

This chapter has a built-in assumption: *very successful nonprofit companies either intuitively or explicitly have a strategy.* At issue is not whether an institution has a strategy operating or not; every nonprofit organization has a strategy operating whether it is explicitly stated or dictated by chance. However, in order for nonprofit organizations to improve their strategic positions they usually need to develop strategies explicitly. The "how" of doing this is what the next few chapters will be about.

SOME DEFINITIONS

Unfortunately, the language of management can seem very imprecise. With the nonprofit community, words like strategy, policies, objectives, and planning have meanings that vary depending on the organization. For purposes of clarity, the next chapters on strategy adhere to the following definitions:

Objective. the end measurable result the nonprofit organization must accomplish.

Strategy. a summary of how objective(s) with major financial or programmatical implications will be pursued.

Planning. predetermining a course of action to which a nonprofit organization anticipates committing resources (financial and otherwise).

Policy. a decision regarding how an organization will conduct its affairs.

THE NO-STRATEGY STRATEGY

There are some companies that are successful without a specific, well worked-out strategy. Ben and Jerry's ice cream is one of them. In starting out their organization, Ben and Jerry's had no defined plan or strategy. And still they succeeded. Part of their success may have been due to the fact that they were just starting out. Harvard marketing professor Michael Porter comments on organizations like Ben and Jerry's that have a *no-strategy strategy* and succeed, and the need for most organizations to have a defined strategy in their future:

> Many companies have been successful without doing so. Ben and Jerry's ice cream, for example, probably never had a strategic plan. They saw a need and went after it. With intuition and luck, they came up with a formula, an image, their positioning, and package. It added up to an interesting strategy.
>
> But in a world where competition is getting tougher every day, there are benefits in having an explicit strategy. Unless you make a strategy explicit, it's very hard for everybody in the organization to know what they should be doing. One real benefit of a strategy is that it unites effort. Everybody in the company, from the salesman to the worker, knows what the fundamental advantage of the company is supposed to be and can act it out in their daily behavior.[3]

Strategy vs. Planning

For sake of discussion, it is important to revisit the difference between *strategy* and *planning*, particularly long-range planning. Many nonprofit organizations have long-range plans but have no strategies to achieve the end result of their plans.

Benjamin B. Tregoe and John W. Zimmerman, senior leaders and management consultants with Kepner-Tregoe, Inc. and authors of the book *Top Management Strategy*, have noted *strategy* is a continuing process requiring it to be separated from normal operations. In their opinion, there is often confusion in management's mind between strategic thinking and long-range planning, with the outcome being an adverse effect on strategy formulation. Long-range planning is viewed as inadequate for strategy formulation. Exhibit 8-1 lists their reasons why.

Nonprofit organizations that purposely build no strategy or seem to operate by chance ultimately have an operating strategy. While it is generally not recognized or explicitly stated, it usually fits into one of the following categories:

- a strategy of hope;
- a strategy determined by crisis;
- a strategy that is subjective in nature; or
- a strategy arrived at through extrapolating today's events into tomorrow.

Strategy by Hope

This is far and away the most popular method of setting a strategic direction. This is the way John Peter in the earlier example set his strategy, by letting events control his outcome. Perhaps this is such a popular method because of the lack of certainty in the nonprofit world. Strategy by hope is often the eventual outcome of the pressure some nonprofit executives feel today that freezes them into inaction. One thing is clear: Strategy by hope is certainly the *easiest* strategy to come up with, with no pressure or associated deadlines.

Doing nothing strategically is a kind of "life preserver" for some nonprofit executives. In a sea of competing courses of action, doing nothing may seem like the safest method of survival. And, for the rare nonprofit executive, doing nothing may work for a while. However, for the majority of nonprofit organizations, embarking on a particular strategic course of action proves to be the most effective tool for not only organizational growth, but maneuvering through a competitive environment.

1. Long-range plans tend to be based on projections of current operations in the future.

2. Plans that companies make determine their direction, rather than a clear sense of direction determining their plans.

3. Where longe-range plans exist to guide planning, they are invariably set in financial terms.

4. If top managers do not have a clear strategy with which to assess the plans that percolate up from the organization, they become locked into allocating resources on the basis of these plans.

5. Long-range plans tend to be overly optimistic.

6. Long-range plans tend to be inflexible.

7. Long-range planning is really more short-range than anyone cares to admit.

Exhibit 8-1 The adverse effects of long-range planning on strategy formulation

Strategy by Crisis

Had a financial crisis threatened John Peter, he no doubt would have moved into this operative mode of thinking. This type of strategy is employed frequently in small organizations where there is what Bill McConkey, Chairman of the Board of the international nonprofit management consulting group McConkey/Johnston, calls *founder's fever*. In this state, the director or founder spends his or her days dealing with "crisis after crisis" as opposed to allocating line supervision and responsibility. In keeping busy, feeling needed all the time, and having the organization revolve around them, directors are gratified, and also have an ever-present reason (or crisis) why objectives are seldom fully reached.

Unfortunately, because so many nonprofit executives are not only competent but work exceedingly long and hard, they can often go for quite a long period of time relying only on themselves. In doing so, they ensure the organization will only grow according to their limits of time and energy. And, they guarantee that the organization will suffer when they leave, get sick, or simply tire out.

Subjective Strategy

This strategy section and the next paraphrases Stephen Brandt's sections "managing by subjectives" and "managing by extrapolation" from his very helpful book *Strategic Planning In Emerging Companies*.[4] In organizations with strategies that are subjective, everyone works hard and does what he or she thinks is right in their own eyes. Every employee is headed somewhere and they all arrive somewhere; however, departments can't agree on the specifics of what "where" means. This type of organizational approach lends itself to dysfunctional operations, internal departmental competition, and accelerated burnout among employees. Never arriving at an institutional objective or destination as a group, this process can destroy the kind of trust among employees needed to help ensure an organization's success. A brand of unproductive splintered attention can develop in this kind of organization. Managers at the top of many for-profit companies work hard to concentrate themselves and fellow workers toward a goal, with the end goal often bringing some kind of value to stockholders. Some nonprofit organizations do not employ this same type of concentration. Instead they engage in activities that carry little value in the eyes of a donor. If an activity cannot be justified *in the eyes of a donor*, it should be reconsidered.

Even though this splintered attention is not a favorable condition, some nonprofit organizations actually thrive in this environment for a period of time. Organizations in this strategy mode rely on salesmanship from the top and in their publications to help ensure trusting donors and nonprofit friends that the organization is embarking on new programs to meet new challenges, while avoiding discussion of how existing programs are faring.

Strategy by Extrapolation

Users of this type of strategy merely go on doing what they have always been doing, keeping in mind the feeling that "tomorrow will be exactly like today." Their nonprofit business will be steady, rigid, and boring. Hence, they achieve tremendous efficiencies in what they do because their routine never changes from day to day.

The inherent problem in this type of operation is that it is distinctly aimed *away* from the needs of clients and donors and is, instead, focused on the organization's desire to *not* change.

Can such a strategy work? It can, and does, especially in environments that are stable and predictable. In addition, there is often the lack of strong competitive pressures. However, should this competitive level playing field change, the nonprofit organization in question can find itself in dire consequences, with little experience in coping with the new competitive realities.

HOW STRATEGIES GROW NONPROFIT ORGANIZATIONS: THREE DIFFERENT ORIENTATIONS

All successful nonprofit strategies must involve themselves in one of two issues: the cause's *services* or *products* in relation to clients and donors (which, together, ultimately comprise the organization's markets). There are many articulated strategies for organizations to use; some designed to enable a defensive posture in light of strong competitive forces at work, others designed to allow offensive posturing to take place, and still others giving an organization a defendable position within its cause-related field. There are many different approaches, each successful one ultimately involving some type of unique construction specific to the nonprofit organization in question. At the broadest level, though, there are some distinct strategic postures that any nonprofit organization can take in coping with its environment and those forces it identifies as competitive.

Three generic marketing strategies in some way or another tend to fit every nonprofit marketing situation. These three strategic postures are:

1. No strategic change.
2. A product strategy.
3. A market strategy.

As part of these three strategies, it is important to look at how strategy relates to competition. There can be little doubt in the for-profit world that the goal of strategy is to beat competition. This sentiment is not always true in the nonprofit world. In fact, some nonprofit organizations are embarrassed at being the strongest within their cause-related field or having clients and donors think their programs are the best.

Herein lies the real difficulty nonprofit organizations can face regarding competition. See the following case study as an example.

CITY MISSION TRIES TO KEEP UP WITH THE COMPETITION

A city mission worked to elevate its direct marketing and funding program. Unfortunately, virtually every strategy the mission undertook in this arena was being dictated by competitors. When competitors produced a brochure, sent an emergency appeal, or introduced a new client service, the city mission imitated them.

The mission's strategy was going toe to toe with other providers of similar types of service. Its strategy was to mirror everyone else and be reactive, with little thought given to how to improve its competitive posture with its clients and donors.

In today's competitive environment, just "keeping up" with the competition is not enough. The key to long-term success is getting ahead of the competition. Allowing oneself to be defined by competition is a small part of strategy. The effectiveness of a strategy is ultimately defined by the value the client or donor feels he or she receives, not by the posturing of nonprofit organizations vis-à-vis other nonprofit organizations.

NO STRATEGIC CHANGE

No strategic change (or the concept of staying where a nonprofit is strategically) is a viable strategy for those conditions that suggest the cost of change is too high. While business periodicals document an endless parade of companies that folded when they did not change to meet changing environmental conditions, some companies feel they flourish by not changing. Consider this for-profit example: The executives of a very successful specialty chemical company in the southeastern United States came to the conclusion that in order to continue their exciting sales growth, overseas expansion and major new equity money would be required. They felt that such moves would drastically alter their lifestyles as scientist-managers, and they decided to alter their sales growth objectives in favor of other objectives that better reflected their professional and personal preferences. The board agreed with the alterations. No change in strategy was initiated.[5]

Though no strategic change is a viable marketing strategy, it seems there are few instances where it is a good strategy. A "good strategy" is usually thought of not in short-term images, but in long-term construction whereby the nonprofit organization, over time, places itself in a position that can be improved over the same time period. Too often in the minds of nonprofit executives, a no-change strategy translates into "no improvement" in the way things are done. There is usually no effort to raise the standards of execution for organizations with a no-change strategy. There is also little cost cutting and creative marshalling of resources. In addition, there is usually little thought given to how the nonprofit organization might defend its market position should a competitor come in and offer the same set of services—perhaps more cheaply—to the same constituency. Quite literally, "no strategic change" often becomes a euphemism for lack of managerial thinking and focus.

Most nonprofit organizations run very hard just to stay in place regarding dollars brought in, maintaining their service share of market, and their return of their fund-raising investment. In times of increased competition in an economy that is very volatile, most nonprofit managers would find a do-nothing marketing strategy as neither particularly enticing nor wise. In addition, this type of strategy seems to ignore a nonprofit organization's needs to strategically self-renew in light of donor and client demands. The lack of strategic choice often causes organizations to focus inward, becoming fixated on long-range planning while ignoring donors, clients, the market at large, and competing nonprofit organizations. The ability to sustain performance becomes lost. There must be a connection between long-term strategy and client/donor/volunteer/constituent needs.

If a no-change strategy is adopted, the organization must not lose sight of its donors and clients. This is where the definition of the client/constituent and donor/volunteer becomes important. Clients and donors are iconoclastic, making and breaking patterns every day, often with very little loyalty to any group. The "yuppie," "baby-boomer" or "post-boomer" markets, for example, and their relationship to philanthropy are often discussed in fund-raising circles and have been a thematic fixture at a number of fund-raising conferences. The following case study is one example of how an established market is breaking apart.

THE "YUPPIE" MARKET IS GONE

Take the much-discussed "yuppie" market and its association with certain branded consumer products, like BMWs. After a stage of high customer energy and close identification, the wave has broken. Having been saturated and absorbed by the marketplace, the "yuppie" association has faded, just as energy does in the physical world. Sensing the change, BMW no longer sells to the "yuppie" lifestyle but now focuses on the technological capabilities of its machines. And "yuppies" are no longer the wave they once were; as a market, they are more like particles as they look for more individualistic and personal expressions of their consumer energy.[6]

As the customers' behavior changed, so did BMW's marketing strategy. Values and technological expertise replaced conspicuous consumption in BMW's messages to its audience, because the audience no longer had the same value structure. A no-change strategy would ignore such signals from the marketplace (clients/constituents/donors/volunteers) and, instead, would rely on hunches and old stereotypes.

It makes sense to move away from a no-change marketing strategy when analysis indicates that the nonprofit organization can no longer meet its objectives the way it intended. Organizations need to look ahead one to three years and project where they will be at the end of the measurement period, contrasted with where they think they should be. If the two are not reasonably within striking distance of each other, the strategy of no change should be reexamined.

One way to move into a more competitively strategic mode is by looking at the causes, services, and products a nonprofit organization offers.

A CAUSE AND PRODUCT STRATEGY

Nonprofit causes and products are items or programs offered to markets that provide not only service to clients but also provide an organization with financial support, volunteerism, and a sense of goal accomplishment. A nonprofit organization's program is that which ultimately benefits or satisfies a particular segment of society. Its products can be more than physical, tangible things. They can also be a person, a service, an event, an idea, or an institution. Sometimes a nonprofit organization's products are defined individually, such as a book on a particular recovery program; sometimes they're defined as a part of a particular grouping, such as a line of recovery books; and sometimes products are defined in broader categories, such as a "book publishing division."

Most nonprofit organizations have used a product strategy, whether knowingly or not. The primary reason for this has been historical. It used to be that all a nonprofit organization seemingly had to do in order to be financially successful was to produce some type of program and a supportive constituency would immediately fall in line with money, enthusiasm, and volunteerism. And while a product strategy can still be a very wise competitive strategy, much has changed in the last several years, particularly in the lack of loyalty exhibited by donors and clients toward nonprofit causes and products, and in the proliferation of causes that mirror each others' operational, promotional, and service activities—what could be termed *generic product approaches.*

Theodore Levitt, amongst others, has said that, "People don't buy products, they buy the expectation of benefits."[7] It is this *benefits cluster*—or the value that donors, volunteers, and clients gain by being involved with any organization—surrounding the organization that is missing from many marketing strategies. An organization, simply put, must provide more benefits for constituent involvement than other nonprofit organizations providing similar services. That, ultimately, will make a difference.

This augmented view of both what a product is and the hidden aspect of competition—forgotten by most nonprofit organizations—has had enormous consequences. As the need for different benefits changes among donors, clients, and constituents, one shift that should occur in the nonprofit marketplace (and should be affecting every nonprofit organization's strategy) is the need for donor, client, and constituent analysis to determine why people will or will not support a cause, and the benefits that accrue to them by their decision to do so.

An organization that opts for a product strategy says, in essence, that the causes, services, and products it produces will be key to the retention and expansion of its supportive constituencies in the future. Its causes will define its markets of clients, support, and help. In a broad sense then, every nonprofit organization that adopts this strategy also adopts the notion that its competition will come primarily from other nonprofit organizations that are producing similar services and products for similar audiences.

A nonprofit organization facing this generic onsurge will try through *differentiation* to create a cause, service, or product that is perceived as unique and different from those offerings of its competitors. This differentiation allows it, then, to create interest among its constituents for the style in which it is pursuing its goals. Differentiation can occur many ways: through targeted audiences, the quality of the service offering, the way (or technology) in which the service is delivered, the donation amounts that are asked for to financially support the operation, the quality of service given back to the supportive clientele, and even the alliances the nonprofit organization has or the endorsements it enjoys.

Typically, there are a number of practical decisions a nonprofit entity needs to make when employing a cause and product strategy. They are discussed more fully in the following section.

Matching the Market

The cause, service, or product needs to match the correct market. There is an interrelationship between what a nonprofit organization offers and what the market wants to buy or support. Ignoring this interrelationship can be detrimental to nonprofit organizations, because they may be producing services or products that the market simply does not want. According to Regis McKenna:

> The environment defines the product. A product can't be viewed in isolation. The elements of the environment—technology trends, market dynamics, competition, social and economic trends—all influence the way customers see the product.

Companies can't just send a positioning message out to the market. They must work with the environment to differentiate and position their products. They must understand who the market influencers are, what the religious issues are, what people are thinking, what their prejudices are, what their likes and dislikes are, what they want to hear. Then companies must position their products to fit in with the attitudes of the marketplace.[8]

The Rules of Performance

A nonprofit marketer should understand basic rules of performance. Certain generalizations about nonprofit causes and products prevail, and understanding them can lead to better marketing decisions. Ignoring them can lead to disaster. Here are a few:

1. A small number of causes and products will bring in the majority of clients, donations, and volunteers.

2. The more marginal a cause, service, or product is in terms of client interest and financial and volunteered support, the more likely it is to drain the organization's finances and personnel.

3. Weak causes and nonprofit products take excessive management time and expenditures.

4. Usually, an increase in management time and in fund-raising expense cannot turn around a cause, service, or product that clients and donors perceive as defective, inferior, or nonattractive.

5. A poor service or product can tarnish the image of other products.

6. Product and service accountability by the nonprofit organization, as well as performance measurability, enhance resource allocation decisions for individual nonprofit products and services.

7. Modifications and repositioning tactics can extend the life of a service or product.

8. Competitors are constantly looking for ways to acquire competitive strengths over others' services and products.

9. Client and donor product and service perceptions may be more significant than the reality of superior or inferior product performance.

10. Very successful nonprofit products and services achieve the highest average gift size or possess the most superior qualities compared to competitive causes and products.

11. Faddish, fashionable, or popular causes can be like Roman candles—quick to light the skies but faster to fizzle out.

Decisions to Support an Image

The goal of daily marketing decisions is to support the overall institutional image desired by the top leadership of the nonprofit organization. In this chapter's opening example concerning John Peter, the actions by his parent organization to subsume him were inconsistent actions, not designed to ultimately set forth a carefully prescribed image. Although it may have been a successful venture, there was little programmatic integration between John Peter and the parent nonprofit organization that seemed strategic. A nonprofit organization must identify its niche and the market segment it hopes to appeal to, and then it must do nothing to destroy the image it is cultivating within that niche. By their own admission, John Peter's nonprofit organization hardly fit with their corporate objectives. They simply did not wish to lose John Peter.

Honing, Rather Than Adding, Services

The goal in producing services is not to be the nonprofit organization with the most services. Many nonprofit organizations feel the need to flood the market with new product introductions to prove to their clients and donors that they are hardworking and diligent. In fact, the opposite often occurs in that clients and donors feel confused and at odds with products that seem to compete for their attention. An organization must determine the optimal number of services and products it can produce, manage, and market effectively to its constituencies. By subscribing to a hodge-podge of diverse operations and a multiplicity of product lines, a nonprofit organization risks alienating a constituency that cannot possibly be interested in all of its offerings, either financially or with their enthusiasm. Enthusiasm is less strong if a cause is too diversified.

A secondary concern occurs with the nonprofit that has many different offerings in the marketplace. Organizations in this situation often have a few services that are financial nightmares internally, and are perceived externally by a supportive constituency as being poorly managed, with few financial or managerial controls.

Understanding Product Life Cycles

Nonprofit marketers must begin to appreciate the powerful relationship between product life cycles and their own marketing strategies. Nonprofit organizations seldom talk about product life cycles and almost never talk about them as an aid in marketing strategy. But indeed they are just that. How might product life cycles be of help in building a marketing strategy?

As described earlier in this text, there are usually four product life cycles. Stage 1 is called *market development*. This stage is traditionally when a new product, service, or cause is brought to a market without there being a proven demand for it. Support by clients and donors at this stage is usually low. Nonprofit organizations sometimes forget demand often has to be created and that demand depends not only on the donor or client feeling a need for the service, but also its complexity, and whether there are substitutes available that will accomplish the donor's or client's same value needs. The fact is that most new nonprofit products or services never leave this stage; rather they do not survive in the marketplace at all.

Stage 2 is called *market growth*. At this stage, the demand for the services begins to accelerate. Some problems can begin at this stage. If the nonprofit organization was the first to introduce the service, it often has to contend with competitors who introduce generic versions or carbon copies. The marketing issue for the nonprofit organization at this stage is to entice the client or donor to try the service and then try to differentiate it from those of the competitors, if all products or services being offered are basically the same.

Stage 3 is called *market maturity*. Demand now begins to level off and growth becomes moderate. Perhaps a better phrase than market maturity is market saturation. Those who are going to respond to the cause or product have done so. If a nonprofit is trying to hold onto donors or clients and keep them from shifting to another nonprofit organization, the organization is probably working very hard to differentiate itself from its competitors. Nonprofit organizations at this stage look for and expect smaller and smaller financial transactions and often resort to premiums, sweepstakes, or other promotional devices to try and continue the differentiation process.

Stage 4 is called *market decline*. The service or product is now losing client and donor appeal and interest or contributions are steadily drifting downward for all nonprofit organizations involved. Some nonprofit organizations will pull much of their fund raising or advertising for the product at this stage. Clients and donors lose interest; fewer and fewer nonprofit organizations talk about the product or cause at all. It's time to go back to Stage 1 and create a unique service or product. One example dramatically traces product introduction all the way to product decline.

EVEN DISASTERS HAVE A PRODUCT LIFE CYCLE

During the Ethiopian famine, a number of nonprofit organizations got involved in providing aid to that country. Some nonprofit organizations viewed this time as an opportunity for donor acquisition. One client prepared to jump into the fray; the planning cycle was very rapid. Television spots, accompanied by direct mail, were used in metro markets where the nonprofit organization had strong, preexisting support. Public relations kits containing videotapes and community involvement strategies were also shipped to religious, civic, and community groups. Press releases and video releases were sent to local media in the designated cities.

In one market, the nonprofit organization identified 11 other groups undertaking basically the same strategy. While there was a relatively strong differentiation element in the organization's appeals, all the appeals from every organization basically talked about the same crisis. In spite of this, there was strong initial acceptance of the direct mail and television test offers and the acquisition tests were rolled out to other cities.

As the promotion campaign rolled out to target cities, other relief groups—both national and regional concerns—did likewise. Acquisition response rates began to fall and the loss-to-profit ratio began to climb. There was also a disappointing second gift response rate from those who had initially come aboard with a gift. Telemarketing efforts were introduced to gain a second gift and were somewhat successful at getting a smaller second gift.

Response rates continued to decline, the national media stopped its coverage of the starving country, and donors were getting bored with the whole affair. Within three years after the acquisition effort, almost 90 percent of the donors acquired by the nonprofit organization from this crisis appeal lapsed in their giving and support to disaster aid. In similar efforts by other nonprofit organizations, the numbers of nonactive names now is even higher.[9]

The following sections explain what lessons can be learned from this case study.

Lesson 1—Market Development.   At the beginning of the chapter, John Peter was essentially bringing a new product to market. How long will it take him to "create" the market demand for his product? That will probably depend on two primary variables: first, is there client or donor demand for the service and, second, are there substitutes for the service already in the marketplace?

Further complicating issues in this market development stage is John Peter's need for resources for his start-up nonprofit organization. Most new products or services never leave the development stage, usually because of a lack of resources. It is simply very expensive and time consuming to launch a new cause that a nonprofit organization hopes will be around for some time.

Lesson 2—Market Growth. In the growth stage, institutions that introduce services that are substitutes for the original often do as well financially as the original. Why? Because substitutes have not had to expend the money or effort required to introduce the original cause, service, or product. They have merely copied the original (or have made slight improvements on it). The consequence of this competitive attack is to truncate the original product's growth because of the presence of so many competitors and choices for client and donor.

This stage is usually marked by a percentage of donors and clients willing to give to the cause or try the service or product. The expectancy of various audiences for the service or product is already latent. By this stage, the original service or product producer worries chiefly about differentiating itself from its competitors, as well as building donor or client loyalty, and getting prospective donors and clients to try the service or product.

In the Ethiopian example, as donors accepted the need to support refugees, the number of channels or options available to donors to give through, or to become involved, increased dramatically.

As an example, in one small community, special famine relief offerings were taken at local places of worship, coin and change collection boxes representing different drives were at the bakery and gas station, the local 4-H sent money, and no doubt some of the community's citizens received direct mail and telemarketing appeals. The consequences of this outpouring of donor and agency response also impacted the competitive situation. Because of a perception of easy profit and heavy donor acceptance, many late-coming competitive nonprofit organizations also jumped into the relief effort.

Lesson 3—Market Maturity. All of the competitive activity quickly moved the market into a maturity stage. The presence of acceptable substitute offerings or ways of giving available to the donor or prospective customer reduces the length of time market maturity lasts; if there are no acceptable substitutes, maturity lasts longer. In the famine example, there were many substitutes.

Larger financial commitments made by donors to the effort early on in the campaign process had begun to dry up; they gave way to requests by nonprofit organizations for gifts of any size. (Most seriously concerned individuals had already given.)

During this stage, nonprofit organizations that had any sort of brand equity or name recognition with a constituency had an advantage over other nonprofits in their solicitation strength and ability to differentiate themselves based on their name's history and previous relationship with the marketplace.

Lesson 4—Market Decline. Of course, in the decline stage, many nonprofit organizations try to reap the benefits of easy money and of being involved in a "glamour" cause. Unfortunately, the decline stage also represents both an over-choice situation among donors ("Everyone is asking for my money for famine relief. Who do I give to?") and an overcapacity situation with too many nonprofit organizations involved in the effort with sound-alike pitches. Donors get bored. Few nonprofit organizations weather a storm like this and solicitation for the project all but ceases. Coming back to the donor, the donor needs a clear pitch and a clear cause; a crowded market dooms everyone.

Implications

Each of these four stages points to the need for an organization to improve its predictive powers when it comes to introducing new causes, service, or products. It is especially helpful to try to discern the profile of the cause being introduced before taking action. Though it is difficult to predict the length and durability of a product, by recognizing some of the pitfalls associated with its profile, a nonprofit organization helps itself rationally and competitively as it introduces the new cause.

A MARKET STRATEGY

Markets refer to any grouping of men, women, and children who share some common characteristics and common needs. The nonprofit organization that looks at a market strategy decides it will provide a range of services, causes, or products that fill, or will fill, client or donor needs. In fact, in this strategy looking for ways to fill this donor or client need becomes the predominant marketing occupation of the nonprofit organization. Organizations which engage in this behavior traditionally spend large amounts of money in market research and donor or client analysis in order to discover these needs.

Of course, developing markets to support a cause or service is very common. Many nonprofit organizations dream about market expansion across this country, and in some cases, the world. To do so successfully requires certain capabilities within the nonprofit organizations that are not always there, such as:

1. Having a system of disciplined, comprehensive, and systematic recordkeeping so an organization knows where it has been and where it wants to go.

2. Identifying the elements through a situation analysis that will shape a strategic plan, in this case, an expansion plan.

3. Looking at a variety of key variables like the seasonality (if any) of the offer, all the variables affecting the costs expended on behalf of the expansion, the expansion vehicle itself (for example, a nonprofit may choose to expand via direct mail list rentals).

4. Developing the system that will take care of new donors or customers once they come aboard.

One good example of a unique capability requirement is the need for comprehensive information systems and management control. Likewise, as a nonprofit grows, it encounters more and more competitors, some in markets where they are entrenched. All of this can lead quickly to problems. Says Stanford Business School faculty member Steven Brandt:

> Many emerging companies grow fairly large without formally thinking through just where they are heading and just what they are becoming. Many emerging companies don't graduate to the major leagues either. Frequently a cause of stopping to succeed is that both product and market-development strategies are undertaken simultaneously.[10]

FIVE GROWTH STRATEGIES

Five overriding market growth strategies must be considered:

1. Getting an existing constituency to either use a service or product more by more frequent interactions with it, getting more financially involved with it, or giving to or purchasing the service more frequently.

2. Allowing the bonding relationship with a market to be reflected in new product features or new services the nonprofit organization introduces that the market feels they have a vested interest in.

3. Expanding into and targeting new audience segments for services or products.

4. Where possible, using vertical integration, whereby a nonprofit organization moves, by its activity pattern, closer to the client, donor, or constituent; for example, a college recruiting high school

students directly as opposed to only talking and trying to persuade guidance counselors of the college's merit.

5. Related and unrelated diversification and the merger of nonprofit companies.

Each of these tactics is addressed separately in the following sections.

Growing Existing Markets

In direct mail fund raising, the four most obvious ways to improve a nonprofit organization's financial performance are to either attract more donors, to encourage existing donors to give more frequently, to persuade donors to increase their average gift size, or to convince donors to contribute to multiple parts of the cause. These same principles hold true in growing a nonprofit organization's general market.

In marketing parlance, "getting more donors" usually is called "increasing market share." And while it is beyond the scope of this book to speak at length of donor acquisition, "increasing market share" is the most obvious way to grow a nonprofit organization and is accomplished tactically by many means.

A nonprofit organization can use a number of different ways to increase its constituents that use its services or support its cause. Each will have its own unique characteristics. For example, the nonprofit organization will experience different donor client drop-off rates depending on the way the clients were recruited. Likewise, the same is true with donors. Depending on the medium by which donors were acquired, a nonprofit organization experiences different lapsing or drop-off rates. For example, donors acquired through television may have half of the donor life of a donor acquired through a magazine advertisement.

Upgrading Involvement. Getting donors to give more frequently, customers to buy more frequently, or convincing clients to avail themselves of the nonprofit organization's services are all a form of *upgrading their involvement.* For-profit product manufacturers ask their customers to use the product more frequently, thereby increasing the likelihood of repeat purchase. Nonprofit organizations take a similar tack in asking their donors to give more than once a year, moving them into programs that require quarterly or monthly gifts, or by asking clients for regular and periodic visits or consultations. Once such a commitment has taken place on the part of the client or donor to an organization, this action causes the individual to be almost impervious to substitute competitor attacks and allows the nonprofit organization substantial bonding opportunities and the luxury of budgeting on committed dollars. In addition, a routinized commitment on the part of the client or donor lessens the chance of their lapsing in their commitment to the nonprofit organization, or stopping their giving to the institution entirely.

Likewise, not only is the frequency of contact or giving increased by the client or donor to the nonprofit organization, but the yearly net value of their involvement is also increased. Similar attempts to accomplish this type of client or donor commitment or bond can be seen being made by book publishers who encourage potential readers to join a book club; or missionaries who seek monthly financial partners; or relief agencies that ask potential donors to feed the same child every month.

A for-profit example gives insight into other ways to increase the utility of a nonprofit organization's services or products in their clients' or donors' eyes:

Arm & Hammer baking soda saw sales go from $15.6 million in 1969 to about $150 million in 1981 largely by finding new applications for its well-known product. After the advertising campaign suggesting using the product to deodorize refrigerators began in 1972, the percentage of households that reported having used the product in this application went from 1 percent to 57 percent just 14 months later. Later campaigns suggested its use as a sink deodorizer, a freezer deodorizer, a cat-litter deodorizer, a dog deodorizer, and a treatment for swimming pools.[11]

Can a nonprofit organization employ the same tactics of increasing its value to different audiences? Consider the following examples:

INCREASING UTILITY

A church normally uses its building just on Sundays. By allowing a day-care organization to use its facilities during the week, the church introduces itself to a whole new group of people.

A camp for young people uses its pool and gymnasium complex heavily during the three months of summer and on some weekends during the course of the year. By allowing the local community to use its gym and pool during slow week nights, it builds a large local support base.

A city mission helps men and women in its programs to finish high school. By offering the help to those who are not in its program, the community begins to view the mission as more than just a service to indigents on the street.

Another way to improve the value from existing donors or clients is to uncover new causes for them to be interested in, or to uncover new applications for causes they're currently interested in.

New Services with Vested Interest

Another tactic is to develop a new service or cause in which donors and clients feel they have a vested interest. This should be done only through direct client surveying and contact.

Someone once said, "Marketing is about having customers, not merely acquiring them." Attracting clients or donors is only the *first* step in the nonprofit organization's marketing program; maximizing their time with the organization and enabling them to enjoy a long-term, multiple-service relationship with the institution is another and, perhaps, equally important goal of marketing. And because today's clients and donors have no need to feel allegiance to any institution, the institution's goal through marketing services is to give these individuals a reason to feel allegiance to the nonprofit organization. This is accomplished in a number of ways.

Keeping a Customer by Adding Features. First, features can be added to existing products to enhance certain constituent members' experience with the organization. A camp begins serving a meatless alternative at evening meals, a convention allows for hearing impaired individuals, a political party adds a plank to their platform aimed at a certain group, an in-bound 800 telephone number is introduced by a counseling center—each of these allows for additional client and donor satisfaction, and the potentiality of additional revenue, client interest, or donor growth.

Nonprofit organizations can also take a cue from for-profit organizations and create product line extensions. A camp has BMX biking for one constituency; for those more advanced, it offers off-road biking. Another organization runs a tri-annual convention for its members; now it offers an off-year regional series of events. A seminary, in addition to its regular classes, now offers a community series of lectures aimed at lay people.

Product line extensions and new product features should come as a *direct result* of donor or client suggestions and, as such, may enjoy a certain amount of built-in support. Before introducing a new service expansion a nonprofit organization usually has to take into account some of the following questions:

• Will there be sufficient numbers of constituents who will benefit from these new additions?

- Can some of the cost incurred be shared or distributed?
- Does the nonprofit organization have the necessary personnel, skill, and resources to do what constituents want them to do?

Not surprisingly, donors and clients can help a nonprofit organization modify existing services and products. They will often, as in John Peter's case, provide the stimulus to create new services or products that, in turn, create new markets or share existing markets. John Peter's new nonprofit offering will hopefully create synergy with the parent company by sharing clients, constituents, and donors, as well as exploiting the parent company's strengths.

Of course, as with all new products or services, a certain amount of testing and analysis is necessary to justify the addition.

Targeting New Audience Segments

This area can actually be an exciting one—that of finding and introducing new constituents and then discovering how their concerns and needs will effect changes upon the organization. (See Exhibit 8-2.) Nonprofit organizations often try to grow by taking existing services, causes, or products and expanding geographically, or by introducing these services, causes, or products into new market segments. Earlier in this text, Spring Hill camp director Mark Olson questioned the need for geographic expansion of his operation.

Geographic Expansion. Geographic expansion can often be achieved by virtually duplicating what a nonprofit organization is doing in one area of the country and just doing it somewhere else. There are numerous

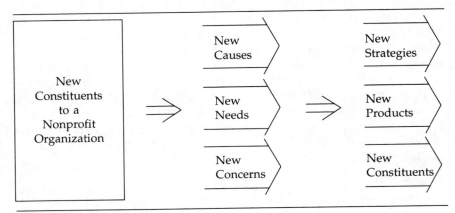

Exhibit 8-2   The constituent-driven nonprofit organization

examples of nonprofit organizations moving from a small operation into a regional operation, and then into a national operation. Sometimes this is done because consumer demand warrants it; sometimes it is because growth does not seem forthcoming unless geographic expansion takes place; and sometimes it seems to make more sense to expose a tested program, service, or product to new audiences rather than look for ways to enhance the program, service, or product to existing audiences.

Nonprofit organizations can expand into *new market segments.* For example, John Peter's organization has a number of options available to it. First, John Peter could design conferences and materials for different industries, thereby using different distribution channels and forming new audience segments.

Second, he could adjust his pricing structure to make his conferences and materials more attractive to certain groups, such as business students.

Third, he could offer a discount to professional organizations within an industry that would tend to use his services more frequently.

Using Vertical Integration

In the for-profit world, companies are often talked about in terms of having a "forward" or "backward" integration policy. Either represents a potential growth direction for nonprofit organizations.

When a for-profit company is said to be involved with *forward integration,* it usually means that a company is moving forward (or closer) with respect to the consumer by taking over or buying the way its product is distributed. If a person made a product that was sold or distributed via a retail chain, he or she would accomplish *forward integration* (sometimes called *vertical integration*) if they bought the retail outlets, thereby allowing the owner of the company to go directly to potential customers as opposed to using a middleman to sell the product.

If the same person was involved in *backward integration,* he or she would be interested in acquiring or buying out the suppliers who supplied the parts for the production of the product. In this way, the owner of the product could guarantee that he or she would always have the suppliers and parts for their product. (See Exhibit 8-3.)

A case study will help to explain the issue of backward and forward integration and also makes clear its application in the nonprofit industry.

A NONPROFIT ORGANIZATION BECOMES A PUBLISHER

A large nonprofit publishing and fund-raising firm used both forward and backward integration with much success. This nonprof-

**Forward
Integration**

(Moving closer to the constituent)

The company actively buys the way a product is distributed
in order to move closer to a constituent group

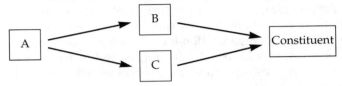

Company A buys outlets B and C to move closer to the constituent

**Backward
Integration**

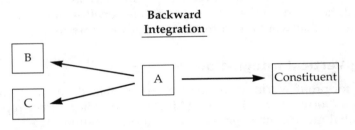

Company A buys companies B and C which are its suppliers
to improve its ease of getting a product to a constituent

Exhibit 8-3   Forward and backward integration

it company integrated backward to buy the printing company that
had serviced its book publishing division, and later created forward integration by introducing its own set of book stores to compete alongside other stores that already carried their products.

There were distinct advantages in this move in relationship to
information passing back and forth between retail outlet, parent
company, and printing house so future demand could be regulat-
ed and measured.

Likewise, there were also technological advantages when a centralized inventory control was initiated among the book publisher
and its stores. This, in turn, helped achieve substantial economies
of scale regarding production questions. On the retail side, the
nonprofit organization's product did not have to compete solely
with other books in the same product category under sometimes
less than ideal circumstances.

Retail outlets were located in key geographic areas. In addition, the number of customers who complained they could not find the nonprofit organization's products at other stores declined to nearly zero because these customers switched their shopping and transportation patterns so as to be able to frequent the new outlets.

Likewise, there were never conflicts with competing firms trying to get their print jobs done at the printing plant, or with having to wait to get print jobs done quickly. Supply and demand was controlled internally.

Negatively, huge costs were incurred by the parent company with the backward-integration purchase of the printing house and the forward integration of opening retail outlets. This enormously increased the nonprofit organization's financial risk.

In addition, while the parent company retained the printing house personnel, they had to hire retail outlet managers which required senior managers to manage in areas in which they had little expertise. The parent company also lost some distribution outlets for its product by reducing its flexibility and committing to the success of its retail outlets.

While sometimes sounding attractive, integration is not always more profitable for a nonprofit organization. Long-term contracts can achieve the same assurances that forward or backward integration can offer.

Diversification and Merger

Diversification means entering into new product markets that are uniquely different from those the nonprofit organization is currently pursuing. According to some, this tactic represents one of the real growth areas for nonprofit organizations in the future.

Previously discussed product modification and expansion of supportive constituencies is one avenue toward diversification. However, diversification can be accomplished more quickly by a nonprofit organization going into a new product arena by acquiring another nonprofit entity or by starting a new venture, where, by virtue of the newly acquired or developed nonprofit products or services, new audiences are introduced to the nonprofit organization in question.

There are, though, almost always some difficulties with a *merger* or *acquisition*. The first difficulty is in the match between the two organizations. Do they have compatible missions or are they extremely diverse? If they're diverse, then the merger or acquisition will often be in trouble down the road. The second area is in management. Nonprofit managers often do not have the background or experience to manage newly acquired organizations. They usually require an extended learning curve. Third, the physical integration time required when two companies merge can mean that either organization will be at risk for some time as the two new partners work out systems together. And finally, there are often huge hidden costs in mergers and acquisitions that both companies have to absorb; whether in new technologies required, new managers that need to be hired, or new audiences that must be sought out.

As with any growth area, there are real threats linked to diversification. Of all of the previously suggested strategies, diversification is the one that can require a management team to move very far afield from its proven area of expertise. Diversification usually implies both the presence of new products and/or services, as well as new markets simultaneously. Even the most accomplished marketing units often have trouble in this situation. For most nonprofit organizations, diversification is the last strategic resort considered after other alternatives are exhausted.

One helpful strategy is to divide diversification into "related" diversification and "unrelated" diversification. A *related diversification* is one in which the two involved nonprofit organizations have meaningful commonalities which provide the potential to generate economies of scale or synergies based on the exchange of skills or resources. An *unrelated diversification* will lack such commonalities.[12]

Related Diversification. Two nonprofit organizations in the same field, often unable to compete effectively with others, may combine their expertise, services, resources, advertising, and fund-raising dollars and, thereby, operate efficiently. Consider a nonprofit book publisher that jointly buys a web press with a small publishing firm; both firms can justify an expensive purchase. Or, a youth camp with a huge indoor ropes course that partners with an executive team-building firm to offer seminars. There are many ways in which nonprofit organizations can work together to pool resources.

Sound farfetched? Not when a nonprofit is interested in achieving economies of scale, like the aforementioned true examples. Each organization gained something important. And, each had related specialties in their field that allowed the whole to become bigger than the sum of its parts. The book publisher had marketing skills and a large talent pool. The small publishing firm had a good service record. The youth camp had experts in ropes courses and a great site location. The team-building firm had business contacts and programmatical expertise, along with an established name.

In each case, the leadership of the nonprofit organizations involved pointed to some or all of the following advantages: new expertise was gained, resources were pooled, skills were learned, new marketing contacts were established, and organizational strengths were exchanged.

What is the marketing risk associated with related diversification? One risk occurs when the two organizations aren't sufficiently related to justify working together. Another would be the difficulty, managerially, of getting into a new field. However, the risks increase in an unrelated diversification.

Unrelated Diversification. Nonprofit unrelated diversifications are primarily financially driven ventures. The goal in such a competitive move is for one nonprofit organization to acquire another that will generate new income, new client streams, a steady supply of cash, or expose a nonprofit organization to new market and product areas.

A nonprofit organization looking at an unrelated diversification usually has a different set of motives than one contemplating a related move. In an unrelated situation, a nonprofit organization's management normally has decided that the venture in question is an attractive "diamond in the rough"; that through managerial or financial restructuring, it can generate new dollars, clients, donors, or markets.

Unrelated diversifications generally develop in one of three ways. The first way is for a nonprofit organization to acquire another nonprofit for nothing or next to nothing. The nonprofit organization potentially receiving the "free" organization may have been selected to be offered the cause because of its reputation, longevity, name recognition, or its leadership. Here's a case study.

FREE RADIO STATION!

A nonprofit organization that works internationally has been offered a radio station for free. Evidently the reason for the offer is the radio station's hope that the much larger nonprofit firm will be able to come in and restructure the radio station for more profitable operations.

Restructuring organizations is the second most popular reason why nonprofit organizations engage in unrelated diversification. A potential downside in *restructuring situations* (and in the previous case study) is, "Does the new owner know anything about managing a radio station?"

Finally, nonprofit organizations enter into unrelated diversifications because they perceive that the cause or the nonprofit market has the potentiality for high growth or great client and/or donor acceptance. This potentiality may outweigh the other two reasons in its importance. The nonprofit's desire to have access to new donors or clients often clouds its perception of the desirability of acquiring an organization that the nonprofit organization may have little or no experience in managerially or have little knowledge of the needs of its donors and clients.

Mergers. Many nonprofit organizations are seriously considering mergers these days. From their point of view, mergers are a quick solution as a growth strategy. Mergers save management and organizational time while acquiring skills and resources not present internally. No doubt the driving force is either financial stresses on the nonprofit organization or pressure from donors.

As an example, a disabled veterans' organization solicited telephone and mail donations last year. In addition, six different organizations with virtually the same mission statement are soliciting funds from the same donor pool, all of which are barely surviving financially. From a donor and personal viewpoint, perhaps some of these organizations are ripe for a merger.

Some specific criteria should be kept in mind when considering an acquisition. Specifically, does the new nonprofit organization have skills and resources that the acquiring organization doesn't currently possess, or will there be a high degree of resource redundancy thereby rendering the merger a very costly venture? Are there specific weaknesses with the organization in question? In addition, it can take considerable time to undo bad strategy and poor client and donor relationships, so the potential acquisition should be carefully considered. In addition, employees should be considered. Who will stay? What is their motivation—their ambition—their productivity level?

In a study reported in *The Chronicle of Philanthropy* on nonprofit mergers, the following was noted in relation to employees:

> The study found a big difference in staff morale at agencies or programs being absorbed and at those agencies that were acquiring other organizations. Staff morale was judged to be high at 73 percent of the organizations that were acquiring another group, but only 45 percent of the organizations that were absorbed reported high spirits among employees.[13]

Finally, will the objectives of the two organizations be worked out in a strategy that will take them both forward?

SUMMARY

This chapter has been about the strategic dimensions nonprofit organizations can use to improve their performance. In today's uncertain, turbulent, and extremely competitive world, lasting marketing success depends on the quality of strategic thinking used by nonprofit organizations. How do organizations take the strategy that is formulated at the top and translate it into operational reality? The difficulty of imposing strategy and making it work is the subject of Chapter 9.

CHAPTER NINE

Types of Strategies

The reality—I think that all of us who have ever been forced through it realize it full well—is that a strategy that is one paragraph long is harder to develop than a 50-page monograph. In 50 pages, you can be all things to all people. In a paragraph or two, you have to figure out just what makes you distinctive.[1]

Thomas J. Peters, INC.

The young lieutenant of a small Hungarian detachment in the Alps sent a reconnaissance unit into the icy wilderness. It began to snow immediately. The snow continued to fall for two days and the unit did not return. The lieutenant suffered, fearing that he had dispatched his own people to death. But on the third day, the unit returned. Where had they been? How had they made their way? Yes, they said, we considered ourselves lost and waited for the end. And then one of us found a map in his pocket. That calmed us down. We pitched camp, lasted out the snow-storm, and then with the map we discovered our bearings. And here we are. The lieutenant borrowed this remarkable map and had a good look at it. He discovered to his astonishment that it was a map not of the Alps but of the Pyrenees.[2]

In a turbulent and unpredictable environment will any map do when one is lost? Extending the analogy to the issue of strategy, will any strategy do when an organization is unsure of which way to go? How does that same organization use strategy and how does it know which strategy to employ? Should the organization adapt to a given strategy, or should the strategy fit the characteristics of the organization? And, given the realities of various competitive situations, are there some organizations for which no strategy will work? This chapter will provide some answers to these questions.

For many nonprofit organizations, using a strategy—even the wrong strategy—can indeed help to focus on its purpose for existence through an intensive review of its plans, positions, and perspectives. This internal analysis is often aided by managers using conceptual frameworks that help organizations identify areas of strength and weakness, and help determine the feasibility and cost of strategy implementation. Depicting such interaction of organizational components has resulted in many framework models by behavioral scientists and consultants trying to diagnose whether organizations can support their particular strategies.[3]

The use of any model is dependent upon a nonprofit organization's situation, with each model designed to key in on particular strategic circumstances.

One of the most important rules to keep in mind is that one cannot separate a nonprofit organization from the strategy it chooses. In short, an organization's strengths, weaknesses, and its particular corporate characteristics—what some would call the "human dimension"—necessitate an ongoing, never-ending internal analysis between its competencies and its strategy desirabilities in order to ensure a fit between the two.

Before looking at some of the strategies available to nonprofit managers and leaders, it is important to first consider how strategies are *interpreted* by managers before they are implemented by their organizations, and then look at how strategies are developed by those who will implement them.

THE NATURE OF STRATEGY AND ITS USES

Given the uncertain economic environment many nonprofit organizations face today, it is important for a nonprofit marketer and/or manager to be able to align the purposes and goals of his or her organization with the changes the environment may be imposing upon it. This often necessitates positioning one's institution in light of an uncertain future and to identify and make the necessary changes within an organization called for by this uncertainty. A nonprofit organization's strategy can help these types of changes to take place if necessary prerequisites are in place:

- The strategy in place must be drawn up to reflect the institution's major goals and policies.

- The strategy must coordinate and control actions in order to achieve a few key targets or goals.

- The strategy must take into account what is both known and unknown (no analyst can so adequately program a strategy as to take into account what will happen once humans get into the act).
- The strategy in question should be supported by other organizational strategies, depending upon a company's complexity.

Given this orientation to developing strategies, any organizational direction can be changed so that the values and ideals of the nonprofit organization in question can be realized. Furthering this notion, Paul Nutt and Robert Backoff in their book, *Strategic Management of Public and Third Sector Organizations,* list three ways in which a strategy can be used in light of its environment:

1. *Strategy as focus*—Because people within organizations have individual goals that can both be competitive and at odds with the organization, strategy can serve to break up personal "fiefdoms," to root and grow by focusing effort which, in turn, helps coordinate activity toward an agreed-upon direction.
2. *Strategy as consistency*—Strategy can reduce uncertainty by offering direction for what is wanted, thereby satisfying the staff's needs for order and predictability in their affairs.
3. *Strategy as purpose*—Strategy also provides meaning to those both inside and outside of the organization by giving them a way to understand what the organization is about and a way to differentiate it from other organizations engaged in seemingly similar activities.[4]

The multiple uses of strategy within an organization have resulted in many books and articles, with the list of its uses seeming endless.[5] At the very basic level, strategy seems to have at least six primary uses within a nonprofit organization:

1. Strategy is, or becomes, a plan by taking the organization in some intentional direction.

2. Strategy also can be used to send signals to competitors. In his popular book, *Competitive Strategy: Techniques for Analyzing Industries and Competitors,* Michael Porter suggests that organizations can give signals which sometimes serve to dissuade another organization from entering the marketplace.[6] For example, if someone runs a food pantry in a town and feels the field is too crowded for others to enter, he or she might institute strong promotional efforts on television, over the radio, and in print ads to give the impression to those considering entering the field that the food pantry already has much of the field sewn up, discouraging new entry attempts.

3. Strategy can be thought of as a pattern, with its stream of actions emerging and connecting those actions with those that were both intended and those actions that were not originally intended. The environment the organization is interacting with changes, forcing new thoughts and discarding the old as the environment provides continuous new information. This type of thinking can be best summed up by the quote from a business executive who said, "Gradually, the successful approaches merge into a pattern of action that becomes strategy."[7]

4. Apart from strategy being used as a plan, perhaps the most popular use of strategy is to create a market niche. Using an organization's strengths in light of its environment, niche strategies try to direct organizational resources into areas where there is little competition, thereby protecting themselves from competitors and maximizing receptivity to its products.

5. While not often discussed in the nonprofit context, strategy can also be thought of as the personality of the organization, what Mintzberg calls "perspective ... an ingrained way of perceiving the world."[8] Strategy defines how an organization will deal with problems and opportunities. In this light, strategy also may be thought of as the protector of the core values of the organization.

6. Finally, strategy is used as promotion. By setting out a direction for the organization, strategy begins the process of shaping action toward the organization's long-term goals through its promotional efforts.

FRAMEWORKS FOR STRATEGY

By viewing strategy through one—or more than one—of the previously mentioned uses, an organization is ready to begin merging its past, present, and future into a coherent strategy. This process begins by taking an historical look at the roots of the company and combining it with the present orientation that promotes and inspires action. This enables the nonprofit organization to target its long-range goals. It is then ready to choose its strategy.

The choice of a strategy is often aided by first using a theoretical framework, both showing structural strengths in an organization, and matching them with the surrounding environment. In undergoing this exercise, an organization begins to shape its structure and systems in anticipation of its strategy. The two are not mutually exclusive, nor do they work independently of each other; rather strategy and organizational structure must exist interdependently.

As discussed in the following sections, the New York-based management consulting firm, McKinsey & Company, in the early 1980s developed *The McKinsey 7-S Framework* designed to show how seven organizational characteristics interact. After we discuss the McKinsey "Framework" and its organizational emphasis we'll turn our attention to the Miles and Snow typology—another framework—which looks at the interaction of an organization and its environment. (We will discuss six other strategy models later on in the chapter.)

THE McKINSEY 7-S FRAMEWORK

The 7-S Framework, though one of the older frameworks used for organizational analysis, is relevant to a nonprofit strategy discussion for a number of reasons. One critical reason is the Framework's assertion that structure and strategy cannot be discussed sensibly without a consideration of the people and skill level of the organization being considered. Nonprofit organizations which enact strategies without first looking at their internal feasibility—and this happens with some regularity in many businesses—will inevitably run into some problems.

Though developed in the early 1980s, the 7-S Framework gained major recognition through two influential books on strategy, structure, and organizations: *In Search of Excellence* and *The Art of Japanese Management*.[9] Tom Peters and Robert Waterman in *In Search of Excellence* identified seven independent variables which interact with each other in an organization:

- Strategy
- Structure
- Systems
- Skills
- Staff
- Style
- Shared values

The first three elements—strategy, structure, and systems—comprise the "hardware" of an organization, while the skills, staff, style, and shared values form the "software," to use a computer-based analogy. When joined together, these seven variables create a managerial system that a manager must balance, with each variable being conditioned by the other six. (See Exhibit 9-1.)

Of particular significance—and a second reason why the 7-S Framework is important to nonprofits and other organizations—is the notion

Hardware | Software

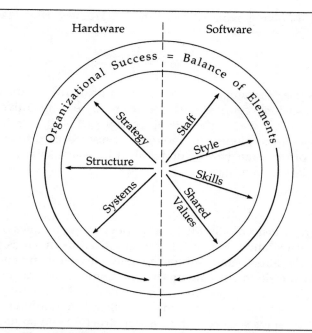

Exhibit 9-1 The seven variables in a managerial system

by Peters and Waterman that the four "soft" elements of the framework must not be assumed. The "soft" skills should be viewed as an indispensable part of a corporate commitment to its long-range plan and strategy, and such attributes must be cultivated, reviewed, and encouraged.

In retrospect, what our framework has really done is to remind the world of professional managers that "soft is hard." It has enabled us to say, in effect, "All that stuff you have been dismissing for so long as the intractable, irrational, intuitive, informal organization can be managed. Clearly, it has as much or more to do with the way things work (or don't) around your companies as the formal structures and strategies do. Not only are you foolish to ignore it, but here's a way to think about it. Here are some tools for managing it. Here, really, is the way to develop a new skill."[10]

Building on Peters' and Waterman's idea, Richard Tanner and Anthony G. Athos, in their book, *The Art of Japanese Management*, used the Japanese corporate giant Matsushita as a way to compare the differences in style between American and Japanese management. Of particular concern to the authors, and one of their major theses in the book, was the meticulous attention paid by Japanese managers to the "soft" S's.

Much of the following explanation of the 7-S Framework is taken from their book.

Strategy

Matsushita's use of strategy—which involved primarily product-market investment decisions, coupled with the desire to be competitively superior to anyone else—was in the role of technological follower. Matsushita did not attempt to pioneer technology but instead tried to emphasize quality and price. Strategy was undertaken by Matsushita in anticipation of its external environment.

Structure

In deciding how tasks are divided and in developing its lines of authority and task orientation, Matsushita decentralized as much as possible, and alternately added and subtracted company-wide functions, like research and development and production engineering, depending on competitive changes in the environment. Within Matsushita, strategy and structure continually reinforced each other. The question asked by Matsushita managers seemed to be, "Is our structure and strategy building on each other's strengths? If not, let's change them so they are."

Systems

Matsushita viewed its systems as powerful procedures and tools in the hands of managers, enabling them to control budgeting, training, accounting and scheduling. These indicators were constantly compared to the organizational plan, and variances with the plan were looked at and addressed.

Systems allow a nonprofit manager to see how well his or her organization is functioning; likewise, they can allow a manager to change an organization from the inside out. Organizations are often reflections of the good or bad quality of their systems. For many nonprofit organizations, the notion of systems is still a new phenomenon.

Skills

The skill level or capabilities allow an organization to perform both efficiently and effectively; in fact, it is the skill level of an organization in particular competencies that usually allows it to have a competitive advantage. Skills are the crucial attributes of an organization. In conversations with nonprofit executives, the realization inevitably arises that the skill level of nonprofit employees needs constant attention.

Style

"Style" refers to both the way an organization and its managers go about making decisions, and the shared values, symbolic actions, and dominant beliefs of the organization that influence its decisions. For example, the "ideal" Japanese leader is often pictured as an elder sitting stolidly above the fray, whereas the American ideal is often younger, kinetic, and a go-getter involved in the fray.

Staff

Referring obviously to people, Matsushita has a centralized training program that attempts and proposes to instill in each employee a core set of values, alongside the specialized skills the company wants. As a consequence, the experience, skills, abilities, attitudes, and expectations of each person are looked at by Matsushita as a benefit to the corporation and lead to individuals being slotted into jobs that maximize their skill mix. In nonprofit organizations, staff are more often talked about by managers in the "hard" way; that is, their pay scales, their training programs, and how they will be appraised. Seldom do managers talk about the "soft" end of the spectrum: employee morale, behavior on the job, motivational systems, and attitude.

Shared Values

For Matsushita, values became both a spiritual and uniting force as they became a belief system whereby thousands of people dedicated their productive lives to the needs of both the company at hand, as well as to society. It was thought, therefore, that one's organizational experience helped to indelibly shape one's character experience. These superordinate goals are concepts that went beyond the formal objectives of the Matsushita corporation.

Examples of these goals for a nonprofit organization could include superior client and donor service while meeting as many of their needs as possible.[11]

Much of the Framework may sound somewhat unusable to nonprofit managers until they realize that by deconstructing an organization, this framework helps a nonprofit manager accomplish four critical tasks:

- First, as an expository device it helps a manager understand his or her organization through a different set of lenses;
- Second, the manager can take a comparative look at the seven dimensions and begin to understand the strengths and weaknesses of the organization;

- Third, this understanding begins to help a manager shape his or her strategy in such a way as to key in on those areas that function as strengths and stay away from those areas that could pose vulnerabilities; and

- Fourth, this framework helps any nonprofit manager focus on the fit and interaction of the strategy he or she chooses and the organization that will implement it.

Nonprofit managers should identify and document the strengths and weaknesses of their organization from most prevalent to least prevalent. The managers should discuss their lists with other co-workers and determine how to both amplify the organization's strengths and minimize its weaknesses.

In order to properly use the Framework, a manager should bear two critical issues in mind: first, the Framework tends to speak organizationally with regard to its attributes and does not really address the personal attributes of those who will implement strategy; and second, the Framework does not place much emphasis on timeliness of action in strategy implementation. A lack of managerial focus on taking action after using the Framework could easily erase its benefits by ignoring opportunities which might be presented, or by delaying the remedying of difficult problems.

The following questions are designed to help a manager work through the 7-S Framework. The goal of asking and answering these questions is to gather the necessary data with which a manager can assess the "fit" between the various organizational components:

- Do the systems fit the structure?
- Do the people fit the culture?
- Do the people fit the structure?
- Does the structure fit the culture?
- Do the people fit the tasks?
- Do the systems fit the strategy?
- Is the organization competent in the tasks required by the strategy?[12] (See Exhibit 9-2.)

THE MILES AND SNOW TYPOLOGY

While the McKinsey 7-S Framework is useful as an internal measure of an organization and the congruence between its parts, the *Miles and*

Assessment of a nonprofit organization requires
discerning how each variable interacts

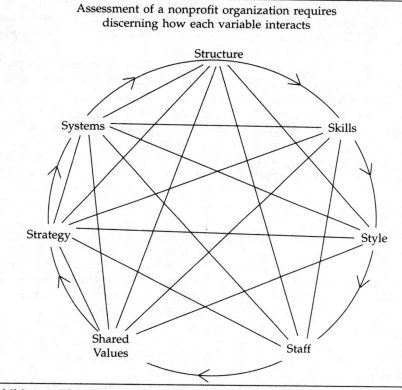

Exhibit 9-2 The interplay of the seven variables in assessing an organization

Snow Typology classifies strategy in terms of shifts in the environment surrounding the organization and, therefore, focuses more externally.[13]

Raymond Miles and Charles Snow looked at 84 for-profit firms and their approaches to environmental shifts. As one might expect (and where there is significant application to the nonprofit world), the more successful companies were able to shift products and services that aligned with significant developments in their environments. As strategies were adjusted to new environmental realities, four strategic organizational patterns emerged which have significance for the nonprofit world.

Defender

Defenders try to protect their "domain" in order to maintain their current level of service. This may be done by either trying to be cost-effective in their operations or by producing products and services that have very high quality. In seeking to protect their "turf" from competitors, they rely on selling franchises, setting up local chapters, developing trade associations, and lobbying.

A for-profit example of this type of defense can be seen in tobacco companies trying to defend smoking products in the marketplace through the Tobacco Institute, an organization founded and funded by companies who wish to sell tobacco and tobacco-related products.[14] A nonprofit industry example is that of many religious denominations who have tried to set up a local parish or meeting hall in as many communities as possible across America as a means to "defend" their faith and develop local advocates or affiliates.

Prospector

Prospectors find new markets and market segments, often while engaging in product innovation. These types of companies spend significant portions of their budget on market research or environmental scanning in order to anticipate contextual shifts. Their entrepreneurial task becomes the search for new products that will fit into particular market segments. To be successful in such an enterprise requires organizations that can move quickly in light of new opportunities, which in turn necessitates organizations with low levels of formalization and flexibility in systems, policies, and management, coupled with a willingness to take organizational risks.

The prospector model continues to be very popular in the nonprofit culture, particularly as nonprofit entrepreneurs move their organizations to popular donor causes, using either intuition or market research to support their movements.

Analyzer

An organization that is both a prospector and a defender is an analyzer; it is looking to both lower risk and take advantage of new opportunities. The strategy that analyzers implement is similar to the Matsushita example previously mentioned. These companies enter into markets after both the products and markets are established. Using an imitation strategy, products are adopted by the company that have a proven track record in the marketplace.

Significantly, the analyzer company often has two organizational cultures comprised of both prospector and defender loyalists, with one group looking to broaden its base of support and another looking to limit its operational focus. This can often lead to organizational friction.

Reactor

Reactors often do not change in the face of environmental upheaval and, if they do change, it can be inappropriate, ineffective, or unprofitable. This lack of change is usually attributable to two reasons:

1. There is either a leadership void or departure, resulting in a lack of clearly defined strategy;
2. The strategy that the organization is articulating is clearly at odds with parts of itself.

Consider the following case study.

FAILURE TO REACT CAUSES LOSS IN MEMBERSHIP

In undertaking a membership research project for a membership predicated nonprofit organization, one of the reasons attributed to declining membership among certain affiliates was the failure of leadership to react to environmental changes in areas surrounding those affiliates. These changes included such events as plant closings, demographic shifts in neighborhoods, and a failure to meet competitive challenges from like-minded nonprofit organizations.

PREPARING FOR THE APPLICATION OF THE CHOSEN STRATEGY

The McKinsey 7-S Framework and the Miles and Snow Typology provide the means to classify—both internally and externally—organizational progress and identify areas of strength and weakness. The organization can then tailor its internal strengths to the external volatilities caused by market environmental conditions. From here, an organization can decide where it needs to innovate, how it must compete with other nonprofit organizations with similar product lines and services, how flexible it needs to be in its orientation, and the modifications in the strategy that need to be made as new market conditions arise.

OTHER STRATEGY TYPES

Having now looked at frameworks for developing strategies, what distinctive strategy types are available to a nonprofit organization? While there are literally hundreds of different strategies available to profit and nonprofit managers, six schools of thought have developed in the private sector. The first of these is conceptual in nature. The Harvard Policy Model looks at the values and obligations of management coupled with the capabilities of the organization in order to find the best strategy fit with the environment that surrounds the company.

The Harvard Policy Model

The Harvard Policy Model came out of the Harvard business school curriculum and, as such, is as much a story of the school's own curriculum development as it is a story of business strategy. The chief function of the model is to help an organization develop a fit between its own capabilities and resources and the environment in which it finds itself. As articulated by Kenneth Andrews, Professor Emeritus of Business Administration at Harvard University, The Harvard Policy Model defined strategy as:

> The pattern of purposes and policies that defines a company and the businesses in which the company is engaged and divides strategy into two problems:
>
> 1. formulation decisions about what to do; and
> 2. implementation decisions about how to execute formulation decisions.[15]

"Strategy" in this definition encompasses both the ends of the corporate activity and the necessary means to achieve those ends. (See Exhibit 9-3.)

In formulating its strategy, a nonprofit organization identifies an intended future that matches both its strengths and market opportunities. Perhaps more importantly, this intended future also needs to match senior management intentions and aspirations. Strategy is formulated through four steps:

1. Analysis of external environment for opportunities and threats.
2. Analysis of internal strengths and weaknesses of the nonprofit organization in question.
3. Analysis of the personal values of the senior management of the nonprofit organization.
4. Analysis of the responsibility of the nonprofit organization to the general public.

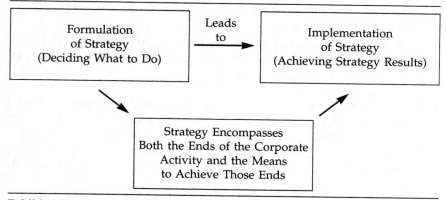

Exhibit 9-3   The Harvard Policy Model

Fundamentally, the Model helps to identify the strengths and weaknesses of an institution, coupled with its value system, and then identifies the threats and opportunities of the environment surrounding the institution as well as the social obligations of the nonprofit organization. As such, the systematic assessment of the strengths, weaknesses, opportunities, and threats (known as the *SWOT analysis*) is the primary strength of the Harvard Model and is applicable to both profit and nonprofit organizations.

External Environment.   The Harvard Model directs managers to first focus on the environmental trends (an activity that benefits nonprofit institutions). Looking at economic, political, social, and technological trends forces a nonprofit manager to undertake the following observations:

1. *Economic trends*—trends in competition, cost, or donation structure in the industry, the seasonality of the clients and donations, and the relationship of the nonprofit organization to the local or national economy.

2. *Political trends*—public attitudes toward the cause addressed by the nonprofit organization; regulations that will affect how the nonprofit undertakes its daily business now and in the future; and the attitude of elected officials toward the organizational mission.

3. *Social trends*—the changing buying, loyalty, and donation patterns of certain age categories in relationship to the nonprofit organization, as well as changing patterns in the family, income, political

identification, and raising of children within the nonprofit organization's environment.

4. *Technological trends*—changes in gathering and retrieving data, the ways new markets are being created through the electronic media, all types of computer technology.

Internal Strengths. An organization looks at its internal strengths (and weaknesses) in order to determine which goals and objectives it is capable of pursuing, versus those that are simply beyond its grasp. Issues such as the pool of talent a nonprofit organization might have, its cash reserves, its material strengths, and the like, all help a nonprofit organization get a fix on its future.

Values. The Harvard Policy Model forces managers to ask: "What are our values and how do they affect the choices for our future strategy?" There is little doubt that the values of those in management play an important part in an organization's goal attainment.

In many nonprofit organizations, there is an implicit assumption or expectation made by management that all employees have the same values, yet rarely do nonprofit organizations undertake a formal values assessment of its top managers, much less all of its employees like the aforementioned Matsushita example.

The General Public. One rising school of thought suggests that clients, constituents, donors, and all relevant stakeholders should be listed on the organizational chart first, with everyone else listed underneath the chart working for this important group. (See Exhibit 9-4.) Clients, constituents, donors, stockholders, employees, suppliers, the community at large—these groups are often not included or thought about as nonprofit managers put their strategies forward.

Implementation. It is very clear in the Harvard Model that strategy without a method for implementation is a "disaster waiting to happen." With its desire to be of use in the everyday world, in the Harvard Policy's view, strategy that cannot be implemented is simply bad strategy.[16]

The Harvard Policy Model has real value to the nonprofit world. First is the aforementioned SWOT analysis and its strong internal and external focus. The Model provides a systematic way for managers to ask questions about themselves, their company, and their environment. In this way, a reasoned approach is prescribed as opposed to a more common entrepreneurial approach. The impact upon particular audiences also is of concern in the model, as opposed to the more unilateral approach taken by the entrepreneur.

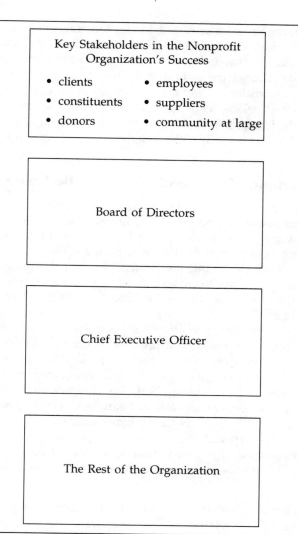

Exhibit 9-4 Nonprofit organizational chart

In addition, by acknowledging that the values of managers play a key role in goal accomplishment, the Model helps to focus on an issue that is usually taken for granted in the nonprofit world; that is, the agreement of key personnel on the direction of the company in question. However, there is also a weakness in the Model because only a handful of senior executives in the Model are assessed, as if the opinions of middle and lower management do not matter.

An additional weakness of the Model for nonprofit managers is that after examination of both itself and its environment, the Model does not provide advice on how to build a strategy from the assessment; except to note that the strategy the institution builds should take into account the strengths of the institution and take advantage of the opportunities that are present. Though taking a strong look at the trends a nonprofit organization might be facing, the Model does not take the next step in prescribing the types of action it should take in light of those very same trends.

The Experience Curve and The Portfolio Framework

The next group of strategies are analytical in nature. Typically, analytical approaches are used to determine how certain product lines are performing; as such, a portfolio approach is usually used. The most widely used such approach is the Portfolio Framework.

The *Experience Curve* and the *Portfolio Framework* strategy are analytical in nature and were developed by Bruce D. Henderson, a man who is less well-known than the organization he started, The Boston Consulting Group.

The Experience Curve strategy suggests that as an institution develops competencies in building a product or running a service costs will go down. The Portfolio Framework is a classification system which determines the value of all services by measuring their market share and potential growth by focusing both on the financial and numerical growth of those services as well as taking an overall view of all of an agency's services. As such, both the Experience Curve and the Portfolio Framework have special significance to those nonprofit organizations that are diversified, as well as those who have been in business for a long time. Our discussion starts with the Experience Curve.

The Experience Curve.   As a nonprofit organization grows, two particular events occur relating to its marketing strategy:

1. The organization's experience in its services or product development allows the nonprofit organization to reduce costs (to not do so usually puts an institution at competitive risk).
2. As the nonprofit organization grows bigger, both financially and through its market share of clients, it accumulates experience in its operations faster (this becomes a subset of reducing your costs).

Both facets, taken together, can lead to significant cost advantages over competitors providing the same service since the Experience Curve grows out of this concern for cost analysis. So the Experience Curve strategy helps explain the pattern of declining costs.

The Experience Curve strategy grew out of the aircraft industry in the 1930s. It was observed that as workers became more proficient in their jobs by performing the same tasks many times, labor costs decreased as efficiency in the job increased. While this was labeled the "learning curve" in the 1930s, it wasn't until the Boston Consulting Group in the 1960s initiated many cost studies that it was discovered that total costs would decline as experience increased. In the quarter of a century since that time, the idea of quality has become an important strategic phenomenon.

The Experience Curve is actually a very specific and predictable function. It says that each time the cumulative production doubles, the value-added cost in real dollars will decline by a fixed percent which will vary from situation to situation. Thus, with an 80 percent Experience Curve, each time the total accumulated production doubles, the cost will be reduced by 20 to 80 percent of its previous level.[17]

Henderson argues that all costs follow a well-known pattern: the unit costs for producing an item drops by one-third every time volume (sometimes called *turnover*) for the item doubles. The Curve's effects are assisted by four overriding factors within an organization: learning, improvements in production, a redesign of products, and scale.

While the *learning* part of the Curve applies to production people and their repetitive tasks, there is no reason to assume it could not apply to other whole groups of workers in the Third Sector. Workers learn to do tasks more quickly and with greater efficiency as the task becomes routinized. Improvements in production and services—especially technological improvements—can also lead to dramatic cost decreases. Even something as simple as a desktop computer, coupled with the "learning" of certain functions, increases one's productivity substantially.

THE EXPERIENCE CURVE IN ACTION

During a development director's tenure with a large nonprofit organization, he saw donor receipting and donor data services move from IBM keypunch cards to a computer tape, which was used by a service bureau, to the nonprofit organization's own hardware and software, with later innovations like optical scanners for donation mail. Each innovation contributed to the organization's, and his, Experience Curve.

Product or service redesign also can lead to dramatic cost reductions by introducing new materials that cost less, or undertaking the same function using a lesser number of steps, people, or pieces of equipment. (A client went from using a stand-alone receipt, thank-you letter, and response envelope as part of its receipting package to combining the receipt and letter into one unit, cutting its costs through redesign.)

Finally, scale—which reflects the natural savings often associated with size—also contributes to the Experience Curve. For example, many nonprofit organizations can benefit through direct mail by receiving a cheaper per piece rate as their file expands. This is called *scale*.

All of these potential improvements in cost savings can positively affect a nonprofit marketer's strategy and implementation. A nonprofit organization can often realize substantial cost advantages by having accumulated more experience in its market than its competitors either in its service, fund-raising, or promotional strategy.

Likewise, an organization's experience can be used to forecast costs in the market or media. Having had experience in certain events (like running a banquet or auction) gives a nonprofit organization advantages over others who have never run the same event. And, knowing its costs then allows the nonprofit organization to set the donation request size they need from their partners, donors, or the philanthropic community, as well as the prices needed for product sales.

The goal of an Experience Curve-based strategy is to drive down costs. However, the Curve does not simply happen by itself. An organizational commitment to making it happen through improved quality, reducing costs, and redesigning effort must take place, as must improvements to increase market share. (Sometimes in their intensity to reduce costs, nonprofit organizations have little left financially for product or service innovation or to deal with shifting opportunities in their environments.)

Gaining market share—another generic strategy proposed by Henderson as a means to building audience and thus facilitating the Experience Curve—also has merit in the nonprofit world, as does his Portfolio Framework. As is demonstrated in the Portfolio Framework in the next section, when a nonprofit organization diversifies its products and services, not all parts of the diversification grow as rapidly as each other, nor can they be strategically managed in the same way.

The Portfolio Framework. Nonprofit organizations with different divisions, causes, or services still have similar problems across divisions: each division is managed differently; each division needs differing amounts of cash; each division differs in its ability to generate clients. In particular, many nonprofit divisions are encouraged to fund their own growth. How does a nonprofit senior manager decide which service, division, or cause gets starved for resources (people, equipment, and money) and which division gets the amount it needs? Does he or she make such a decision based on potential, on loss, on the need for cash, or on the division's ability to fund other divisions through its ability to stimulate cash?

Portfolio strategies force decisions regarding cash, service, opportunity, and growth strategies for these different causes, services, and divisions through an overt analysis as opposed to default decision making. In addition, this methodology appraises the financial potential of each division and leads to marketing and management recommendations regarding the future of each division.

There are as many portfolio models to look at as there are reasons why nonprofit and for-profit organizations diversify. The focus here will be on the Boston Consulting Group's Portfolio Framework and Growth Share Matrix. More often than not, most for-profit and nonprofit managers allow diversification to take place either for opportunity reasons or to spread financial risk over different parts of the organization.

A RETREAT CENTER COULD BENEFIT
FROM THE PORTFOLIO FRAMEWORK APPROACH

A large retreat center both runs corporate-sponsored programs and allows groups using their own programs to rent its facility; both strategies bring in revenue but appeal to different parts of the market and have different managers for each part of the business. A Portfolio Framework approach to this organization's strategy would take a look at both of these endeavors and decide what the nonprofit organization does best and where the opportunities are the greatest.

In the retreat center example, the nonprofit manager looks at his diversified nonprofit with its various causes, services, and products and thinks of it as a portfolio of businesses, with each business having varying degrees of client potential and cash flow. The manager may choose to keep both programmatical emphases within his retreat center; he or she will have a different strategy, cost, audience, and expectations—service, financial, and otherwise—for each.

As stated previously, Henderson postulated a relationship known as the Experience Curve. And from this postulate grew the Boston Consulting Group Matrix, outlined in his 1979 book, *Henderson On Corporate*

Strategy.[18] Henderson said that any business could be categorized into one of four types:

1. *High growth/high market share businesses*—which he called *stars*—generate substantial cash but also require large investments in order to either maintain their share of market or to increase it.

For a nonprofit organization, these are causes or divisions that are in a growth mode or in a strong competitive position. Normally, they have a strong Experience Curve and are able to generate sizable sums of money. These "star" divisions are generally self-supporting and are usually capable of commanding resource infusions from management.

2. *Cash cows* are low growth/high share businesses which not only generate large cash flows but require low investments and, therefore, generate profits that can be used elsewhere in the business.

In a nonprofit organization, a "cash cow" normally represents a mature cause or service and client and donor market, with the "cash cow" division requiring little in the way of cash infusion from the corporate office.

3. *Low growth/low market share businesses*—called *dogs* by Henderson—produce few clients and little cash and offer little prospect that their market share will be increased. Because they are presumed to be weak in their Experience Curve, divisions that are classified as "dogs" are often seen as "bottomless pits" for cash and usually represent both a management and financial drain to the nonprofit.

4. *High growth/low market share businesses*—called *question marks* by Henderson—normally require substantial investment in order to become a "star" or "cash cow" and, therefore, their future is often undecided. If they continue to need heavy cash infusions they will become "dogs"; if they show promise and their market position can be changed, then these "question marks" can become "stars."

Many nonprofit companies today consist of multiple causes or services that are only marginally related primarily because of entrepreneurism on the part of the founder or institution. One nonprofit organization, for instance, is a multimillion dollar company with over 40 different divisions, with some divisions only slightly related to the purpose of the organization.

On a daily basis, some nonprofit managers make decisions about resource allocation to different causes or services. This is where strategic portfolio models can help. The strength of the portfolio method is that it provides a means of measurement against dimensions of strategic import.

Using the Strategic Business Unit. Central to the idea of portfolio management—and an idea the nonprofit world could embrace more fully—is the concept of a *strategic business unit* (SBU). An SBU is one way to identify those nonprofit operations where a distinct set of products or services is offered by the organization to an identifiable group of clients, constituents, or donors.

SBUs CAN HELP DEFINE GOALS

A nonprofit organization has many divisions, but is very concerned about two of them. One of the divisions is dealing with a problem that all of society has yet to fix because of lifestyle issues, a target market that is horizontal in nature with many different age and ethnic groups, different sexual persuasions, and a population mix that is all over the map. Because of the unwieldiness of the problem, the division's goals are unclear.

The other division deals with a problem that has a history of being able to be treated, a population that is relatively the same age, clearly defined target groups, and thus clearly defined goals.

In the previous case study, the division of the nonprofit organization that deals with providing the treatment for a problem that has a history of being treatable, and deals with clearly defined target groups, could be considered an SBU within the nonprofit organization. The function of the SBU is to completely service the defined target group, including the tailoring of its products (in this case, treatment options), the tailoring of its strategy, and the fulfillment of customer service.

The concept of the SBU grew out of the diversification of organizations and the needs of its managers. The more a company diversifies, the more a for-profit or nonprofit manager needs to be able to adapt his or her strategy to the market they serve. This necessitates the management of various strategies on a market-by-market basis.

As a consequence of diversification, competition increases. Given the idea of the SBU within the Portfolio Framework, the manager's job is to find those products where a company can realize distinct advantages *in areas where their competitor may be vulnerable.* Another consequence of diversification in larger nonprofit organizations is organizational in nature. In order to maximize profits or donations, a for-profit or nonprofit organization must decentralize to make SBU managers more accountable to their markets and strategies. This focus on SBUs and the ability to also monitor their performance then has implications on the allocation of resources. Decentralization and adequate control are two important values and strengths of the Portfolio Framework.

The strength of the portfolio approach is that it provides a method of measuring nonprofit business options against dimensions of strategic importance. For example, let us say we are nonprofit organization executives trying to determine into which of many divisions to invest our time, energies, and resources:

- First, we take a look at each product, or SBU, and the plans for each.
- Second, we look at the business strengths of the SBU. Strengths may include our size, growth rate, the amount of revenue that is generated by the SBU, our image in the community, the quality of our leadership; each, or any combination thereof, may be a strength. In each category we try to attach some measure, such as strong, average, or weak. If we are looking at the growth of our SBU, we must ask whether our growth in comparison to others is strong, average, or weak. By virtue of looking at the strengths of each SBU, we also look implicitly at our weaknesses.
- Third, we do the same for the market attractiveness of our product. What is size of the market for this product? Is the market diversifying rapidly? Are there legal problems in the market regarding our product? Is the audience for our product relatively stable? Is there strong competition in the market for this type of product? Our goal is to rate our answer to each question against some type of measure.
- Fourth, what are the strategy recommendations that come out of this type of analysis? For example, those nonprofit divisions and products that consistently rank strong or above average should embark on an aggressive attempt at growth. Those in the middle must seek ways to make themselves more profitable. For those products and divisions that rank poorly, the organization should consider a minimal investment of resources.

The Portfolio Framework is a relatively easy way to make some claims and recommendations for those nonprofit organizations with diverse operations. Its weaknesses include the difficulty of knowing where the appropriate strategic dimensions should lie.

The Competitive Strategy Framework

The next strategy is specifically geared toward looking at industries and the forces that shape that industry. Professor Michael Porter of Harvard Business School developed a competitive analysis using industry norms that can be described as a *managerial model*.[19] In such a model there is a strong linkage between strategy and the financial returns of the company in question. According to the model, managers only have to listen to the signals emanating from the industry that they are a part of.

Michael Porter is viewed by many as the leading strategy theoretician in North America today. His first major work, *Competitive Strategy: Techniques For Analyzing Industries and Competitors*, developed an industry competitive model suggesting that the underlying forces that shape an industry can be used to predict the success of a strategy. In other words, Porter suggests that certain forces at work in an industry may help predict whether an organization will be successful within that industry. The forces Porter cites are:

1. The relative power of buyers
2. The relative power of suppliers
3. The threat of substitute products
4. Industry competitors
5. Potential entrants (See Exhibit 9-5)

How do these factors affect a nonprofit organization? An example may help. Assume we want to open a youth camp in Colorado. One industry force would be the presence of competitors and substitutes for what we hoped to do. Given that Colorado has more camps per capita than any other state in the nation, this fact may prove to be a problem in getting to our goal. Likewise, with so many camps and with large unpopulated regions in Colorado, will we have a large enough pool of clients or customers for our camp?

A manager's job (in both the for-profit and nonprofit organization) in all of this is to pay close attention to the five forces that govern industry; the strategy's job is to allow the organization to find a position where it can defend itself against these forces or influence them in an institution's favor. Let's consider each force.

Relative Power of Buyers. By "buyers" Porter means "clients and constituents." His sense is that they are not all alike. An example from the nonprofit world illustrates this: The marketing director for a nonprofit publishing house knows that selling books to individuals is a very different proposition than selling them to bookstore chains. Individual buyers come into a store and buy the book they choose. They do not negotiate price. They pay the stated price. If the cost of the desired book is too much, they have little recourse. They may be able to find it cheap-

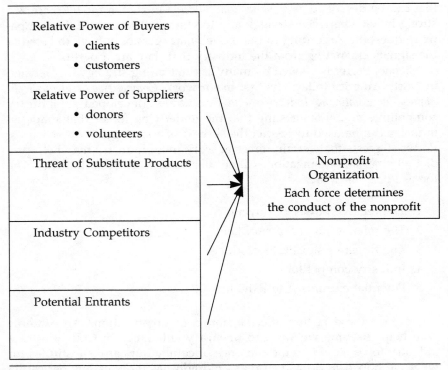

Exhibit 9-5   Competitive strategy framework: Five industry forces

er elsewhere, or they may choose to save their dollars until they have the required amount.

The bookstore chain, on the other hand, is in a better position to negotiate price because of the volume of books it will purchase. If the chain encounters a price that is too high it has significant recourse; it can threaten to take *all* of its business elsewhere. In fact, when substitute products are available from several publishing houses, the bookstore chain negotiates among several publishers for the best price. It has stronger buying power than the individual consumer.

Buying power is usually most significant for standard or undifferentiated products (i.e., products where there are many substitutes to be found). Extending our publishing example, consider publishing houses that publish Bibles. There are literally hundreds of different Bible publishers available, with most products being substitutes for each other. In this example, buyers constitute a major force because of the sameness of the product and the ability of the buyer to shop around for the cheapest product. (See Exhibit 9-6.)

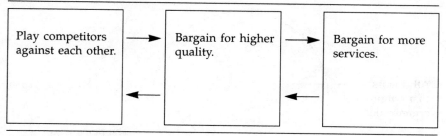

| Play competitors against each other. | → | Bargain for higher quality. | → | Bargain for more services. |

Exhibit 9-6 Relative power of buyers

Relative Power of Suppliers. "Suppliers" have a very general application in Porter's Competitive Strategy Framework. Suppliers provide the means for an organization to continue. They include almost anyone from financial institutions to material goods dealers. In the for-profit world, suppliers exert pressure upon an industry by raising prices or reducing the quality of goods. Thus, they literally can squeeze the profit out of some industries. A supplier group becomes powerful if:

- it is dominated by a few companies;
- its product is unique or if it has built up switching costs (switching costs are fixed costs buyers face in switching suppliers);
- it does not have to contend with other suppliers in selling to a particular industry;
- it poses a threat of integrating forward into the industry's business; or
- the industry is not an important customer of the supplier.[20]

On face value, Porter's supplier group may not sound like it has much to offer the nonprofit world. Consider, though, donors for one second. Many nonprofit organizations are dominated by just a few donors, upon whose gifts the organization relies heavily. What's more, even though many nonprofit organizations resent being dependent upon just a few individuals or foundations, they have very little choice but to continue. (See Exhibit 9-7.)

Nonprofit organizations in this situation tend not to try to find new donors to reduce their reliance upon the few. The psychological and pragmatic cost of undertaking such a task is too great. (In the for-profit world, these costs would be called *switching costs*. In the nonprofit industry, switching costs are just too high to be reasonable.)

In addition, because some donors waver today in their loyalty to nonprofit causes, especially with so many different groups doing essential-

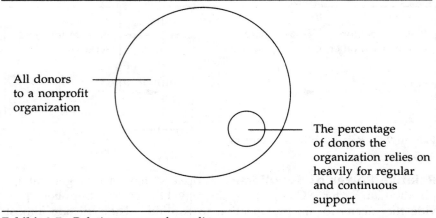

All donors
to a nonprofit
organization

The percentage
of donors the
organization relies on
heavily for regular
and continuous
support

Exhibit 9-7   Relative power of suppliers

ly the same task, the importance of some supplier groups puts many
nonprofit organizations' financial future at risk.

Threat of Substitute Products.   In many nonprofit situations, more
than one cause or service can perform the same function for the client.
The presence of substitute products limits not only the amount of service or profits an industry can enjoy, but also its potential. A case study
further explains Porter's notion.

SUBSTITUTE PRODUCTS AND SUMMER CAMPS

The children's camping industry has numerous competitors with
many of the camps being roughly the same size and having the
same disposition. Industry growth is slow and many of the camps
lack any differentiation. In order to build camp traffic they often
resort to cutting prices. Unfortunately, for many camps fixed costs
are also high and, because their debt load is often high too, they
are left with no choice. They can't leave or exit the business so the
camps keep competing even though they may be earning low or
even negative returns.

Industry Competitors.   Porter's Competitive Strategy Framework
requires that the nonprofit executive remember that strategy within his or
her organization is a matter of interdependence. The success of one's strat-

egy often depends as much on what the other guy does as what the non-profit organization does strategically. Porter puts the point succinctly:

> In most industries, competitive moves by one firm have noticeable effects on its competitors and thus may incite retaliation of efforts to counter the move; that is, firms are mutually interdependent.[21]

And as seen in Exhibit 9-8, rivalry within an industry is usually a function of a number of factors including competitors that are equally balanced, slow industry growth, a large number of substitute services or products within the industry for clients and buyers and little differentiation among them, and high strategic stakes.

Rivalry intensifies when one of the competitors feels the need to seize an opportunity or feels pressure from other areas of expense within their firm. Such rivalry often leads, then, to new marketing moves and retaliation by other members of the industry.

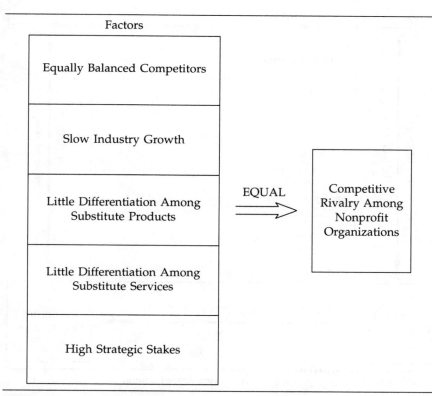

Exhibit 9-8 Industry competitors

For example, an initiative by a city mission to start working with women on the street enables the mission to get new funding dollars and good local press. The mission's strategic move prompts the other two mission competitors in town to retaliate strategically by starting their own special services for women. Likewise, a church in a community starts a day-care as part of its growth strategy, in order to be seen as providing needed services to the community, while allowing the church to introduce itself to new community populations it might not normally contact. Other churches in the area, facing the same marketing dilemma, open their own day-care centers. In each example, action by one organization creates a response in other organizations. (See Exhibit 9-9.)

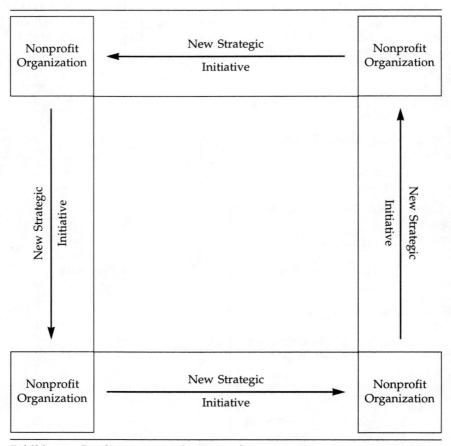

Exhibit 9-9   Retaliatory moves by nonprofit organizations

Potential Entrants. The key to understanding how potential entrants come into an industry is to understand what Porter calls *entry barriers*. These barriers serve to prevent new competitors from both entering and then succeeding in an industry. Porter identifies seven barriers that limit industry access by for-profit firms, some of which very much apply to nonprofit organizations:

1. The lack of strong economies of scale; some nonprofit organizations simply cannot afford to enter some causes, even if they feel strongly about them.

2. Product differentiation (by which Porter means that some existing products within the industry enjoy high degrees of customer loyalty). Though there are many organizations involved in building affordable housing, Habitat For Humanity enjoys a high degree of client, volunteer, and donor loyalty.

3. Capital requirements, especially when they are large and risky. By some estimates, it costs close to two million dollars to build a youth camp. Not many nonprofit organizations can afford this expense.

4. A lack of access to distribution channels. Small, independent publishers often have a problem getting their books to a buying public.

5. The switching costs absorbed by a firm in moving from one industry to another, especially for new equipment that is needed or new training of employees.

6. Cost disadvantages that may arise if competitors enjoy either proprietary product technologies or are receiving sizable subsidies from some entity. A nonprofit marriage counseling organization is able to offer its seminars very cheaply because a donor and client has endowed the organization's marriage seminar division.

7. Government policy—whether licensing or regulation—that limits certain types of organizational operations. Some aspects of Operation Rescue's work has been put at risk by government regulations.

Industry Forces and Their Strength

The identification of these five industry forces and their comparative strength is key in determining what an organization's strengths and weaknesses are in relationship to other nonprofit organizations within the industry. By knowing an institution's strengths and weaknesses, a marketing manager can then establish a strategy position with respect to each of the forces with possible approaches being:

1. Positioning the nonprofit organization so that its capabilities provide the best defense against the existing array of competitive forces. For example, a nonprofit organization in a highly competitive market puts its most experienced manager in a position of leadership in a division experiencing a strong competitive backlash from competitors.

2. Influencing the balance of forces through strategic moves, thereby improving the nonprofit organization's relative position. An example of this type of strategy is the local college that announces its capital campaign early before its crosstown rival, in hopes that the early announcement will help it capture local community foundation and corporate gifts.

3. Anticipating shifts in the factors underlying the forces and responding to them, thereby exploiting change by choosing a strategy appropriate to the new competitive balance before rivals recognize it.[22]

A recent example of this type of strategic move is the number of international disaster relief organizations now using television as a vehicle to get support from constituents, having seen the power of disaster and hunger news footage to move television viewers into action quite on their own.

It is not a nonprofit organization that solely defines a marketing strategy; instead, it must also decide how it wants to compete with respect to the industry forces. Consider how the industry forces of competitors, new industry entrants, and the bargaining power of donors are affecting the nonprofit organization in the following case study and its need to change its strategy.

ENVIRONMENTAL LOBBYING GROUP STRUGGLES TO KEEP UP WITH THE COMPETITION

An environmental lobbying group has for years resorted to a door-to-door canvas to solicit its funds. Today, the costs of canvasing eat up about two-thirds of the dollars raised. This is not the only problem the nonprofit organization faces. New lobbying groups are also entering the field, using sophisticated direct mail and television appeals. And, they are wooing away the organization's donors by offering them a type of membership package they are more comfortable with.

Porter's Three Competitive Strategies

The structural analysis of an industry and its forces is Porter's first major thesis; his second is the notion that there are three generic competitive strategies that can be applied as a way of coping or in response to the industry forces. These three strategies are mutually exclusive and an institution cannot pursue, according to Porter, more than one at the same time for the same product or service and still succeed. Nevertheless, Porter's three strategies—overall cost leadership, differentiation, and focus—are useful for nonprofit organizations.

Overall Cost Leadership. A nonprofit organization gains leadership in this area by deciding to "manage away" its expenses as much as possible. As a result of such a move, the nonprofit organization can:

1. often remain profitable when rival organizations are not only trimming expenses but margins;
2. remain more competitively flexible as a nonprofit entity even though costs of providing services may increase;
3. deter other nonprofit organizations from entering an industry— called *entry barriers*—by not allowing them to achieve sufficient economy of scale; and
4. allow the nonprofit organization in question to compete with others that might also produce substitute or similar products.

As with any strategy, there is also a downside to Porter's cost leadership position. Cost increases in materials or services can wipe away any financial advantage to a nonprofit organization, even when it reduces its expenses as much as possible. Likewise, changes in technology can render past investments obsolete, again limiting the effectiveness of the strategy. Finally, an organization can simply cut too much expense or cut in strategically wrong areas, thereby hurting the overall mission.

Differentiation. Michael Porter's second generic strategy is one of "... differentiating the product or service offering of the firm, creating something that is perceived industrywide as being unique."[23] As you may recall, Porter's definition of industry is a "group of firms creating products that are close substitutes for each other." The process of differentiation can take many forms. The design, look, and feel of a product or service can be different from others in its categories; the technology can be different as can the emphasis on client service; or the method by which funds are raised can be unique.

Differentiation is exceptionally valuable to a nonprofit organization because:

1. It isolates the nonprofit organization from different types of rivalry by developing loyalties between the service or product and clients, based on the product's differentiation.
2. Such a loyalty creates an entry barrier for a new nonprofit organization trying to enter the same field.
3. If the differentiation is successful in a client's or donor's eyes, then the seller can charge higher fees for its purchase as customers become insulated from substitutes, or raise more dollars as donors get less sensitive to the cost of the service being provided.

However, there are some dangers to this strategy as seen in our economy today. Consumers—when perceiving or experiencing financially difficult times—often forsake product loyalty and instead purchase products based on price. In addition, a product or firm's differentiation strategy is wide open to imitation by any number of competitors. When this happens the advantage for the differentiated product disappears.

Focus. Unlike Porter's first two generic strategies, focus is not an industrywide strategy but is concerned with a particular client or buyer group, a segment of the cause, or a geographic market. The goal of a focus strategy is to serve a particular group very well and in thus serving this strategic target, the nonprofit organization can operate more efficiently and effectively.

Potentially, the nonprofit organization which runs a focus strategy can often achieve above-average financial returns because it offers to its market superior client and donor service, as well as producing specialized services and products meeting specialized needs.

Of course, once a nonprofit organization embarks on a focus strategy, it necessarily limits its overall market share achievability and service potential.

Summary of Porter's Competitive Strategy. Porter's Competitive Strategy theory serves as a comprehensive framework upon which a nonprofit organization can build its strategy. Just like for-profit companies, nonprofit organizations are affected by industry focus. Certainly donors, constituents, and clients can exert pressure upon a company, as can a nonprofit organization's own labor supply. And, many nonprofit organizations are aware of how intensely they must compete for dwindling resources.

Unlike the Portfolio and Harvard Policy frameworks, which do not always provide a clear picture of the actual way a strategy must interact with its environment, Porter provides a clear picture of how an industry operates. By understanding industry forces, a manager can better decide how to interact with each "force." In addition, Porter goes beyond simple strategy concepts such as "build on your strengths" and "reduce your risk" which are implicit in both the Harvard and Portfolio frameworks, and instead gives the reader very specific plans of attack (as can be seen in Exhibit 9-10).

Unfortunately, there are many major problems with the Competitive Strategy. First, it can be difficult to identify what forces are affecting a particular industry. And second, some nonprofits do not fit easily into one "industry."

Step 1
Look at the five fundamental forces determining the nature of competition in a business
Step 2
Look at the three generic competitive strategies for coping with industry structure
Step 3
Recognize and act on market signals from competitors
Step 4
Forecast how the industry will evolve
Step 5
Determine if there are new industries to enter

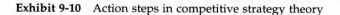

Exhibit 9-10 Action steps in competitive strategy theory

Applied to city government or state departments, the industry model has much less value. In other cases, industry types can be misleading. For instance, hospitals fall into three categories: the voluntary nonprofit segment, the for-profit segment, and the government segment. The forces in each segment are more different than alike. However, examining homogeneous segments may be useful using the Porter model.[24]

In addition to this problem is the fact that Porter's Framework focuses exclusively on the industry and not on the managers who manage in the industry. Even though the Framework conveys the feeling that managers will perform the analysis tasks, we see no managers at work in the Framework, nor do we see them interacting with each other.

Finally, this may be in an age where some nonprofit organizations—in order to survive—are going to have to look at collaboration instead of strong competition. Given both the numbers of some nonprofit organizations producing substitute products and the inability of many nonprofits to receive the funding they really need, a strategy model based on competition may be wrong for them.

The Stakeholder Management Framework

Thus far our look has been at strategy models that assume a basic status quo in nonprofit operations and the environment in which they operate. The previous four models have not been specifically designed to accommodate new trends in the environment nor the emergence of new ideas and groups. The governing assumption for the previous strategy models has been that the rules are the same for everyone in each industry, and that these rules are relatively stable. What happens when this is not the case?

The roots of stakeholder management grew out of the Stanford Research Institute in 1963 with the term "stakeholder" used to generalize the notion of "stockholder" as the only group to whom management need be responsive.[25] Thus, the stakeholder concept was originally named for the groups without whose support the company would cease to exist. The Stanford Institute researchers felt that unless corporate executives understood the needs and concerns of the key stakeholder groups they would not be able to formulate corporate objectives which would receive the necessary support for the survival of the company.

There was much criticism later generated for this notion, especially by H. Igor Ansoff who argued in his book *Corporate Strategy: An Analytic Approach to Business Policy for Growth and Expansion* and in other articles that the "objectives" of a firm and those who were "responsible" for implementing those objectives were not synonymous terms as the stakeholder theory contended.[26] Conflicting stakeholder objectives could serve as constraints upon the corporation's growth and survival, and a manager's job within this framework was to try to balance conflicting objectives. (See Exhibit 9-11.)

Today, the basic idea behind the Stakeholder Management Framework involves the presence of a stakeholder—a person who can affect or is affected by actions taken by managers of a nonprofit organization or business—and the setting of objectives that takes their presence into account. Clearly in this two-way relationship the very notion of how a business is run takes on a new meaning. Still included in this notion is the idea that potentially conflicting stakeholder objectives must be managed into a stable pattern of objectives if the nonprofit organization is to succeed. In his book, *Strategic Management*, R. Edward Freeman writes, "The point of strategy is to chart a direction for the firm. Groups which can affect that direction and its implementation must be considered in the strategic management process."[27]

Who are the nonprofit stakeholders? They are the individuals or groups that have or hold a stake in the institution and its results: clients, management, unions, constituents, suppliers, community, and public government, the board of directors, and donors. The emphasis upon these groups means that the first step in stakeholder strategy is to identify the relevant stakeholders and determine how performance in each service or product area will affect them and the nonprofit environment as a whole. The ultimate operational goal here is to determine minimal needs, the expectations and the desired outcomes for each group.

In for-profit and nonprofit organizations, different stakeholders compete for attention, resources, and priorities of the organization. Key groups must be identified first.

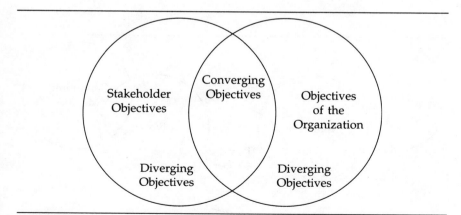

Exhibit 9-11   Stakeholder objectives and organization objectives can both converge and diverge

Second, this identification of key groups must also be balanced with the notion that some stakeholders wear multiple hats: a nonprofit organization's employee may also be a donor to the organization; a volunteer may give of his or her time and also may be a voluntary member of a group that designates money to the nonprofit organization; and a volunteer also may be a member of a community benefitted by the non-profit organization's efforts. With each "hat," this stakeholder also may wield differing levels of power, influence, and the ability to influence different objectives in the nonprofit organization. (See Exhibit 9-12.)

The third step is for the organization to determine how the stake-holders will measure its performance. This becomes important for two reasons. One is for the organization to estimate its own vulnerability; some stakeholders may simply expect outcomes from the organization that it has no intention of providing (at this point). Second, by asking stakeholders what their expectations are for the organization, managers move away from guesswork and into a realistic criterion.

The fourth step is a process step; generating objectives with the like-ly outcome that different groups of stakeholders will have different objectives and different outcomes. (See Exhibit 9-13.) Analyzing each role the stakeholder plays within the organization helps prioritize objectives. (See Exhibit 9-14.) It also forces the organization to develop a plan with the stakeholders in mind at the outset of the planning mode.

The punch line for the process level is simply this: if managers routinely have to answer questions about their stakeholders, they will likely pay attention to managing stakeholder relationships.[28]

The fifth and culminating step could be considered a negotiation step; satisfying the organization and the stakeholders regarding the direction

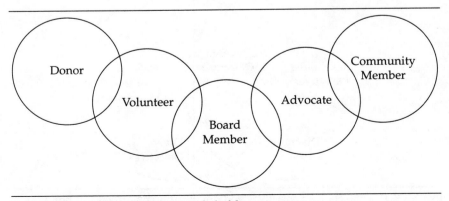

Exhibit 9-12   Different "hats" a stakeholder may wear

Objectives sought	#1	#2	#3	#4
Stakeholders				
Clients				
Management				
Unions				
Donors				
Constituents				
Local government				
Community				
Suppliers				

Exhibit 9-13   Defining the effect of objectives on stakeholders

of the firm. It is here that managers—both in for-profit and nonprofit organizations—often find themselves in unfamiliar waters. In the stakeholder relationship, managers do not, by definition, control their own fiefdom; they carve out a future in conjunction with others (stakeholders) who also must be taken as having a legitimate voice for the future. This is contrary to the security most nonprofit managers enjoy by having the ability to control their own destiny. When nonprofit managers are questioned about stakeholder input, the usual responses are either: "We know what they like" or "They do not have the same level of expertise in this area as we do; therefore their opinion—while important—is not really necessary." (See Exhibit 9-15.)

Such transactions with stakeholders only work if the organization and its management view stakeholders as having legitimate concerns, and give the various stakeholder groups regular and periodic input into the planning and strategy process.

How Does this Framework Differ from Others Looked At?
The Stakeholder Management Framework differs significantly from the Harvard Policy, Portfolio Strategy, and Competitive Strategy Frameworks on a very basic issue: *how to interpret the modern corporation.*

From the stakeholder perspective, the corporation is a social institution whose walls are permeable by a host of persons and groups with a stake in corporate action. From the managerial perspective, which underlies the other three frameworks, the corporation is an institution that is meaningfully separable (that is, different in kind) from other

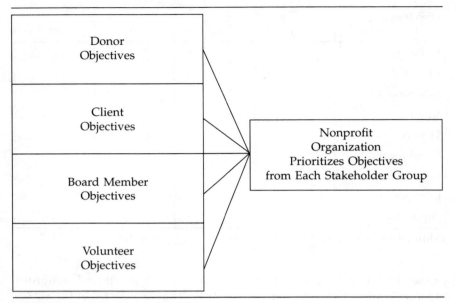

Exhibit 9-14   Prioritizing objectives

social institutions such as government, family, and schools. The distinc-
tion can be carried further.

From the stakeholder vantage point, the corporation is a fragile institution, continually subject to revision as stakeholders come and go.
Accordingly, strategy is an uncertain, dynamic process of juggling
diverse and conflicting stakeholder relationships that make up the corporation.[29]

Interestingly, the Stakeholder Management Framework sounds most
applicable to the nonprofit world according to many individuals

Step 1	Identify the key stakeholders in the organization
Step 2	Determine the roles each stakeholder group plays in the organization
Step 3	Determine how each stakeholder group measures its performance
Step 4	Generate objectives from each stakeholder group as an aid to organizational planning
Step 5	Begin the process of satisfying both organizational and stakeholder mandates

Exhibit 9-15   Five critical issues in stakeholder management

Pitfall 1	Individual concerns take priority over organizational concerns
Pitfall 2	Organization can be so encompassing in its reach that issues of profitability and performance are lost or relegated to the background
Pitfall 3	The need for timely action can be jeopardized due to the organization's desire to listen to everyone
Pitfall 4	An organization has a difficult time building everyone's opinions into its objectives
Pitfall 5	Trying to please everyone can leave an organization directionless

Exhibit 9-16   List of potential pitfalls in using the Stakeholder Framework

because of its emphasis on individual stakeholders meeting together to develop strategies and analysis that take into account the needs of all the various stakeholder groups. If an organization does not know who its stakeholders are, how they will judge the organization's performance, and how the organization is actually doing in light of these criteria, then there is no chance for a company to really say it works on behalf of its supporters.

Individual people being concerned about their own stakes is one of the cornerstones of this framework. It is here also, in its desire to be truly all-encompassing in its reach, that stakeholder philosophy can run into problems. Central issues of profitability and performance can easily be crowded out by stakeholder agendas that are peripheral in nature. In addition, given the need to hear from many different points of view, the need for timely action in the Stakeholder Framework can be paralyzed by the equal need to analyze many different points of view. How, for example, does one take advantage of a special strategic business opportunity in this framework if everyone's opinion must not only be solicited but somehow built into a firm's objectives? (See Exhibit 9-16.)

We now move into a final strategy model which is really not about strategy at all. It is called the Planning Process Framework.

The Planning Process Framework

Annual plans or strategies generally take the form of the Planning Process Framework. For many nonprofit managers, strategy and planning are interchangeable concepts. By planning, you achieve or derive a strategy.

The main idea behind the Planning Process Framework is that the most important part of any strategy is the way or process by which decisions are implemented. In this framework, managers make, implement, and control decisions across various functions and levels within a nonprofit organization. Planning process systems typically address four questions:

1. Where are we going? (mission)
2. How do we get there? (strategies)
3. What is our blueprint for action? (budget)
4. How do we know if we are on track? (control)[30]

The key notion in the Planning Process Framework is to link mission, strategy, resources, and direction so that their interrelationship can be identified and carefully managed. There is a certain face value logic to the planning process. For most nonprofit managers, it makes sense to concentrate on the core mission of the organization, acknowledging where it is going, how it is getting there, and accomplishing its mission while correcting any performance that does not contribute to the same mission. Many nonprofit managers agree that this is precisely what they want to accomplish in their organizations.

However, to work properly, the Planning Process Framework must be characterized by a high degree of organizational formality, tight controls with very precise goals and objectives, clear performance indicators, and strong centralized authority. While some nonprofit organizations may operate under these conditions, they are by no means universal. And as a result of this fact, most nonprofit organizations and their plans typically concentrate on a few areas of concern, and rely on decision-making apparatus where politics play a preeminent role both in getting the plans accepted and in controlling other outcomes like budget expenditures and resource allocation.[31]

Organizations using such a framework often use a linear strategy, employing checklists and step-by-step procedures; strategies that might emerge because of competitive or environmental shifts are all but ignored. The effectiveness of the framework depends on how well managers devise and carry out procedures for fitting their organizations with the environment surrounding the organization.[32] Behind this strong emphasis upon procedures and process discipline are two basic assumptions about managers:

1. managers have limited reasoning capabilities; and
2. managers do not always opt for the "best" way to act.[33]

The Planning Process Framework's rigidity leads frequently to two shortcuts by nonprofit managers:

1. they do not consider alternative solutions to problems, nor do they gather the background information on the alternative solutions; and

2. given the then limited set of alternatives, managers often accept the first convenient and satisfactory solution available to them.

The obvious strength of such a framework is its desire to control the outcomes of many systems and functions across an organization. There is tremendous benefit to nonprofit executives and managers, with well-defined responsibilities, to think out and consider strategic questions. And should an organization contemplate a change in its operations or experience a change in its environment that is both complex and larger than normal, formal planning systems are useful.

The profound weakness, though, of the formal planning system is that in rigid organizations with strong centralized authority, strategy can be lost, as can attention to mission. In fact, strategy is treated quite differently in this framework, as opposed to those strategy models we have discussed previously. Strategy is only incidental in the Planning Process Framework. The planning process is centrally concerned with its own maintenance as a process, not the strategy produced by the process.

The Planning Process Framework believes that managers can imagine both desirable futures and can plan in anticipation of the future competitive environment. The Planning Process Framework users believe they can see the world in sufficient enough detail to make correct strategic choices. Typically, formal planning as part of the framework is done in a planning cycle, usually addressing five issues:

1. set objectives;

2. generate alternative strategies for achieving objectives;

3. analyze the pros and cons of each alternative;

4. select the best strategic alternative; and

5. prepare appropriate plans, budgets, cash flow statements, and so on.[34]

While there are literally hundreds of different formal planning frameworks, all tend to work in a linear manner, building upon the answers to specific questions until a full-fledged strategy has evolved. And in doing so, a nonprofit organization loses its ability to act quickly or take advantage of economic opportunities because of its commitment to the "system."

James Brian Quinn, a Dartmouth policy professor, realized that even the best laid plans go awry and the environment sometimes dictates strategy. In studying 10 companies and how they dealt with change, Quinn discovered that most of the strategies were precipitated by external or internal events over which management had little control. The organizations responded to these events with incremental decisions, from which Quinn developed "logical incrementalism."[35]

In logical incrementalism—and the reason for including it as part of the formal planning frameworks—Quinn did not deny the importance of the planning process. In fact, his process is far more complex than the Planning Process Framework; however, his system is flexible enough to take the environment into account in planning through a series of feedback systems and consensus building as part of the planning framework. Quinn positioned his logical incrementalism not in contrast to the Planning Process Framework, but in support of it. Sometimes incremental decisions were formally part of the planning framework and were often inserted. Then sequential decision making took over. (An example of this would be testing a new service; once the test was finished, sequential decisions could be made regarding service refinement and introduction to the public.)

Without Quinn's input, the formal planning process becomes a private affair between members of management within a single company. The public is really not included, nor their opinion asked for. Hence, the presence of "control" as a management imperative; soliciting opinions outside the organization would sacrifice some of this control.

EVALUATION OF THE EIGHT MODELS

The reader has now considered eight different models of strategy analysis and planning. And as demonstrated, each is unique and brings different strengths and weaknesses to a strategic situation. In the following case study, a nonprofit organization encounters a series of problems and opportunities. How would each strategy planning model deal with this situation?

UPDATING THE AMERICAN ALCOHOL REHABILITATION UNION

The American Alcohol Rehabilitation Union was founded in St. Louis 50 years ago. It grew out of the old Temperance League. The original purpose of the organization was to rid society of alcohol abuse. Its current director, Curt Johnston, was hired four years ago when the organization had 15 employees. However, the nonprofit organization is now down to six employees, primarily because the funding to the organization is drying up. A number of donors give to the organization, but the organization itself does no active fund raising. Unfortunately, demand for the organization's services has never been larger. Curt Johnston and his team also face another difficulty; most of the organization's donors are very old and remember the Temperance League days. They are not really acquainted with the new services the Union offers, such as drug counseling, anti-drug and alcohol presentations at high and junior high schools, as well as one-to-one and family counseling. Curt Johnston and his team need to determine which strategy would be best to solve their problems.

Quite apart from actually erecting a marketing and service strategy for a nonprofit organization, the evaluation of each strategy is critical for a number of reasons. The immediate one is, "What does the organization do if its strategy is wrong?" Let's use the case study and plug in each strategy to see which one is best for this nonprofit organization. Looking at the problem using the eight models presented in this chapter, how would each model help solve this organization's problems?

The McKinsey 7-S Framework

The McKinsey 7-S Framework suggests that the strategy and structure of an organization must be considered together when planning, with both components taking into account an organization's staff, their skill levels, and the systems and style of the organization. Combined, they interact with each other in light of the organization's goals. The McKinsey 7-S Framework would propose the following solution to Curt Johnston's problems:

First, the Framework would take into account the organizational structure looking at how tasks are divided between Curt and his team, as well as the skill level of each employee conducting those tasks in light of the organization's needs.

Second, because the lack of money is threatening the very existence of the organization, Curt Johnston and his team might create a superordinate goal that becomes a rallying point for each of the other six factors in the Framework. In other words, if the goal is to accumulate more of a specific resource (i.e., money), then the strategy must fit this goal. The structure of the organization may change in light of this goal, as might its systems and staff should the organization find no one on staff with the ability to raise the needed funds. The organization may decide instead to change its fee structure or begin charging for some services that used to be free. Each of these decisions will bring changes into the organization's systems and structure.

Third, Curt Johnston and his team will have to decide if the style of the organization in the past (not charging for services and no fund raising) is a style they are content with or whether must it be changed. Because change seems inevitable, the way in which they create a new organizational culture spurred on by fund raising or charging for services will be important.

Finally, because the 7-S Framework does not require Curt Johnston and his team to interact with key stakeholders other than themselves, they can use the Framework and make the changes within the confines of their organization.

The Miles and Snow Typology

Unlike the 7-S Framework, which looks internally at an organization, the Miles and Snow Typology classifies strategy in terms of shifts in the environment surrounding the organization. Berkeley Organization Theorists Raymond Miles and Charles Snow, in their research, concluded that organizations could be grouped into one of four groups:

1. *defenders,* who try to protect their domain;
2. *prospectors,* who find new products and markets while engaging in constant product innovation;
3. *analyzers,* who try to discover new markets while keeping old ones alive; and
4. *reactors,* who do not change in the face of environmental upheaval.

The Miles and Snow Typology would suggest the following course of action:

First, the American Alcohol Rehabilitation Union needs to realize that it has been in a reactor mode for some time, without a clearly defined method of meeting the many changes the organization has encountered. This fact may cause the organization to ask itself if the problems it faces have occurred because the Union has not had an articulated strategy in the past or if it has just been employing the wrong strategy. In either case, much of the blame will fall on Curt Johnston; being cast as a *reactor* may prove harmful to his leadership.

Second, the organization must figure out how to move from a *reactor* to an *analyzer* as quickly as possible. As part of this move, the organization needs to shore up its financial support with the older, loyal donors in order for it to be able to survive financially while it makes other strategic decisions. As part of this analyzer strategy, the nonprofit organization will need to ready itself emotionally and pragmatically for two different types of strategies: one aimed at reassuring the established clientele that the Union is still holding up those values dear to them, and the other strategy aimed at securing new markets of interested individuals who appreciate the Union's products and will either pay for them, or help support them financially.

Harvard Policy Model

The chief function of the Harvard Policy Model is to help an organization create a "fit" between its own capabilities and resources and the environment in which the organization finds itself. This strategy is divided into two parts: formulation and implementation.

In formulating its strategy, the company in question identifies its intended future and matches both its company strengths and market opportunities. The Harvard Policy Model would suggest the following course of action for The American Alcohol Rehabilitation Union:

First, Curt Johnston and his associates must identify opportunities where the Union can be successful, particularly as these opportunities relate to issues of money. For example, what services does the organization provide that they could charge for? In undertaking a task of this nature, the team must also identify the risks associated with these opportunities.

Second, in identifying opportunities, Curt and his team must determine the capabilities of the organization to achieve these opportunities in regard to managerial, financial, technical, and material resources; they must discount those opportunities beyond the capabilities of the organization.

Third, Curt and his six-person team must decide what personal aspirations they have for the organization and its future. Do they want to continue together as a team or not? Can they pursue the organization's goals and their own simultaneously? Both questions will need to be answered by all concerned.

Fourth, they have to decide if the future they agree upon as an organization will continue to have a positive bearing upon society at large. One issue they will need to face here is that the perception by the public of what they do is different than what they actually do operationally. This difference in the actual operational goals of the organization versus the goals the supportive constituency have for it will ultimately need to be resolved.

These first four steps taken by Curt and his team have involved the formulation of their strategy. The next three steps involve the implementation of their strategy.

Having decided what they want to do, the fifth step in this process is for the group to structure the organization so that it can achieve its intended objectives.

With new jobs and role definitions will also come the need for new systems. In step six, the organization should concern itself with developing the necessary systems to support the new strategy. For example, if the Union is going to charge for its services, then a billing and receipt system must be set up.

Step seven is perhaps the most crucial. That is deciding if the leadership is right in the organization given the objectives it wants to achieve.

The Experience Curve

In using the Experience Curve for The American Alcohol Rehabilitation Union, the first critical question for the organization is, "Are there any services that you currently offer or undertake that can be produced at a cheaper rate than any of your competitors producing the same service?" Given that the organization has a long history in the field, but a relatively short one offering its newer services, the question may be hard to answer. On the other hand, if the entire industry is relatively young, then the Rehabilitation Union may have some slight, competitive advantage.

There are two compounding problems associated with this strategy. First, any advantage accrued by the organization through its experience in providing services relies on the notion of where financial breakeven occurs in its work. Given that the nonprofit organization has never offered services for a fee, it will take a minimum of one year to establish a financial trend line. Second, the drug and alcohol rehabilitation industry may be an industry where experience is not an important selling tool, but reputation is. With the lack of a strong organizational marketing culture designed to cultivate a strong image in the minds of the public, the Union may get competitively outclassed.

The Portfolio Framework

The Portfolio Framework is a classification system which determines the value of the different services organizations like The American Alcohol Rehabilitation Union offers. It does this by looking at both the numerical and financial growth of these services, as well as by taking an overall look at the organization. The Portfolio Framework's recommendations and action steps regarding the American Alcohol Rehabilitation Union are as follows:

First, the nonprofit organization must view the services that it offers as distinct from each other in a management, marketing, and financial sense. Each service needs to be evaluated as to its financial worthiness. The reason for taking this point of view is so Curt Johnston and his team can know which services to continue, which to expand, and which to offer less of. Each service offered is to be called a *strategic business unit* and the ultimate objective for each unit is to have a significant financial return to the organization.

Second, Curt and his team have to decide who takes strategic and financial responsibility for each of the services offered, particularly as they relate to other similar services competitively. In addition, the leadership team will have to decide what opportunities (if any) exist for some of the services and how best they can be grown.

Third, in undertaking this evaluation they may wish to use the following typology in making decisions about their services:

- Those services that show high growth potential are in a strong competitive position and can be self-supporting.
- Those services that will not grow much more but are extremely lucrative to the organization should be maintained.

- Services that produce little cash and offer little prospect of growth should be seen as unsuitable for the future.
- Services that might be growth-oriented for the nonprofit organization, but currently have a small market, should be evaluated as to what will happen if resources are invested.

Competitive Strategy Framework

The Competitive Strategy Framework is concerned with five forces that shape an organization and the organization's industry, in general. The Strategy Framework believes these forces can be used to predict the success of an organization's strategy. This underlying structure of industry forces then determines the nature of each organization's strategy and the constraints with which it must operate. In particular, these five forces are:

1. the bargaining power of buyers (in this case the users of the American Alcohol Rehabilitation services);
2. the bargaining power of suppliers (those who enable the group to continue such as donor and volunteers);
3. the threat of new entrants into the industry;
4. the threat of substitute products (other groups whose services could be used instead of the Rehabilitation Union's services); and
5. the current rivalry amongst competitors.

Given these five industry forces, the Competitive Strategy Framework would propose the following steps to Curt Johnston and his team:

First, because there is significant demand for the organization's services, the relative power of buyers of the services could become quite strong. Of particular note are those groups or schools using the Union's services frequently. When, and if, the Union begins to charge for its services, large user groups, like schools, will be in a position to negotiate a lower price with the Union, especially if it has an alternative source of services.

Second, the suppliers (donors) to the nonprofit organization also have the potential for great power because they are few in nature and are relatively concentrated. These donors can withhold their giving if they don't like where the organization is going and can use their financial support to severely restrain or empower the organization.

New entrants seem likely in this field because of the apparent high demand for the types of services being offered by the Alcohol Rehabilitation Union. The threat of new competition will force the Union to begin to move strategically in a way that will ensure it has a supportive constituency in the years to come.

Fourth, in many cases, more than one type of service will perform the same function as another for the buyer of the service. The threat of substitute services being offered is real for the Alcohol Rehabilitation Union. Should substitutes be offered, no doubt the Union will get in a pricing war for use of its services, thereby driving its prices down and further exacerbating its financial condition. Strategically, the Union needs to look at services not currently being offered.

Finally, the Alcohol Rehabilitation Union may not be aware of other organizations offering similar services. This is an area where it needs to do research in order to find out who its competitors might be, the tactics they are using to compete, and the signals they may be sending the marketplace, such as relocating to different areas, hiring more counselors for its practice, and so on.

The Stakeholder Management Framework

The Stakeholder Management Framework is concerned with two issues: The first concern is for the groups without whose support company operations would cease. The second is setting corporate objectives that takes their presence into account. The first operational goal for Curt Johnston and his team using this framework would be:

To identify those groups that have a critical bearing upon the operations of the American Alcohol Rehabilitation Union. This group would no doubt include people like donors, staff, clients, users of the services offered such as schools, families, board members, and local interested community residents.

The second operational goal would be to identify the minimal needs of each group, the expectations of each group, and the desired outcomes of each groups vis-à-vis the nonprofit organization. In other words, what does each group want the American Alcohol Rehabilitation Union to be and how do they fit in the picture?

Third, Curt Johnston and his team would have to work with each identified stakeholder group in helping them decide how they would measure their performance in relationship to the organization. This would help the organization know its vulnerabilities and would move the organization towards realistic criteria.

Fourth, generate objectives with the likely outcome that different groups of stakeholders will have different objectives and want different outcomes. Analyzing each role the stakeholder plays within the organization will help to prioritize objectives.

The culminating step is a negotiation step—satisfying the organization and the stakeholders regarding the direction of the Alcohol Rehabilitation Union.

The Planning Process Framework

The main idea behind the Planning Process Framework is that the most important part of any strategy is the way or process by which decisions are implemented. Planning process systems typically address four questions:

1. Where are we going? (mission)
2. How do we get there? (strategies)
3. What is our blueprint for action? (budget)
4. How do we know if we're on track? (control)

The mark then of effective managers using this framework would be how well they carry out their procedures in fitting the organization into its environment. The Planning Process Framework would suggest the following types of actions for the American Alcohol Rehabilitation Union:

First, the nonprofit organization must set objectives for itself, particularly as they relate to finances, people and their roles, and the direction of the organization.

Second, they need to generate alternative strategies for each objective. For example, the need for money may suggest a fund-raising strategy, a fee for services strategy, a takeover strategy in which the Union tries to be bought out, or the like.

Third, Curt Johnston and his team need to evaluate each objective as to its suitability, strengths, and weaknesses.

Fourth, they need to select the best strategic alternative in order to develop the necessary tactics and prepare the necessary budgets, resource allocations, new job descriptions if any, and so on.

There are, though, other, more subtle questions and observations that indicate implementation problems.

SUMMARY

The reader has now been provided with a number of theoretical strategy frameworks to choose from. Each allows the nonprofit manager to manage his or her organization from a different perspective; each has a different set of strength and weaknesses; and each can help an organization create a coherent strategy. Chapter 10 explains how a nonprofit organization's image and its strategy should go hand-in-hand.

CHAPTER TEN

Improving the Nonprofit Organization's Image

A nonprofit organization can produce an extremely satisfying array of programs for its clients that both helps and satisfies them; it can have excellent relations in its work force; it can even have a strong and successful marketing and fund-raising program; but if it fails to communicate this information on a regular basis to the various stakeholders who comprise its support base, then the nonprofit organization's management and marketing team is making an error that could hurt the organization long term.

Barry J. McLeish

No discussion of marketing for nonprofit organizations can be complete without addressing the large, and often overlooked, topic of managing the exterior image of the organization. The *public relations* or *image management* function serves to let the public know of the organization's successes, its high points, its goodwill, and the functionability of its internal finances. Image management has grown out of the nonprofit organization's realization that it can no longer afford to sit back and assume that its good performance among clients will automatically generate resources and support amongst certain audiences.

In these times of the skeptical (and overwhelmed) volunteer and/or donor, a marketing manager or nonprofit marketing director must be sure that potential supporters know the exact purpose of the organization, its workings, and its financial situation, especially if there is a high percentage of money directly applied to a specified cause.

WHAT COMPRISES A NONPROFIT ORGANIZATION'S IMAGE?

The need for a good image or identity is one of the most generally agreed to, yet least understood, aspects of nonprofit marketing strategy. At its most simplistic, a nonprofit organization's image is seen as its logo; similar to the way its stationery or brochure are designed. At the other end of the organizational image spectrum is the idea that a nonprofit organization's image is best understood in light of its communication strategies, the nomenclature it uses, its relationship with donors and volunteers, its programmatical implementation, and the general way in which it carries on its affairs.

Yet in the minds of many nonprofit executives the way in which a nonprofit organization projects its image is little more than a "cosmetic" issue, something that is done to dress up the organization for public consumption. To these nonprofit executives there is nothing of substance within the organization that is worth portraying to the general public through a sustained image campaign or coverup.

However, to many other nonprofit marketers a nonprofit organization's image is a very positive tool. An "image" becomes a sophisticated way to both speak to, and hear from, an organization's constituency. The image a nonprofit organization wants to project should start from its objectives and reason for being. From this starting point, a tactical strategy should be developed and implemented that takes into account all of the nonprofit organization's programs, services, and operations; including the way these are portrayed to the public through the organization's communication tools. Over time, an accumulation of a nonprofit organization's images slowly begin to impress themselves upon its various constituencies, building an awareness that results in attitudes—either positive or negative—being formed toward them. The end result is an "image" that is associated with the organization.

To be effective, a nonprofit organization's image program has to be planned for and should include one or more of the following attributes:

1. A nonprofit organization, through its image, needs to educate or inform its supportive publics and constituencies regarding the organization's goals, objectives, and role in the community (or communities) in which it operates.

2. An organization's image program is designed to build up the nonprofit organization and to garner favorable opinions about its work, service, and community relationships.

3. Given the skepticism of donors and volunteers today, a nonprofit organization's image should project confidence in how the organization spends its money, utilizes its resources and takes care of its clients.

4. Finally, a nonprofit organization's image ought to convey that the organization is a good place for volunteers to work, as well as for qualified individuals who may be contemplating long-term employment.

Primarily, a nonprofit organization needs to view its image as a major resource and asset. As such, it needs to be carefully planned for, developed, nurtured, and controlled. Consider the following example of how a good image can be an asset:

IMAGE IS EVERYTHING!

The nonprofit Museum of Native Americans serves both Native Americans and non-Indian audiences as well. Its design is to pay special tribute to Indian cultures that once thrived as well as to Indian culture today. The museum features Indian artifacts, sells homemade Indian crafts, conducts a special Native American lecture series, and is a place where Indians can come together for meetings and ceremonies. The museum has received several community and national awards and has a very good financial rating.

However, donations and new visitors are down numerically. The museum's director is seeking to improve donations and the number of new visitors to the museum with two marketing campaigns. One is a direct mail campaign, coupled with telemarketing to potential visitors and donors. The other is a public relations campaign designed to key in on the museum's good name and reputation through newspaper, magazine, radio, and television coverage. In both campaigns the strong points of the museum have been stressed: its assistance to Indians, its awards, and the importance of the museum culturally.

THE ADVANTAGE OF A FOCUSED IMAGE GOAL

The goal of an image program can often be muddled into an all-encompassing, unfocused "good image." Instead, as in the museum case study, a very focused campaign, coordinated with direct mail, telephone, and/or advertising media carrying the same message can prove to be much more useful, and often will yield more favorable results.

There are three primary reasons for a nonprofit organization to focus upon a goal in developing its image program:

1. First, a nonprofit organization has to decide how it wants to "be seen" by the consumer. Having created a goal allows the organization to monitor all of its external operations under this goal. There are always pressures within a nonprofit to change the way it presents itself to the public. To not comply with this goal often means a nonprofit organization presents a fragmented image to the public.

2. A goal allows a nonprofit organization to avoid the inefficiencies and confusion often associated with a fragmented image. In particular there are benefits gained in the promotional arena (by allowing various publics to know precisely who the organization is, what it stands for, and, therefore, what they are responding to).

3. A focused image goal also facilitates growth in a nonprofit organization by projecting an image that can be memorable and distinctive, thereby creating a competitive advantage over those nonprofits who have a fragmented image.

Obviously, in order to arrive at one's goal for an image program, the nonprofit marketing director must first look at what are the strengths of the organization, and what would encourage a potential donor or volunteer to give of either time or money. Consider the Girl Scouts of America.

THE GIRL SCOUTS WORK AT THEIR IMAGE

The Girl Scouts' goal is to have something to offer to all young women. In the more than 300 Girl Scout Councils around the country, they have studied the needs of young women and their families and have developed programs for ages five and up. They are market-driven and routinely look at the needs and wants of the communities they serve and develop programs to fit these needs and wants. An example of this is the recently created Daisy Scouts program aimed at the needs of a five-year old.

In addition they train their leaders thoroughly not only to deal effectively with their clients in an educationally sound manner, but also with the ups and downs of managing the councils and interfacing with its large volunteer work force, community leaders, donors, and council management staff. In particular, volunteers are targeted for special service and consideration because their numbers within the Girl Scout organization determines to a large measure how many young women can be served. This in addition to the enormous financial savings these volunteers contribute to the organization.

Finally, this high standard of operation is communicated to the public through high-profile events like its cookie sales, and through its constant emphasis on a quality operation and interface with communities from which it draws its clients and volunteers. In addition, the Girl Scouts partner with organizations like Nike in order to not only help their client population, but also to benefit from the joint efforts of nationally recognized corporations.

Consider the possible strengths a nonprofit organization like the Girl Scouts could communicate to its various publics about its programs:

1. Recent recognition or rewards.
2. Favorable financial ratings or results.
3. The benevolent programs they run for young women and their families where no charge for services is imposed.
4. The programs they run in different ethnic environments aimed at their particular population.
5. The reading programs and mentoring programs they offer to their clients.
6. The leadership training they provide.
7. The ethnic diversity of their leadership.
8. The nature of their volunteer programs, the type of volunteer they attract, the benefit they play in the lives of young women, and the benefits the volunteers receive themselves.
9. Being a part of corporate events that benefit the Girl Scout clients like Nike's fitness training events.
10. The nature of the Girl Scouts' volunteer board.
11. Current leaders in America who have benefitted from the Girl Scouts' programs.
12. The overseas Girl Scout programs, particularly the ones benefitting entire communities.
13. The skills that are taught to young women through the broad diversity of the programs the Girl Scouts offer.

14. The Girl Scout cookie drives, the number of cookies sold, the benefits received by young women in selling the cookies, and the benefits received by participants who buy the cookies.

15. The manner in which special needs young women can participate in Girl Scouts.

After identifying the possible strengths of an organization, and those that are likely to elicit favorable feelings from potential donors, clients, constituents, and volunteers, these strengths should be converted into goals. For example:

1. Announce the receipt of a recent reward and seek to gain coverage of the award in 10 national newspapers.

2. Publicize favorable financial ratings and results in 5 to 10 national magazines by convincing editors to write stories which mention or feature the organization in question.

Exhibit 10-1 takes the 15 strengths noted for the Girl Scouts and translates them into potential goals through which the Girl Scout image program could be enhanced. As can be seen from the exhibit, having taken the strengths an organization has to offer, a nonprofit marketing director or manager has, in written form, some very focused goals that he or she can attain.

---

1. *A recent public recognition or award* can be used towards the goal of announcing the recent award to 10 national newspapers in order to use the coverage to posture the organization in a good light.

2. *Favorable programmatical results* can become a means to achieving the organizational goal of attracting new volunteers and/or donors who desire to be involved with a program that gets results.

3. In showing that *certain programs run at no charge,* the nonprofit organization can be seen as a caring organization who desires to be differentiated from those organizations perceived as always having their hand out.

4. *Demonstrating ethnic programming* as a goal postures the organization as one that is not interested in cookie-cutter programs and seeks to treat each person as an individual.

5. *Reading and mentoring programs* are exceptionally strong tools in demonstrating to a constituency that the organization is very interested in issues of morality and the social concerns of this country and has goals in these areas.

Exhibit 10-1   15 strengths of the Girl Scout program developed into 15 goal statements for an image program

6. *If the Girl Scouts' leadership training programs are strong,* they can then have the goal of demonstrating to the general public that the organization is very interested in the issue of this country's future leadership and is willing to do something about it.

7. *Ethnic diversity of leadership* says to all interested that the Girl Scouts have the goal of promoting individuals based on their abilities and talents, regardless of background.

8. Detailing *the nature of the nonprofit organization's volunteer programs* allows the nonprofit organization to develop goals of attracting more competent volunteers.

9. *Being a part of a corporate environment* has the goal of demonstrating that the oganization is well thought of, partners with the community at large, and is viewed by corporations as being a legitimate force for good in the environment.

10 *Showing a nonprofit organization's board* is done for the goal of garnering trust for the organization from its supportive constituency, as well as to demonstrate that it is well managed.

11. If a nonprofit organization has the goal of trying to convince their constituency that they have strong leadership programs designed for young people, they might *show current American leaders who benefitted from the nonprofit organization's training.*

12. If the Girl Scout organization has the goal of being seen as an international operation, it should then *detail its international programs.*

13. *Looking at skills that are taught to clients* can mean the nonprofit organization has the goal of demonstrating the competency of its programs, as well as its desire to attract more individuals to its programs.

14. *Announcing Girl Scout cookie time* is so programmed into the American psyche that, at this stage in its product life cycle, the goal is to remind individuals across the country that the decision they made last year to buy cookies was the right decision and they should make it again this year.

15. If the goal of the nonprofit organization is to show that it includes everyone, then *showing special needs individuals* demonstates powerfully that this is a reality in the organization's life.

Exhibit 10-1 (continued)

ATTAINING THE IMAGE GOALS OF THE CAMPAIGN

Nonprofit management has the obligation to communicate regularly with its various constituencies. An ongoing managed image program results in a stronger bond between the organization and these same constituencies. It is essential that the nonprofit organization's management always remember that even the smallest financial donor or least willing volunteer still owns a part of the nonprofit organization and will tend to remain loyal as long as the nonprofit shows it cares for them by not only communicating to them, but reminding them that their choice of being involved with the organization was the right choice.

Putting image goals into action can be relatively simple as long as the implementer first understands the five overriding rules used in the development of an image campaign.

Rule 1: Know the Intended Audience

The first rule is to know who the image campaign is to be directed at and who it should influence. For those organizations that are not in a regular habit of listening to their supportive constituencies on a regular basis, it is doubtful that a strong image campaign can be mounted to influence and inform individuals without prior research of their opinions, values, information about the organization in question, as well as their attitudes toward it. There are various ways to collect this type of information:

1. mail and phone surveys;
2. including a questionnaire in an organization's annual report or donor and/or volunteer publication; and
3. do the survey with appropriate constituents face to face.

Exhibit 10-2 contains a list of possible questions a nonprofit organizations' director or marketing manager would want to know in order to develop a sound imaging program.

Rule 2: Determine Who is Running the Campaign

Who should be involved in the image program and what is the role of each person? In some organizations, this role falls naturally to the marketing manager, development director, or resources manager. For some smaller nonprofit organizations, this job will fall to the members of the management team. To help achieve the necessary effectiveness, particularly in public situations, a spokesperson needs to be chosen who will have the appearance of credibility and be seen as a suitable representative of the organization.

1. Personal data as to the average age, education, income level, and years of supporting the nonprofit organization.

2. Opinions and information levels on programmatical aspects of the organization.

3. What needs the mission of the organization must address this year and within the next three years.

4. What are the areas of most satisfying involvement for the constituent at this point in their lives.

5. The extent of involvement of the constituencies in the organization:
   (a) Are they donors?
   (b) Are they volunteers?
   (c) Are they both?
   (d) Do they recommend the organization to others?

6. What does the organization do or provide for the constituent that is most helpful?

7. What are the biggest obstacles to the organization accomplishing its goals in the next three years?

8. What are the three biggest strengths of the organization in the constituents' minds?

9. What are the three biggest weaknesses of the organization in constituents' minds?

10. What information that the organization sends out do they see?

Exhibit 10-2   Types of constituent questions whose answers will influence a nonprofit organization's imaging campaign

Rule 3: Determine the Best Type of Program

An image campaign can last from two months to much longer. Typically, there are five generic types of programs that can be executed singly or in any combinations in an image campaign. Each is listed here and then briefly discussed in the following sections:

1. individual contacts with members of a supportive constituency;

2. group meetings, often involving extended question and answer sessions;

3. formal presentations to corporations, foundations, the media, or local legislative bodies;

4. mailing of printed material; and

5. general publicity, including all aspects of public relations and advertising.

Individual Contacts. Obviously, the most important consideration for individual contacts is the selection of who is representing the non-profit organization in question. Not only must this person be an effective communicator, they also need to understand the organization's inner workings and its goals for the services being offered. Often these types of qualifications place the spokesperson fairly high up the organization's ladder.

Group Meetings. Informal group meetings are a very effective method of getting information across to large numbers of people in a cost-efficient manner, as well as gaining information as to the public's attitudes towards the nonprofit organization on a variety of issues. The best group meetings are often kept fairly small and informal with about 20 to 40 individuals in attendance. There is a minimum of prepared presentation with the bulk of time devoted to questions and answers. Of critical importance in meetings like this is to have a representative whom the group members feel has not only the ability to hear their concerns, but also take these concerns and deal with them appropriately.

Formal Presentations. Formal presentations can either be small and intimate or large in nature. The goals of such a meeting are often to announce something, take a stand against someone or some issue, or to petition for a group (like a legislative body) to act in some way beneficial to the nonprofit organization. Usually such meetings involve the presentation of carefully prepared materials that often detail new programs or initiatives. Visual aids and displays often accompany such a presentation.

Mailing Programs. Much of the supporting constituency of a nonprofit organization often feel swamped with mail. Nevertheless, most organizations in North America have well-oiled mailing programs that seek to attract favorable attention and achieve the best impressions on behalf of the mailer. Mailing programs can include everything from news releases, new program announcements, information newsletters, annual reports, quarterly results, and other timely information.

General Publicity. Any publicity a nonprofit receives—whether good or bad—has some type of effect upon its supportive and interested constituency. The relationship a nonprofit organization wants with its supporting groups should be factored into the planning and preparation of all of its news releases, promotional material, advertising, or other printed communication. For the uninitiated, it is often advisable to hire a small public relations firm to coordinate the placement of relevant articles into publications that potential donors, volunteers, clients, and constituents will read. Oftentimes, this includes newspapers on the local and large metropolitan scale. How might an image campaign involve all of these points? Let's look at a fictitious case study.

Your nonprofit organization wishes to announce to the press that the services it provides to a particular client group is a part of a growing trend among other nonprofit organizations in this country. Specifically, you are looking for an angle that will net your organization and its story coverage. What are the key steps you must take?

First, you must have a clear idea of the group you are working with, their demographic information, and the benefits your program provides. In addition, you need to know the prevailing feeling of the organization's supportive community towards this type of programmatical activity.

Second, as you are the spokesperson for the organization, you decide to inform a city desk editor of the city's daily newspaper, a suburban editor of the weekly newspaper, the three news editors of the television stations in town, and the five community affairs directors of local radio stations. Prior to calling the various press officers, you have assembled a ready-made group of interviewees for the reporters among your nonprofit clients. In addition, you also handpick other nonprofit representatives that are noncompetitors or that are in alliance with you, to verify the trend to the media.

Third, you create a press kit for each media representative you are going to see, containing important facts on your nonprofit organization as well as details on the trend your organization is a part of, how your organization got where it is, and the implications of the trend to the organization in the future.

Finally, you also mail press releases to other media officers in town, as well as mailing them to those representatives you called in order to make sure they get the information should the planned meeting go awry. Along with the release is a letter detailing how the media might play the information about the trend into a story that helps to highlight your nonprofit organization's part in the story.

Rule 4: Determine an Appropriate Image to Convey

One way in which to develop an organizational image is to recognize the strengths and limitations of the desired image strategy at the beginning.

Listed here are 10 generic image campaign strategies that a nonprofit organization can try to implement, depending on its strengths and goal desires:

1. **"You may not know us, but you know the services we help provide for this community."** This is a favorite of nonprofit organizations that serve as an umbrella for many different nonprofit initiatives. The best example of this type of imagery is United Way, with its multiplicity of programs under its umbrella. The goal of such an image campaign is to try and promote recognition for not only the individual initiatives but for the parent company as well.

2. **"Look what we're doing for our city!"** Some nonprofit organizations believe it is important to spend their time, money, and effort to be loved by a community. Though this strategy could appear to be self-serving, it is sometimes helpful for a nonprofit organization anxious to broaden its constituency. An ideal candidate for this strategy would be an old-line nonprofit organization that has done very little advertising of its services in the past, though providing strong programs. This campaign would be a way for the organization to get recognition from the community.

3. **"Here's what we ought to do on behalf of _____."** Advocacy campaigns usually point out opinions that fit the objectives of the nonprofit organization running the image campaign. This type of image campaign is only successful up to the level of interest in the particular subject matter by the community at large. The goal in this endeavor is often to become a spokesperson on behalf of the issue.

4. **"Here's why we're in the news."** News can be potentially the most interesting thing you can offer to a reader or prospective supporter. While it is hard to plan when the media is going to run a newsworthy piece on your organization, this type of image campaign can be very persuasive to newspaper readers and television viewers. An ideal time to run this type of campaign is when the nonprofit organization has won some type of civic or national award.

5. **"Meet the new nonprofit organization."** Perhaps this is better titled, "Here are the steps we have taken since our problems." Unfortunately, some organizations go through crises and have to try to recover from them. Constituents are fans of improvements, efficiency, and new developments. This strategy is meaningless unless you can demonstrate to your audience that by rebuilding your nonprofit organization, you are going to provide better services, help more people, spend the donors' dollars wisely, and try to ensure that whatever happened to the nonprofit in the past will not happen again.

6. **"Have you seen our new services?"** The inherent advantage in this type of image campaign is that people are intrinsically interested in

new products and services. This interest allows a nonprofit organization to present its new services as benefits to not only the user of the services, but also to the supportive constituency who will fund the services. Ideally, this type of image campaign will not only detail the new services but do so in light of the characteristics of the organization that is bringing the new services to the public.

7. **"Have you met the types of individuals who are our donors, customers, and volunteers?"** This type of image campaign supports the interests of an organization's donors and volunteers and shows itself to be solidly on their side. This campaign is an ideal opportunity for a nonprofit organization to advertise for individuals who fit the organization's profile of donors, customers, and volunteers by showing the profiles through character portrayals in the campaign.

8. **"By using this celebrity spokesperson, we hope you feel us to be a credible organization."** The obvious goal in this image campaign is for the credibility of the spokesperson to be transferred to the organization. Indeed, a well-known face may attract some attention to the organization. The best example of this type of campaign today is Habitat For Humanity's use of former president Jimmy Carter as spokesperson in much of their printed material.

9. **"From the stature of our board chairman or chief executive officer as spokesperson for this organization, we hope you will feel more trust in putting your faith—and hopefully resources—in us."** The use of a board president or chief executive officer in an image campaign is usually reserved for a very serious campaign where lots of credibility is needed. Perhaps the need is to discuss a new building program or the influx of clients that is straining an organization's budget. The goal here is not to convey that the organization is in trouble; rather, that the issue is serious and warrants the readers' or listeners' attention.

10. **"Meet one of our employees."** Featuring one or more employees can often be a better strategy than using an outside spokesperson, especially if the employee represents the message. For example, a city mission may feature someone who has been rehabilitated from the street, who now works in some capacity in the mission.

Rule 5: Proactive Image Management

The single most important issue in image management is to be proactive as a nonprofit organization. Basically, image management is simply a method of thinking ahead and planning a long-term program of image activities. The program should provide a plan and schedule for handling more or less predictable activities the nonprofit organization is engaged in, such as announcements of new services on behalf of clients or new products being introduced to customers.

An image campaign should involve a written document upon which everyone can agree. Agreement on objectives, general strategy, the spokesperson (if any), and specific activities of the campaign can save considerable frustration later on. Essential items that will need to be thought through by the marketing director for the image campaign are:

- Organizational goals for each service or product including geographic distribution, increases or decreases in the use of the service by clients, and the future importance of the service to the nonprofit organization.

- Trends for each service or product that would include a recent history of the service or product, its markets and users, competitors to the product or service, and expected demand for the product or service in the future. In addition, note any expected new product or service introduction by the nonprofit organization in the near future.

- The reputation of the nonprofit organization in relationship to competitors, vendors, donors, volunteers, and clients.

- Significant achievements of the nonprofit organization, or achievements by its management, or client alumni.

- Important donors, volunteers, alumni, board members, constituents, or advocates.

WRITING THE IMAGE CAMPAIGN PLAN

The writing of an image campaign plan (which is really a strategy in writing) is an important task both for management's sake, as well as for all members of the image team to have access to it in order to evaluate its progress. The written plan ought to include some basic items.

Current Situation

This section, taking into account any marketing research the organization has gathered specifically on behalf of the plan, comes at the beginning of the plan. Using all relevant information, this section's goal is to let management know the reasons "why" regarding the image campaign, what market research information has shown the organization as to the attitudes of its supportive communities, and the generally expected timing and results of the proposed campaign.

Program Objectives

Once the "current situation" has been described, "program objectives" can be presented. This section can be divided into "immediate" and "long-range" objectives. This division of objectives is important because the net effect of an image campaign may be cumulative and over time past the scheduled running of the campaign. A typical objective list may read as follows:

- Heighten the credibility of a particular program.
- Increase the exposure of the nonprofit organization.
- Provide the organization with media exposure in its market area.
- Generate inquiries from volunteers to the nonprofit organization.
- Support an advertising campaign the nonprofit organization is engaged in.

While it is often hard to predict the success of an image campaign, a nonprofit organization should expect the campaign to move the organization closer to its overall marketing goals.

Rationale

Following the "objectives" portion of the plan, it is important to state the reason why the image campaign approach is being recommended at all. Some organizations do not see the need for such a campaign. The purpose of this section is in part, to point out what will be accomplished over and above the normal marketing programs of the nonprofit by pursuing an image campaign. Issues such as cost effectiveness of the campaign, its ability to reach many people, the credibility of its message, and the inexpensiveness of this style of campaign in reaching new donors, volunteers, and interested parties.

Vehicles

The final section of the plan—the section that can come before the closing statements—deals with the image campaign itself. This section details the media vehicles to be used, as well as their function in the campaign. How each fits into the strategy should be detailed. It is often helpful to divide this section up into subunits such as "Press Release Program," "Generating Inquiries," "Formal Presentations," and "Feature Article Program."

SUMMARY

As the reader has seen, having a great strategy is only part of the equation in building a strong nonprofit organization. The concept of an organization's image and its ensuing public relations program are also critical to its acceptance within various constituencies. Chapter 11 ties both strategy and public relations together as it demonstrates how a nonprofit marketing practitioner can begin to think strategically while implementing strategic choices.

PART FOUR

Strategic Marketing

CHAPTER ELEVEN

Implementing Strategic Marketing Choices

As governments, we stumble from crisis to crash program, lurching into the future without a plan, without hope, without vision.[1]

Alvin Toffler
The Third Wave

The third reason IBM has been so successful was that once I had a picture of how IBM would look when the dream was in place and how such a company would have to act, I then realized that, unless we began to act that way from the very beginning, we would never get there.[2]

Tom Watson
Founder of IBM

Naomi Huntsperger, the new Executive Vice President of Development for a public broadcasting television station, was brought into the position from another city following the reassignment of her predecessor, who had been on the job for five years. The former development director was highly thought of inside the organization and was well respected throughout the city. Naomi's new staff are proud of what they accomplished under the previous development director and were loyal to the traditions he established. Naomi also admired the former executive but feels there is a need for new program directions. In particular, she wants to address improved customer service through the receipting and direct mail departments. But when she talks of the need and her vision with senior staff members, they raise endless objections. She senses their objections are not just to her, but to any change within the institution.[3]

Similarly, Harry Kouns runs the development department for the Civic and Art Center in his city. During the past 25 years, the center has built up a growing reputation, coupled with audience and community support. This year Harry and other staff members welcomed a new center director. Unlike the old director, the new director does not like to meet donors or visit corporate sponsors with Harry. Likewise, the new director has canceled some popular programs run by the Center that have been running on a yearly basis for the last eight years. There have been several heated discussions with the board by Harry and others, but the board is keeping the new director in place. At last count, donations were down 13 percent and some corporate sponsors were wondering out loud if they would be back the following year as sponsors.[4]

In yet another example, Al Scanlon, director of City Center Food Cooperative, is getting under-bid by the food pantry down the road. He can't prove it, but judging from the new vans they have, and their ability to keep their facility painted, clean, and neat, Al feels his job, his food pantry, and, ultimately, those he serves are all in jeopardy. When he thinks about the situation, all he can really see doing is just working harder. But, he can't give much more emotionally or physically.[5]

In all of these cases, those charged with directing these nonprofit organizations face the same issue: How do you implement a marketing strategy within an organization that is either resistant, or flat out refuses to change?

This chapter presents some practical ideas a nonprofit practitioner can use in revising an organizational strategy, and reviews some of the barriers many practitioners face in setting their strategies in place.

STRATEGY AS A NEW IDEA

For some nonprofit organizations, the notion of having an organizational strategy is a new one and takes getting used to. How will an organization deal with the changes such a strategy might impose upon it? To deal with the changes that often come with strategy it is important to first look at why nonprofit organizations have such a hard time with the notion of strategy to begin with. Once these "barriers" to strategy have been looked at, the chapter will then focus on implementation and evaluation considerations.

OPTIMUM CONDITIONS FOR CHANGE

Bringing a marketing strategy into a nonprofit organization, especially an organization that has operated without one, is hard work. Accepting change is difficult for the nonprofit organization. During the process, some individuals may express that their "freedom is gone," or "they no longer feel like a vibrant, contributing member," when a marketing strategy is announced. In addition to the personal discontinuities some express, developing an organization-wide strategy requires tremendous management energy and time, in an environment of scarce organizational resources.

In *Managing Change in Nonprofit Organizations*, Jacquelyn Wolf offers these practical suggestions for remembering how organizations tend to change:

- Organizational change must be seen as a process, not an event. It is difficult to pinpoint when change begins—with vague "readiness" or coherent intent. Change is integrated over a lengthy period, ranging from an optimistic 18 months to three years and more.

- Change must be approached as a people-centered process. It may involve physical alterations in site, technology, and structure but the managers' concern ultimately should be with the involvement, commitment, resistance, and acceptance of those involved as stakeholders.

- Support from the top—someone very senior in the organization must have a vision of what life will be like after the change effort is undertaken. That vision must serve as the driving force behind the strategy. If implementation is attempted without motivation from the top, a strategy can become rudderless and quickly lose direction.

- Change and its outcome must be flexible—It is not possible to anticipate all of the steps and potential outcomes. Indeed, to do so would preclude adequate participation by those whom the changes will affect—both internally and externally.

- Beware of emulating too closely the success of other nonprofit organizations. Effective change is highly contextual. What worked at the Children's Aid Society may not work at the ballet.

- Persuasion and participation are far stronger tools than brute force in implementing change.[6]

THE SIX MAJOR BARRIERS TO CHANGE

There are six major barriers nonprofit organizations generally must cross to begin the process of putting a strategy in place. They are:

1. the nonprofit culture;
2. the large scale of their goals and purpose statements;
3. the environment;
4. their staff and volunteer interaction;
5. the mixing of revenue- and nonrevenue-generating activities; and
6. the need for a strong performance culture.

The Nonprofit Culture

The average nonprofit "culture" can be an obstacle to implementing new strategies. Usually, the typical nonprofit organization is made up of a highly committed office staff that is somewhat underpaid and understaffed. The office furniture is often old or used. Sayings related to the nonprofit organization's mission adorn the wall. The office leaders are typically articulate, highly educated and motivated, especially in areas of the core mission relating to the organization. And because most nonprofit organizations produce services, most office staffers can talk in detail about the types of services the nonprofit provides.

In addition, there exists one more important piece of the nonprofit culture: the policies and programs the nonprofit organization generates, and the corresponding values that emanate from the organization, are often more important to the organization's personnel than achieving the end results or goals of the organization. What comes to mind are the workers in soup kitchens, in hospitals, in the Boy Scouts of America, in the alcoholic rehabilitation centers, in mental health facilities. These are individuals who are dedicated to the *cause;* not focused on the *bottom line.*

Naturally, certain rites and ceremonies of the organization become intermingled with the programs it is running. As such, a performance-predicated marketing strategy whose goal is to take the organization "somewhere" to accomplish some end result is often unsuccessful, not because it is the wrong strategy, but because it is simply *not accepted as one of the core values of the organization.* For example:

- A nonprofit organization does not use direct mail because it does not want to appear too "Madison Avenue" in its fund raising.

- A religious college's beliefs about women does not allow it to put women on its board, even though its curriculum is coed and the bulk of its donors and volunteers are women.

- An environmental group refuses to discontinue its "canvas" style of fund raising—even though it costs $.65 to raise a dollar—because it believes it is educating the consumer through the canvassing process.

- A food pantry refuses to work with other groups that distribute food in an effort to build a citywide food distribution network because it has always worked alone.

Within these organizations, the culture of the nonprofit organization, including their means of action, *esprit de corps*, and history are more important than reaching financial goals. However, financial goals are ultimately important to survival in an increasingly competitive nonprofit environment.

Goals and Purpose Statements

The unfortunate truth is that many nonprofit organizations set goals for themselves that they can never accomplish (i.e., eliminate all smoking from the state of Wisconsin). Such organizational purpose statements are too sweeping in their breadth (i.e., "To help all residents in the State of Michigan get involved in the plight of the homeless"). They also are self-defeating for two reasons: first, they cannot reach everyone—"all smokers," "all residents"—and, second, such missions (or goals) do not state specific enough goals. With nothing tangible to strive for, the nonprofit organization has no method for meeting its progress. In addition, without specific fund-raising goals—in dollar amounts, in usefulness measures, in profit percentages—there is no effective measurement for use of funds, raising those funds, and so on. Without a barometer, the organization has no way of knowing how high or how low it is going.

How does a marketing practitioner navigate between both organizational culture and financial mandates? By returning to four basic principles. They are:

1. establishing long-term service goals and mission;
2. evaluating the objectives to reach these goals;
3. developing potential action plans to achieve the goals; and
4. working within approved budgets and timelines.

Statements like this have several negative effects. First, they allow the nonprofit organization too much latitude in the types of programs and services it can offer the public, thereby making organizational service parameters very difficult to establish. To overstate, almost any program can seem acceptable.

Second, such broad and overreaching goals make the task of personnel and programmatical performance evaluation by the board and senior organizational directors almost impossible. If the organization does not have a target, it is easy to criticize it.

Third, service priorities become almost impossible for managers to establish; each ends up fighting over the merits of his or her ideas.

Fourth, it is very hard to find and establish an all-encompassing strategy for an organization that is trying to accomplish the typically broad agenda that many nonprofit organizations try to address.

Much of this book has been devoted to defining succinct, practical goals and missions. Take a final look at your mission and your goals:

1. Is your mission statement brief (i.e., more than a paragraph)? If not, try to rewrite it.
2. How many goals does your organization have?
3. Do you have one broad goal or many small goals or both?
4. Are your goals measurable?
5. How can you measure, on a quarterly basis, how your organization is meeting its many goals? How is it meeting its
   - service goals?
   - financial goals?
   - overall goals?

Dealing with the Environment

Some equate working in the nonprofit world to working in a fish bowl—everyone cannot only see what you're doing while you're inside the bowl, but also has an opinion on it. Consider the nonprofit development director's pressures today:

- The demand for nonprofit services has increased.
- Contributions in some sectors are down.
- Operating grants are on a decline.
- There is a need for nonprofit organizations to operate more "businesslike."

- The public gets worried if a nonprofit organization operates in a way that seems too "businesslike."
- Donors expect efficiency and demonstrated competence.
- Competition is increasing.

It's no wonder nonprofit organizations seem to have such difficulty implementing change: they must show a hard-hitting business capacity, accompanied by compassionate concern and advocacy for the needy! As such, the development director must interface with many different environments. It may be helpful, at this point, to fill in a worksheet formally defining the environments in which the development director and each employee must interact. (See Exhibit 11-1.) The simple act of defining your environment can make clear what kind of orientation you wish to undertake for each.

Staff and Volunteers

There is great respect for volunteers in the Third Sector and many can testify to their tremendous contribution to the nonprofit world. (The conventional taxonomy divides society into three sectors: the government, business, and the public or "third sector.") In fact, the more volunteers the organization can attract, the better. An effective marketing director in the nonprofit world is a consummate organizer and motivator of volunteers.

However, some marketing directors have mixed feelings about volunteers. On the one hand, there is a tremendous advantage to having volunteers within the organization when the task that needs to be accomplished can be handled adequately. On the other hand, the needs that volunteers have in relationship to the organization are not the same as the needs of a paid, full-time staff. The two are sometimes at odds with each other. For example, volunteers usually want to undertake tasks that they either have appreciation for or that validate their own feelings of contribution to society. These sought-after tasks are sometimes in short supply and are oversubscribed by volunteers. Rebuffing a volunteer's attempted efforts at helping pit the pragmatic needs of the organization to get a wide variety of tasks done as opposed to the volunteer's desire to participate in a task. This clashing of needs (and sometimes cultures) is a task for the nonprofit marketing team, since the nonprofit organization's success depends on integration of the two groups into a smooth working relationship.

An operating strategy can serve to enhance integration; or it can completely stymie it by positioning both groups—paid staff and volunteers—with no common ground.

| *Job Title* _____ | *Current Date* _____ | |
	Completion Date _____	
Current Environment	Immediate Concerns	Goal

Exhibit 11-1   Staff environment worksheet

How Do You Avoid Such Conflict?   First, an organization must evaluate why it is currently allowing volunteer involvement and its purpose in doing so. The outcome of such a question should lead to the development of a policy statement articulating both the mission of the organization and its goals in using volunteers.

Next, an organization must develop particular staffing policies that it wants volunteers to fill and subsequent position descriptions for its volunteers. Depending on the size of the volunteer force, an organization may also want to create the position of "volunteer coordinator" to manage the volunteer positions across the organization. Finally, an organization must constantly assess whether its volunteer program is performing in the way it should and up to the performance level that is required. (For example, one organization tried to get their volunteers to eat their lunch at their desk and not with other employees in order to try and maximize their contributions to the organization.)

Volunteers generally want an outlet in which to work where their presence reinforces the goals of the mission, does not necessarily challenge it, and likewise does not serve to negatively influence the performance of the paid staff. Paid staff need to see volunteers in a new light as people whose skill mix can, in the right situation, work to reinforce goal accomplishment and the organization's mission.

For many organizations, accomplishing this integration has meant the hiring of a D.O.V.E. (Director Of Volunteer Efforts) to help bring the two cultures together. A Director of Volunteer Efforts or Volunteer Administrator not only demonstrates the need for the volunteer program, but integrates it into an organization:

1. By evaluating the entire process of the organization's volunteer efforts—its coordination of tasks, its selection of people, its perceived and actual effectiveness, the budget available for it, and the methodology behind its volunteer training.
2. By publicizing the benefits of the volunteer efforts throughout the organization on a regular basis.
3. By assessing how their organization's program is affecting the community at large, both through the lives of those in the program, and the lives touched by volunteers to the nonprofit organization.

Revenue and Nonrevenue Activities

A nonprofit television production team has begun to sell studio time to for-profit advertisers doing commercial work. Other nonprofit organizations also seek to derive income from profit-generating activities. As nonprofit organizations look to improve their bottom line, more and more are venturing into for-profit activities; making a profit in one area allows the nonprofit organization to provide services in another. This organizational duality in purpose and methodology, however, can be problematic, as the following case study suggests.

RUNNING FOR-PROFIT AND NONPROFIT OPERATIONS WITHIN THE SAME ORGANIZATION

An interdenominational nonprofit organization, seeking to promote ethical work patterns in today's workforce, had both a for-profit publishing division as well as a nonprofit division that employs counselors to work with mainstream for-profit business people. The organization is engaged in both nonprofit and for-profit activities simultaneously. As a consequence, this practice has produced two completely different cultures and staff at the organization. One group has a strong altruistic culture where service and one set of core values are preeminent, while the other is completely immersed in its bottom line and marketing focus with another set of core values. Both organizational cultures work with different constituencies, requiring staff with skills that mirror each culture. Both cultures are often at odds with each other.

Should this organization run two strategies? Should it devise two different sets of performance criteria, one for each group? One way for an organization like this to coexist is to develop strong shared values among the two divisions. However, the organization needs to decide first that it is willing to tackle the problem. To do so and to correctly change this explosive environment by putting the two disparate cultures back together is a function of building shared attitudes for each division and second, building a shared strategy for the two divisions.

Performance Culture

"The difference was, we executed."[7] This statement by Jan Carlzon, president of Scandinavian Air System, is significant because the *execution* of plans, for many nonprofit organizations, is the biggest obstacle they have to overcome. Many nonprofit organizations simply do not have a history of goals, plans, implementation, and evaluation of such plans. They can be lax in measuring their progress with a plan; the only controls in place tend to be accounting controls.

Robert Waterman, author of *The Renewal Factor,* relates an interesting experience with the San Francisco Symphony. Having volunteered his time to introduce this West Coast symphony to the concept of long-range planning, he discovered that in order to do this, he first had to help the symphony measure its own performance as compared with other great symphonies. This was accomplished through a *fact pack.*

> We measured as many parameters as we could find. First we tackled the financial state of the orchestra, then our own past and that of some of the world's "great" orchestras. We looked at things like the long tenure of great conductors with the great orchestras. . . . We compared the average weekly salary of our musicians with the great orchestras. . . . We contrasted the utilization of our symphony hall (83 percent at the time) with that of the others (all running in excess of 90 percent). . . . We measured our subscription ticket sales (70 percent) against those of the others (most running over 85 percent). . . . We evaluated factors like average ticket revenues and income from broadcasting and recording.[8]

To build a great nonprofit organization means to move away from a short-term preoccupation to a long-term approach in every aspect, with multiple goals and measurement systems. What Waterman and the symphony members did first was to separate fact from fiction. A fact base was the starting point for bringing in change. How could any of the board or interested parties know what constituted a world-class symphony without first examining some type of fact base.

What was measured were indicators that would help the symphony know whether it had a chance at becoming a great symphony. The numbers focused attention on the issues and values that were important in achieving the symphony's goal, which was to become a great symphony. Part of the process of implementing change is in realizing that with every aspect, a constant analysis of effort and the efforts of others in the same industry or business requires a "performance evaluation" of some sort.

MOVING INTO AN ACTION PHASE

Sustaining the process of developing, refining, and, later, changing strategies (if need be) is one of the great tests of nonprofit leadership. In doing so, the leader of the organization must not only address the goals and aims of the organization, but must also carry out a process that includes the major stakeholders and the exterior world in a timely manner.

The leader or director of the nonprofit organization should be the driving force behind the implementation of a marketing strategy. He or she should decide when the process should go ahead, as well as how long the process should take. Often there is a group of men and women who help the organization's leader in developing the process of strategy refinement. This group can be called many things—from the strategic management group or task force, to a name which may have special significance for the organization, such as the ALPHA group. This group is not only in charge of strategy, but serves as the driving force behind its effectiveness. The following sections describe common problems with implementing a new organizational strategy.

A Lack of Commitment to the Strategy Itself

Most nonprofit marketing directors have seen strategies sitting on office shelves in their original three-ring binders collecting dust, unused. Sometimes these strategies are simply too vague for real relevance in everyday operation; or management may have agreed initially to the strategy but really did not integrate it into its daily operations. Some strategies suffer from a lack of clear-cut objectives and performance criteria, while others never really get evaluated by the senior leadership because they were not included in the original strategy planning process.

How do you prevent this from happening? First, senior executives have to be convinced that the old methodology—for whatever reason—is not working. A new strategy must replace the old one. Second, successful change usually involves more than changing job descriptions. Instead, it involves changing behaviors. Therefore, old habits or stereotypes will have to be altered. Third, senior leadership will absorb the changes at various levels of speed and understanding. The marketing manager must realize that the change in strategy will not be instantaneous.

Top Management was not Involved

The first attempts at building a marketing strategy often go very well. But it is up to management to truly implement the plan. Here's one example of a nonprofit director's opinion on his organization's leadership:

> Senior management had been observers to our department's process and had a passive role. I was naive to think that they were going to allocate resources to a program that did not take into account their particular, vested interests.[9]

Change must be led by line management and preferably senior leadership in order to ensure that the necessary commitment and resources for such a change are available. And while top leadership should lead the effort, sometimes outside experts provide additional impetus to both the leadership and management that the change is right.

The Objectives are Very General and Short-Term

Some nonprofit marketing directors have a difficult time engaging in the strategy-making process because they are constantly required by accountants and senior managers to perform against short-term financial goals. No marketing officer with this kind of pressure will develop a long-range strategy if the focus is always on the short term.

Can a marketing officer compensate for an organization that is always focusing on the short term? It is very hard because a change in strategy ultimately involves those inside the organization. The marketing manager must be consumed with the involvement, commitment, and resistance of those who will help implement the change. Can they incorporate a vision of what the organization will be like in the future? Often a planning framework like those discussed in Chapters 7 and 8 is very helpful in nurturing this process.

Inadequate Projections

On their first pass at building a marketing strategy, many nonprofit marketing managers develop their strategy by merely projecting their budget and subsequent financial increases to it. Their strategy is internally focused and quantitative rather than projecting the necessary breadth, trend analysis, and depth that a strategy requires.

A marketing manager overcomes the predilection of some nonprofit executives to evaluate only financial data by first gathering high levels of participation in the change process. Second, the marketing officer must use his or her informal network to gather intuitive information about the environment, particularly from key stakeholders or support communities. Third, as part of the diagnosis, the officer also looks at statistics, charts, available data, and so on.

The marketing manager and the senior leadership of the organization need to be aware of all of the forces operating upon the nonprofit organization, many of which are not purely financial.

The One Plan for One Situation Scenario

Some strategies do an excellent job of conceiving a scenario that works perfectly within one section of the environment surrounding the nonprofit, while missing huge chunks of other environmental imperatives. The strategy's challenge is to develop a sweeping look at potential changes in the environment while conceiving of strategic and timely organizational responses to these changes. The organization can respond more perceptively when a strategy is developed for a much bigger task.

As part of the diagnosis providing the rationale for change, the marketing officer often discovers that one strategy is not sufficient to solve every problem. As a consequence, the officer should develop a series of steps or stages that deal with certain opportunities, problems, or audiences over a period of time. In addition, he or she should articulate the additional resources that will be needed at each step, the new data that may need to be researched, and the cost of each step.

The Planning System and Strategy

Sometimes, marketing directors from larger nonprofit organizations are so constrained that he or she is never quite sure how many strategic questions are simply overlooked and never answered. These systems can be exceptionally complex and bureaucratic. Forms tend to dominate the process, whole strategic alternatives are often not discussed. In addition, not only are alternatives not discussed, when a strategic opportunity presents itself to the organization, the organization has a hard time taking advantage of it because of their excessively rigid system.

The key means to overcoming a rigid system is to involve and motivate others to consider new directions for the organization. Though not always easy—especially in organizations where the strategy process has gone on before with little or no change in the organization—this becomes the most viable solution. Often, the inclusion of individuals whose opinions are different than others, leads the organization to a reduction of its rigid system.

TAKE THE FINAL STEP

The final step in this long process is the development of an *action plan*— a "to-do" list—from which to work out the necessary details to complete all of the required activities to bring the nonprofit organization's services or products successfully to their respective markets.

A sample to-do list could be the following:

1. Define the strategy needed.
2. What alternatives does the organization have? What alternatives do other members of the leadership like?
3. How will the organization go about making the strategy choice amongst alternatives? Who must agree to the process?
4. Define the selection process. Who makes the final decision on the selection?
5. Research the implementation phase. Who is already involved? Who should be but is not? Is anyone offended by the new director? Can we compensate anywhere in the strategy to minimize offense?
6. Evaluate the strategy. Consider the time frame; income and expense considerations; and people.

Such a plan is often projected out for 6 to 12 months. Included in this plan, and supporting its conclusions, are all the client, constituent, volunteer, or donor surveys performed, any environmental statements or analysis undertaken, all strategy documents related to meeting both client and donor service and product requirements, as well as the timeline and budget for each step of the process. Costs should be tracked continuously, across project and service, in order to monitor them carefully. Exhibit 11-2 is a sample marketing plan for a nonprofit institution.

A leading hospital in the Midwest is seeking to intensify its rehabilitation program through a 30 bed subacute facility that is apart from its main hospital, where intensive training, mentoring, and support for nonacute patients in its rehabilitation program can take place cost effectively.

Summary

By means of purchasing—or leasing—a separate subacute facility (known as a *step-down* facility) in the adjacent community of Deerfield, the XYZ Hospital Corporation will create the "Deerfield Rehabilitation Center" for purposes of further serving its rehabilitation population. The goal is to provide for its medically stable population more intensive care, therapy, mentoring, encouragement, and training by rehabilitation technicians on behalf of the rehabilitation patient population in an environment that allows time for more hands-on training and support.

The primary reasons for taking a *step-down approach,* and the method by which this marketing plan has evolved is:

1. The hospital can no longer afford to keep new rehabilitation patients in its facility for as long as is required in order to give them adequate coping and support skills necessary to re-enter society.

2. The hospital overhead costs for maintaining a rehabilitation step-down unit inside its own walls is prohibitive.

3. An analysis of recent patients' attitudes regarding hospital care once the patient has been discharged, the problems they encounter, and their perceived ability to integrate back into society, suggests the need for this facility.

4. A review of longitudinal studies covering all aspects of successful rehabilitation patient treatment suggests the need for a step-down facility.

5. In-depth interviews with rehabilitation physicians, technicians, administrators, and outside experts concur with this need.

6. The current per-diem cost for physicians to constantly monitor this type of population is too great.

The choice of a step-down facility will present a more attractive option to patients who choose the XYZ Hospital by demonstrating both an intensive rehabilitation approach not found in most hospital situations our competitors offer, as well as an opportunity for the hospital to offer patient continuity programs in our treatment options—not currently offered—which will help foster a more satisfied patient and will create new income streams for the Hospital.

Profile of Target Populations

This marketing campaign will target three overall groups of potential population segments: current and recent rehabilitation patients (within the last six months) that the hospital has served or is currently serving; long-term rehabilitation patients (and their parents if patient is still a dependent); and potential referral populations including doctors with rehabilitation or related academic credentials, insurance companies, educational counselors, and selected corporations.

Review of the Product

The product is both an idea and a facility. The idea is that the XYZ Hospital wants to be involved with the rehabilitation patient in a meaningful way from the day the acute patient is first diagnosed as needing rehabilitation therapy, and then throughout the patient's subacute life as his or her modality changes over time. The institution is designated as a place where patients can come to receive help and encouragement, counseling services, and hands-on help in integrating their rehabilitation condition with the lives they wish to pursue.

Benefits to be provided through this product:

1. The chance for ongoing relationships to develop between doctor and patient.

2. One-step shopping convenience.

3. Community with patient and caregiver.

4. Patient's access to answers.

5. Heavily supportive environment.

6. Accessible location to Mid-Western patient population.

Competitive Alternatives

There are competitive caregivers for almost every type of problem our rehabilitation patients may have. This product will not necessarily be offering new—or even better—care. What it will be offering is the ability for the new, acute rehabilitation patient to overcome the shock and trauma of the injury by promising that the primary caregiver will be with the patient on every step of his or her new journey. The patient will not have to shop for services, will not experience the discontinuity of having to reintroduce one's self to new caregivers, and will have a sense of being noticed and cared for.

Scan of the Environment

Projections show that insurance companies and government funding programs will increasingly pressure hospitals to turn their rehabilitation patients over faster. As a consequence, the hospital will be blamed for not providing adequately on behalf of the patient. Nor can it . . . the per-diem costs of doctor and patient will not allow long-term care between both of them. The patient will either shop for new services, or not seek them out.

The step-down option allows for the opportunity of providing care on behalf of the patient, meeting their physical, social, and psychological needs, while reducing the costs associated with providing this service by having a stand-alone facility that does not suffer from excessive overhead, provides technicians as opposed to physicians doing the work, and allows then rehabilitation unit to discount its services because of the savings associated by having a steady stream of patients.

Opportunities and Threats

The ease with which the step-down facility can be incorporated and made ready to service its population represents its most pressing opportunity and threat. The opportunity is that the Hospital can capture significant market share rather easily and at minimum start-up expense by pursuing this idea. The threat is that the facility will be easily replicated by other competitors. The marketing issue is to be the first to provide this type of service.

Objectives

1. To introduce the facility no later than July 1, 1995 and fill minimally 30 beds per day with patients for the first six months of operation.

2. For referral audiences to the facility; (a) to introduce the facility to them by means of a short video; (b) to provide a personalized tour; and (c) to secure their agreement to refer the facility to their target populations.

Strategies

1. Research through focus groups and panels the attitudes of target adopters to the idea, their perceived use of it, their willingness to be a part of such an operation.

2. On the basis of market research, define target segments. The projected initial target segments will be existing XYZ rehab patients, current individuals whose patient history would make them open to the services the facility will offer.

3. Communication and advertising messages will be positioned to fit each target segment with the projected messages emphasizing personal care, community, support, and cost reduction.

4. A variety of media channels will be used: XYZ data base, vertical magazines aimed at rehab population, and personal calls on referral agents.

5. High levels of publicity will be sought through open house events, photo opportunities, high profile community endorsements, and a PSA campaign through television and radio.

Budget

Apart from the costs of the facility and staffing, we project spending approximately $400,000 through related media, and sales expenses in the first six months.

Action Required

Seek approval for all budgetary items, timetable for market rollout, and go-ahead for implementation of the plan.

*Source: This description and marketing plan of the Deerfield Rehabilitation Hospital is based on a real-life hospital, though the name "Deerfield Rehabilitation Hospital" is fictitious.

Exhibit 11-2   Marketing plan for Deerfield Rehabilitation Hospital*

CHAPTER TWELVE

Putting the Plans
Into Action

I saw a sweatshirt that had written on its front: "Don't sweat the small stuff." On the back of the sweatshirt were these words: "It's all small stuff."

For nonprofit marketing directors, the building of a marketing strategy for their nonprofit organization is made up of hundreds of "small" steps. The "small stuff" that makes up an effective strategy will continue to become clearer to you as you go over the notes you may have made while reading this book, or as you spend time in reflection on your own institution's strategy, or lack thereof. The book's themes on what strategy-driven, for-profit and nonprofit organizations are undertaking to succeed are summarized in this chapter.

USE COMPETITIVE BENCHMARKING

There are better ways to run your organization and produce your services and products. For years, the best-run for-profit organizations had looked only within their industries, searched out the competition, and investigated how they produce their products and run their service systems. In the 1990s, the concept of *benchmarking* (the same technique of searching out the best in competitor processes and systems and then emulating them), expanded outside the bounds of the for-profit industry.

Identifying superior performance in particular functions—whether personal or organization-wide—means nonprofit organizations must rely not only on trade journals, company publications, annual reports, consultants, and professional presentations, but literally need to go and visit other nonprofit organizations to find out how they are engaging their various environments strategically. One suggestion is to contact a successful, noncompeting organization. In addition, nonprofit organizations must seek out for-profit companies that engage in activities similar in nature to its own (i.e., customer service systems, taking care of clients, and so on.)

Here's an example that shows the benefits of benchmarking: for years, a competitor's development director exchanged processes in direct mail and foundation systems with another noncompeting director in order to not only speed up the "learning curve," but to improve each other's revenue procurement. It worked for both organizations.

> If you want to maintain the status quo, then don't benchmark. If you want to remain where you are . . . don't benchmark. Competitive benchmarking will open the organization to change, and to humility . . . and provides the stones for building a path toward competitive excellence and long-run success.[1]

PLACE MORE EMPHASIS ON MARKET RESEARCH

Over the years, market research had been used by the for-profit sector as an excellent, if not primary, means of learning about their customers. The need for this type of research is no less important in the nonprofit sector. Because the nonprofit organization's goal is to establish relationships with donors and clients in order to maintain their continuity of involvement, it is crucial to the organization's growth and effectiveness to know its supportive constituencies.

Too often, nonprofit organizations measure many variables but gain little understanding from the measurement process. There are three things that must be measured constantly in a nonprofit organization:

- Donor, client, and constituent satisfaction;
- The organization's employee satisfaction;
- Cash flow in and out of the organization.

A case in point of the benefits of market research: The National Museum of the American Indian in Washington, scheduled to open in 2001, mailed an appeal to its constituency that included a survey. The letter promised the responses to the survey would be kept confidential, with the survey asking a broad range of questions including the kinds of displays and exhibits contributors and interested parties wanted. The survey resulted not only in very concrete suggestions for how the Museum should be planned and structured, but also resulted in an outpouring of gifts and enthusiastic support.[2]

Marketing directors must continue to push for more and more monies for market research in their organizations. Techniques such as *cluster group analysis,* where data is combined from a nonprofit organization's donor list with geographically based computer modeling to target mailings to those most likely to donate to the organization, *simple tracking tests* measuring overall procurement of services and giving of donors involved in certain services of the nonprofit or fundraising initiatives, and long-term *client and donor continuity graphs* all are techniques that need to become tools used daily by nonprofit managers as they shape their strategies for the future.

FOCUS ON THE CLIENT, CONSTITUENT, OR DONOR

Jerre Stead, the CEO of National Cash Register (NCR), has a rule regarding his customers and their relationship to NCR: Aggressively, even militantly, he focuses on customers and results. "I say if you're in a meeting, any meeting for 15 minutes, and we're not talking about customers or competitors, raise your hand and ask why. If it goes on for half an hour, leave! Leave the meeting!"[3] Stead illustrates a critical point: the value of market research pertains to the methodology of getting information on clients, constituents, and donors. This is a critical organizational task that must be seen as a top priority item in every work setting.

RESEARCH IS KEY TO SUCCESSFULLY FILLING CLIENT, CONSTITUENT, AND DONOR REQUIREMENTS

James Emery White built his new church in Charlotte, North Carolina, based on the research responses of three zip code areas. The research showed him what kind of support services the church needed to offer, when to schedule services, the types of sermon material that would be helpful . . . in fact, the research also showed him what the unchurched were feeling about this new church and eventually helped White and his congregation to reach out into the community.

Many donors to nonprofit organizations are reining in their spending and justifying every purchase and donation transaction in order to maximize the value of each dollar that is spent. Shouldn't nonprofit organization get to know these individuals better, in order to serve them better and allow them to serve the organization better?

KNOW THE COMPETITION

Getting control of a marketing strategy doesn't involve a lot of "what if" scenarios. A good marketing strategy often starts with what competitors are doing. It starts with an intense evaluation of what they are doing right and what they are doing wrong. It continues with the nonprofit organization's program and marketing teams investigating a competitor's literature, programs, advertising, volunteer, and solicitational strategies in order to not only benchmark their organization, but also to find those areas of vulnerability that the organization's ability and expertise will allow it to exploit in the marketplace.

Frederick the Great said, "It is permissable to be defeated, but never to be surprised."[4] The push for competitor intelligence is so intense in some for-profit companies that salesmen are not reimbursed for expenses until they have filled out a form detailing the competitive information they uncovered in a sales outing.[5] Other organizations interview their competitor's customers through focus groups. Still other organizations have employees who do nothing else except go to trade shows in attempts to find out more about their competitors' strategies.

Your nonprofit marketing strategy only makes sense in light of *what your competitors are doing*. Competitor intelligence must become a priority for nonprofit marketing managers, especially those who are interested in developing strategies aimed at gaining market share in the marketplace.

ITS STILL THE ECONOMY!

A decade or more of galloping expansion is over for most nonprofit organizations. "We haven't crashed and burned yet," says one spokesman, "but we've had to slow down the train."[6] This is continuing to be felt in a number of ways:

1. *Slow growth.* Slow growth may be with nonprofit organizations for a very long time. As the availability of financial resources increasingly

constricts the organization, nonprofit managers tend to change their operating style. It drastically limits the margin of error managers can make. "Low growth amplifies the painful consequences of strategic mistakes. Suddenly the market no longer forgives errors of judgment. This is why companies in which an ingrained skepticism toward accepted assumptions, the habit of analysis, and where the practice of strategic thinking has become a way of life are the companies that seem to prosper so remarkably in bad times as well as good."[7]

2. *Strategic stalemates.* Some nonprofit markets have reached maturity. Their market share has become fixed, as have their competitors', and their strategy has become stalemated. It becomes hard for a nonprofit organization to stimulate new demand in this situation; change is also hard, and usually expensive.

3. *There are usually few options for nonprofit organizations.* One option is to diversify. In Chapter 7, a study was mentioned about a Methodist denomination. One church that was part of the study illustrates a diversification strategy: Through market research it was found that parents within a one-half mile radius of the Church had no day-care options available. One was started in a Church basement with a program neighborhood parents helped create that not only proved financially positive, but has encouraged 16 percent of its users to try the Church services at least one time.[8]

4. *Uneven distribution of resources.* Nonprofits have differing supplies of labor, land, resources, materials, and technology. Not every program can be made successful; nor can every competitive strategy have the necessary resources it needs for success. Nonprofit strategists have to begin to decide which programs will provide the greatest boost to their organization's overall effort. Without doing so, allocations of resources and materials often take on a bureaucratic nature, with little regard to the overall balance of a nonprofit organization's goals and opportunities.

NEW TACTICS ARE NEEDED TO STAY COMPETITIVE

Nonprofit institutions must move faster these days to outrun the shortening life cycle of many of their services and products. Service and product development time must be shortened, competitor information must be more factual, and service and product launches and introductions must be more carefully crafted. Needless to say, a nonprofit organization's services and products should be of the highest quality because fixing or correcting them in a crowded marketplace usually dooms the service or product.

Whenever and wherever possible, nonprofit institutions must automate and computerize. This is especially important in maintaining a data base area where strategic segmentation is the major key to success with donors, and in the systems area, particularly in tracking the relationship and continuity of clients, service users, and donors.

Finally, nonprofit organizations must stop assuming they don't have to evaluate their performance. For many organizations, a worker's pay is directly dependent on performance. This will be hard medicine, though, for most nonprofit organizations. "The majority (of nonprofit organizations) still believe that good intentions and a pure heart are all that are needed," wrote management expert Peter Drucker in December of 1991 in *The Wall Street Journal*. "They do not yet see themselves as accountable for performance and results."[9]

Leaders and managers of all types of institutions face violent upheaval: demographic changes; the shift in the United States' value structure; the decline of organizational and product loyalty; the reduction in federally funded programs; a shift in spending priorities by both public and private sector companies; and the obsolescence of international boundaries have all contributed to this volatility.

This increased uncertainty and ambiguity of roles and borders requires nonprofit organizations to think and act as never before. For some nonprofit organizations, this means using a strategy to help reach the end goals that their organizations have put forth; a strategic effort that is disciplined and designed to produce certain fundamental decisions and actions that ultimately help guide it into becoming the institution it envisions. The question of what it envisions for itself, though, will be reconsidered totally.

Other questions remain for those embarking on a new marketing effort. "How should marketing directors think about their nonprofit's long-term direction?" "Is a marketing strategy an essential part of this thought process?" Based on the arguments presented here, one certainly hopes so.

A good marketing strategy not only matters but is the essential or critical ingredient to an organization's goal completion. A marketing strategy takes an organization's goals, policies, and action sequences and guides the nonprofit organization in allocating resources—time, people, and money—to achieving its goals.

Back in 1960, Theodore Levitt wrote a classic article in the *Harvard Business Review* called "Marketing Myopia." One statement from this article was, "We've forgotten the needs of our customers. We must get back in touch with them."[10] What was true then is even more true now. In a nonprofit world that is desperate for solutions, the use of the simple tools offered by "marketing strategy" could allow hundreds, if not

thousands, of nonprofit organizations to improve not only their financial performance, but also the services they provide. At a time when
nonprofit services are desperately needed, the installation of "marketing" thinking in a nonprofit organization could offer a revitalized hope
to not only these institutions, but also the people they serve.

SUMMARY

In our best conscience as providers of nonprofit services, we should
make our goal first to listen to what is needed; second, to determine
where the gaps are in this service that are not being filled; third, to
deliver unique nonprofit services; and, fourth, to find a way to communicate all of the above to the world, to both regular constituents and new
constituents. If our goal is truly to fill a need, then let's go forward, listen to clients and donors to identity that need, and then provide a service to fill in the blanks in an otherwise profit-oriented and self-moti-
vated world. Nonprofit doesn't have to mean we can't make money or
have a good bottom line: It simply means that we provide services in
good conscience at the lowest possible cost.

Notes

ACKNOWLEDGMENTS

1. Frederick Buechner, *The Sacred Journey* (New York: Harper and Row, 1982), p. 107.

PREFACE

1. Peter F. Drucker, *Managing for the Future* (New York: Truman Talley Books/Dutton, 1992), p. 203.
2. "Strategies for Introducing Marketing into Nonprofit Organizations," Philip Kotler, taken from Philip Kotler, O.C. Ferrell and Charles Lamb, *Strategic Marketing for Nonprofit Organizations: Cases and Readings,* 3rd ed. (Englewood Cliffs: Prentice-Hall, Inc., 1987), p. 5.

CHAPTER ONE

1. James M. Greenfield, *Fund Raising: Evaluating and Managing the Fund Development Process* (New York: John Wiley & Sons, Inc., 1991), p. 2.
2. Rosabeth Moss Kanter, *The Change Masters* (New York: Simon & Schuster, 1984), p. 17.
3. Barry McLeish, *The Donor Bond* (Rockville: The Taft Group, 1991).
4. "Japan's American Prophet," Hobart Rowen, *The Washington Post Weekly Edition,* July 29–August 4, 1991, Volume 8, Number 39, p. 5.
5. *Ibid,* p. 5.
6. "Strategies for Introducing Marketing into Nonprofit Organizations," Philip Kotler, taken from Philip Kotler, O.C. Ferrell, and Charles Lamb, editors, *Strategic Marketing for Nonprofit Organizations: Cases and Readings,* 3rd Ed. (Englewood Cliffs: Prentice-Hall, Inc., 1987), p. 5.

7. This section adapted from the following articles: "Marketing for Nonprofit Organizations," Benson S. Shapiro, *Harvard Business Review,* September/ October, 1973, and "Corporate Identity and Directions," Siri N. Espy, taken from David L. Gies, J. Steven Ott, and Jay M. Shafritz, *The Nonprofit Organization* (Pacific Grove: Brooks/Cole Publishing Company, 1990), pp. 143–155.

8. Thomas Wolf, *Managing A Nonprofit Organization* (New York: Simon & Schuster, 1990), p. 126.

9. Armand Lauffer, *Strategic Marketing for Not-for-Profit Organizations* (New York: Free Press, 1984), p. 20.

10. *Ibid,* p. 18.

11. "Marketing for Nonprofit Organizations," Shapiro, *Harvard Business Review,* p. 263.

12. The author recommends the following books on nonprofit resource attraction: Barry McLeish, *The Donor Bond* (Rockville: The Taft Group, 1991); James M. Greenfield, *Fund Raising* (New York: John Wiley & Sons, Inc., 1991).

13. Houston G. Elam and Norton Paley, *Marketing For Nonmarketers* (New York: AMACOM, 1992), p. 7.

CHAPTER TWO

1. Al Ries and Jack Trout, *Bottom-Up Marketing* (New York: Plume Books, 1990), p. 82.

2. "Giving Out," *The Wall Street Journal,* Volume LXXI, Number 58, January 8, 1990, p. 1.

3. "DATE News," *DATE Newsletter,* December 1990, p. 1.

4. Personal phone conversation with Mark Olson, Director of Spring Hill Camps, January 15, 1991.

5. David L. Gies, J. Steven Ott, Jay M. Shafritz, *The Nonprofit Organization* (Pacific Grove: Brooks/Cole Publishing Company, 1990), p. 138.

6. John M. Bryson, *Strategic Planning For Public And Nonprofit Organizations* (San Francisco: Jossey-Bass, Inc., 1988), p. 4.

7. *Ibid,* p. 1.

8. "NonProfits in a Shaky Economy," Stephen G. Greene, *The Chronicle of Philanthropy,* Volume II, Number 23, p. 1.

9. "Dealing With a Shifting World," Lawrence N. Smith, *NonProfit Times,* Volume 1, Number 1, p. 1.

10. Barry McLeish, *The Donor Bond* (Rockville: The Taft Group, 1991).

11. "Tougher Customers," Rosalind Klein Berlin, *FORTUNE,* December 3, 1990, p. 37.

12. *Ibid,* p. 37.

13. George Barna, *The Frog In the Kettle* (Ventura: Regal Books, 1990), p. 176.

14. Thomas J. Peters and Robert H. Waterman, Jr., *In Search of Excellence* (New York: Harper and Row, 1982).

15. McConkey/Johnston client correspondence received November 27, 1990.

16. Peter Drucker, *Managing For Results* (New York: Harper and Row, 1964).

CHAPTER THREE

1. Geraldine A. Larkin, *12 Simple Steps to a Winning Marketing Plan* (Chicago: Probus Publishing, 1992), p. 4.

CHAPTER FOUR

1. Sun Tzu, *The Art of War,* translated by Thomas Cleary (Boston: Shambhala Publications, 1988), p. 81.

2. John O'Toole, *The Trouble With Advertising* (New York, Chelsea House, 1981), p. 90.

3. Fred Setterberg and Kary Scholman, *Beyond Profit* (New York: Harper and Row, 1985), p. 2.

4. "How Can So Many Professionals Have So Little Effect on Increasing the Growth Rate of Philanthropy?" Irving R. Warner, *The Chronicle of Philanthropy,* January 20, 1991, p. 37.

5. "Back To Basics In Direct Mail," Holly Hall, *The Chronicle of Philanthropy,* January 29, 1991, p. 22.

6. "Recession Catches Up to Ministries," Joe Maxwell, *Christianity Today,* June 24, 1991, p. 57.

7. John Lyons, *Guts* (New York: AMACOM, 1987), p. 10.

8. Michael L. Rothschild, *Marketing Communications* (Lexington: D.C. Heath and Company, 1987), p. 42.

9. McConkey/Johnston client file, June 24, 1991.

10. Rothschild, *Marketing Communications,* p. 44.

11. Judith E. Nichols, *Changing Demographics: Fundraising in the 1990s* (Chicago: Bonus Books, 1990), p. 8.

12. Joel Garreau, *The Nine Nations of North America* (Boston: Houghton Mifflin, 1981). Michael J. Weiss, *The Clustering of America* (New York: Harper and Row, 1989).

13. Weiss, *The Clustering of America,* introduction, p. xii.

14. Nichols, *Changing Demographics: Fundraising in the 1990s,* p. 19.

15. *Ibid,* p. 19.

16. Rothschild, *Marketing Communications,* p. 56.

17. Nichols, *Changing Demographics: Fundraising in the 1990s*, pp. 28–29.

18. *Ibid*, p. 28.

19. Dr. Thomas J. Stanley, *Marketing to the Affluent* (New York: Dow Jones-Irwin, 1988), pp. 137–138.

20. Philip Kotler, *Marketing for Nonprofit Organizations* (Englewood Cliffs: Prentice-Hall, 1975), pp. 108–109. See also Philip Kotler, *Marketing Management*, (Englewood Cliffs: Prentice-Hall, 1984).

21. David A. Aaker, *Strategic Market Management* (Toronto: John Wiley & Sons, Inc., 1984), p. 57.

22. *Ibid*., p. 56.

23. Personal conversation with Dr. Curt Scarborough, President and Chief Executive Officer for Christian Civic Foundation, in June of 1989.

24. Steven C. Brandt, *Strategic Planning in Emerging Companies* (Reading: Addison-Wesley Publishing Company, 1984), p. 68.

CHAPTER FIVE

1. Fred Setterberg and Kary Schulman, *Beyond Profit* (New York: Harper and Row, 1985), p. 2.

2. "Disaster Fatigue," Tom Post, Jeffrey Bartholet, and Jane Whitmore, *Newsweek*, May 13, 1991, p. 38.

3. "What's the Matter With Kids Today?" Paul Taylor, *The Washington Post National Weekly Edition*, July 15–21, 1991, p. 34.

4. "Taking Risks in Hard Times," Special Report Team, *The Chronicle of Philanthropy*, January 15, 1991, p. 1.

5. David A. Aaker, *Strategic Market Management* (Toronto: John Wiley & Sons, Inc., 1984), p. 70.

6. Peter F. Drucker, *Managing the Nonprofit Organization* (New York: HarperCollins Publishers, 1990), p. 17.

7. *Ibid*, pp. 10–11.

8. Michael E. Porter, *Competitive Strategy* (New York: The Free Press, 1980), Chapter 7.

9. Burton A. Weisbrod, *The Nonprofit Economy* (Cambridge: Harvard University Press, 1988) p. 109.

10. *Ibid*, p. 109.

11. Aaker, *Strategic Market Management*, p. 78.

12. J. Donald Weinrauch, *The Marketing Problem Solver* (New York: John Wiley & Sons, Inc., 1987), p. 25.

13. "Falling Company Gifts Test Environmentalists," Keith Schneider, *The New York Times*, December 23, 1991, p. A8.

14. George Barna, *The Barna Report* (Ventura: Regal Books, 1992), pp. 131–132.

15. J. Donald Weinrauch, *The Marketing Problem Solver*, p. 56.

16. Adapted from Peter Drucker, "What Businesses Can Learn from Nonprofits," *Harvard Business Review*, July–August 1989, p. 90.

17. Theodore Levitt, *Marketing for Business Growth* (New York: McGraw-Hill, 1974), pp. 152–153.

18. Timothy Burgess, speaking at the Evangelical Development Ministry 1991 conference in Orlando, Florida, October 20–24.

19. Michael E. Porter, *Competitive Strategy* (New York: The Free Press, 1980), p. 48.

CHAPTER SIX

1. Edward de Bono, *Sur/Petition* (New York: HarperBusiness, 1992), pp. 12–13.

2. "Is Your Company Vision-Driven?" Tom Brown, *Industry Week*, May 18, 1992, p. 11.

3. "What Intelligent Consumers Want," Faye Rice, *FORTUNE*, December 28, 1992, p. 57.

4. *Ibid*, p. 57.

5. James M. Greenfield, *Fund-Raising: Evaluating and Managing the Fund Development Process* (New York: John Wiley & Sons, Inc., 1991), pp. 8–9.

6. This section on internal analysis has benefitted from two fine books on the subject, James M. Greenfield, *Fund Raising* (New York: John Wiley & Sons, Inc., 1991), and Philip Kotler, *Marketing for Nonprofit Organizations* (Englewood Cliffs: Prentice-Hall, 1984).

7. The American Association of Fund-Raising Counsel Trust For Philanthropy, Nathan Weber, Editor, *Giving USA*, (New York: AAFRC Trust For Philanthropy, 1991), p. 9.

8. Personal conversation with a development director of a city mission in March of 1993 at the annual International Union of Gospel Missions convention in Memphis, Tennessee. The story and comments are real but the name of the development director and of the mission are disguised.

9. The American Association of Fund-Raising Counsel Trust for Philanthropy, Nathan Weber, Editor, *Giving USA* (New York: AAFRC Trust For Philanthropy, 1991), P. 8.

10. Greenfield, *Fund Raising*, p. 39.

11. Adapted from Greenfield, *Fund Raising*, pp. 43–47.

CHAPTER SEVEN

1. Theodore Levitt as quoted by Regis McKenna, *Relationship Marketing* (New York: Addison-Wesley Publishing Company, 1991), p. 1.

2. "Question: Every Company Has One. It Exists, Even If Only In The Head Of The CEO. It is Created, Either Explicitly, Or In The Shower. Very Good Companies Develop It Assiduously. What Is It? Answer: Strategy," *Success*, June, 1989, p. 32.

3. Theodore Levitt, *Marketing for Business Growth* (New York: McGraw-Hill, 1974), p. 189.

4. "Planning and Management in Nonprofit Organizations," John O. Alexander in *The Nonprofit Organization*, ed. David L. Gies, J. Steven Ott, and Jay M. Shafritz (Pacific Grove: Brooks/Cole Publishing Company, 1990), p. 160.

5. Thomas E. Broce, *Fund Raising* (Norman: University of Oklahoma Press, 1986), p. 20.

6. Peter Drucker, *People and Performance: The Best of Peter Drucker* (New York: Harper's College Press, 1977), p. 119.

7. J. Donald Weinrauch, *The Marketing Problem Solver* (New York: John Wiley & Sons, Inc., 1987), p. 28.

8. Personal survey of clients done by Barry McLeish in early 1994.

9. Tom Peters and Nancy Austin, *A Passion for Excellence* (New York: Random House, 1985), p. 10.

10. Robert H. Waterman Jr., *The Renewal Factor* (New York: Bantam Books, 1988), p. 125.

11. Peters and Austin, *A Passion for Excellence*, p. 71.

12. "Turning Around the Lord's Business," Rodney J. Irwin, *FORTUNE*, September 25, 1989, p. 116.

13. *Ibid*, pp. 116–117.

14. *Ibid*, pp. 116–128.

15. Fred Setterberg and Kary Schulman, *Beyond Profit* (New York: Harper and Row, 1985), p. 7.

CHAPTER EIGHT

1. Theodore Levitt, *Marketing for Business Growth* (New York: McGraw-Hill, 1974) p. 156.

2. While names have been changed, this story is built on an actual client example.

3. "Question: Every Company Has One. It Exists, Even If Only In The Head Of The CEO. It Is Created, Either Explicitly, Or In The Shower. Very Good Companies Develop It Assiduously. What Is It? Answer: STRATEGY," Don Wallace, *Success*, June, 1989, pp. 32–34.

4. Steven C. Brandt, *Strategic Planning in Emerging Companies* (Reading: Addison-Wesley Publishing Company, 1984), pp. 11–14.

5. *Ibid*, p. 21.

6. "Marketing is Everything," Regis McKenna, *Harvard Business Review,* January–February 1991, p. 73.
7. Theodore Levitt, *Marketing for Business Growth* (New York: McGraw-Hill, 1974) p. 8.
8. Regis McKenna, *Relationship Marketing* (New York: Addison-Wesley, 1991) p. 57.
9. From the personal files of Barry McLeish, Vice President, McConkey/Johnston, 1986.
10. Steven C. Brandt, *Strategic Planning in Emerging Companies* (Reading: Addison-Wesley Publishing Company, 1984) p. 22.
11. David A. Aaker, *Strategic Market Management* (New York: John Wiley & Sons, Inc., 1984) p. 235.
12. *Ibid,* p. 252.
13. "Financial Stress Found to Prompt Non-Profit Mergers," Jennifer Moore, *The Chronicle of Philanthropy,* January 15, 1991, p. 36.

CHAPTER NINE

1. "An Excellent Question," Thomas J. Peters, *INC.,* December 1984, p. 162.
2. "Substitutes for Strategy," Karl E. Weick. In David J. Teece (ed), *The Competitive Challenge,* (New York: Harper and Row, 1987), p. 222.
3. See Harold J. Leavitt, *Managerial Psychology,* 4th ed. (Chicago: The University of Chicago Press, 1978).
4. Paul C. Nutt and Robert W. Backoff, *Strategic Management of Public and Third Sector Organizations* (San Francisco: Jossey-Bass Publishers, 1992), pp. 58–61.
5. For one of the more popular lists of how strategy can be used within an organization, the reader is urged to see "The Strategy Concept I: Five Ps for Strategy," Henry Mintzberg, *California Management Review,* Fall 1987.
6. Michael E. Porter, *Competitive Strategy: Techniques for Analyzing Industries and Competitors,* (New York: Free Press, 1980).
7. "The Strategy Concept I: Five Ps for Strategy," Mintzberg, p. 12.
8. *Ibid,* p. 16.
9. Thomas J. Peters and Robert H. Waterman, Jr., *In Search of Excellence* (New York: Harper & Row, 1982). Richard Tanner Pascale and Anthony G. Athos, *The Art of Japanese Management* (New York: Warner Books, 1981).
10. Peters and Waterman, *In Search of Excellence,* pp. 10–11.
11. Pascale and Athos, *The Art of Japanese Management,* pp. 1–86.
12. "A Model for Diagnosing Organizational Behavior," David A. Nadler and Michael L. Tushman, *Organizational Dynamics,* Autumn 1980, pp. 35–51.
13. Raymond E. Miles and Charles C. Snow, *Organizational Strategy, Structure and Process* (New York: McGraw-Hill, 1978).

14. Cited by Nutt and Backoff, *Strategic Management of Public and Third Sector Organizations*, p. 76.

15. Kenneth R. Andrews, *The Concept of Corporate Strategy*, 3rd ed. (Homewood, Illinois: Irwin, 1987), pp. 18–22.

16. Daniel R. Gilbert, Jr., Edwin Hartman, John J. Mauriel, and R. Edward Freeman, *A Logic For Strategy* (New York: Ballinger, 1988), p. 48.

17. David A. Aaker, *Strategic Market Management* (New York: John Wiley & Sons, Inc., 1984), p. 171.

18. Bruce D. Henderson, *Henderson on Corporate Strategy* (Cambridge: ABT Books, 1979).

19. Gilbert, Hartman, Mauriel, and Freeman, *A Logic for Strategy*, p. 105.

20. Porter, *Competitive Strategy: Techniques for Analyzing Industries and Competitors*, p. 27.

21. Gilbert, Hartman, Mauriel, and Freeman, *A Logic for Strategy*, p. 88.

22. J.I. Moore, *Writers on Strategy and Strategic Management* (London: Penguin Books, 1992) pp. 44–47.

23. Porter, *Competitive Strategy: Techniques for Analyzing Industries and Competitors*, p. 37.

24. Nutt and Backoff, *Strategic Management of Public and Third Sector Organizations*, p. 110.

25. R. Edward Freeman, *Strategic Management* (Boston: Pittman, 1984) p. 31.

26. H. Igor Ansoff, *Corporate Strategy: An Analytic Approach to Business Policy for Growth and Expansion* (New York, McGraw Hill, 1965).

27. Freeman, Strategic Management, p. 31.

28. Gilbert, Hartman, Mauriel, and Freeman, *A Logic For Strategy*, p. 115.

29. *Ibid*, p. 118.

30. Bryson, *Strategic Planning for Public and Nonprofit Organizations*, p. 32.

31. A. Wildavsky, *The Politics of the Budgetary Process* (Boston: Little, Brown, 1979) as quoted by Bryson, *Strategic Planning for Public and Nonprofit Organizations*, p. 32.

32. Peter Lorange, *Corporate Planning: An Executive Viewpoint* (Englewood Cliffs: Prentice-Hall, 1980), pp. 280–282.

33. Gilbert, Hartman, Mauriel, and Freeman, *A Logic for Strategy*, pp. 128–132.

34. *Ibid.*, p. 132.

35. "Logical Incrementalism," James Brian Quinn, *Sloan Management Review*, Fall, 1978, pp. 7–23.

CHAPTER 11

1. Alvin Toffler, *The Third Wave* (New York: William Morrow and Company, Inc., 1980), p. 18.

2. Tom Watson as quoted by Michael E. Gerber, *The E Myth* (New York: Harper Business, 1986), p. 39.

3. Based on personal client files. The names of the facilities and the names of individuals have been changed.

4. *Ibid.*

5. *Ibid.*

6. "Managing Change in Nonprofit Organizations," Jacquelyn Wolf. In *The Nonprofit Organization,* ed. by David L. Gies, J. Steven Ott, and Jay M. Shafritz (Pacific Grove: Brooks/Cole Publishing Company, 1990), pp. 246–247.

7. Peters, "Strategy Follows Structure: Developing Distinctive Skills," p. 17.

8. Robert H. Waterman, Jr., *The Renewal Factor* (New York: Bantam Books, 1988).

9. Client comment contained in the body of a letter received by Barry McLeish in the month of January 1994.

CHAPTER TWELVE

1. "Bettering the Best," Jesse Cole, *SKY* (January 1993), p. 22.

2. "A Museum Attracts Gifts by Asking Donors How It Should Be Run," Tracy A. Fine, *The Chronicle Of Philanthropy,* June 1, 1993, p. 30.

3. "Could AT&T Rule the World?" David Kirkpatrick, *FORTUNE,* May 17, 1993, p. 55.

4. "The New Race For Intelligence," Richard S. Teitelbaum, *FORTUNE,* November 2, 1992, p. 104.

5. *Ibid,* p. 105.

6. "Battle for the Bottom Line," Beth Spring with Thomas Giles, *Christianity Today,* April 6, 1992, p. 66.

7. Kenichi Ohmae, *The Mind of The Strategist* (New York: Penguin Books, 1982), p. 167.

8. Client files of Barry McLeish.

9. Spring with Giles, "Battle for the Bottom Line," p. 67.

10. Theodore Levitt, "Marketing Myopia," *Harvard Business Review,* July–August, 1960.

Index